Fundamentals of Microsoft Fabric

Designing End-to-End Analytics Solutions

Nikola Ilic and Ben Weissman

Fundamentals of Microsoft Fabric

by Nikola Ilic and Ben Weissman

Published by O'Reilly Media, Inc., 1005 Gravenstein Highway North, Sebastopol, CA 95472.

O'Reilly books may be purchased for educational, business, or sales promotional use. Online editions are also available for most titles (*http://oreilly.com*). For more information, contact our corporate/institutional sales department: 800-998-9938 or *corporate@oreilly.com*.

Acquisitions Editor: Michelle Smith	**Indexer:** Ellen Troutman-Zaig
Development Editor: Shira Evans	**Cover Designer:** Susan Thompson
Production Editor: Ashley Stussy	**Cover Illustrator:** José Marzan Jr.
Copyeditor: Penelope Perkins	**Interior Designer:** David Futato
Proofreader: Paula L. Fleming	**Interior Illustrator:** Kate Dullea

July 2025:   First Edition

Revision History for the First Edition

2025-06-25:   First Release

See *http://oreilly.com/catalog/errata.csp?isbn=9781098172923* for release details.

978-1-098-17292-3

[LSI]

Table of Contents

Part II.   The Features: A Deep Dive

Part III.   Putting Fabric into Production

Foreword

In this new era of generative AI, every organization is racing to figure out how to make its teams more productive, to empower its customers, and to reinvent business processes. Data is the fuel that powers AI—now, more than ever, it is critical to ensure that organizational data is accessible, structured, and ready for AI. This is where Microsoft Fabric comes in, making it easier than ever for data teams to land their data in one place, collaborate across this data, and get it in a state where it can be served to the business so that they can make better decisions.

The vision of Microsoft Fabric revolves around three main pillars.

Fabric is an end-to-end data platform.

Data is a team sport. To get a solution up and running takes collaboration among many people with different skills. Before Fabric, these solutions required numerous products to get the job done. This often meant moving data from one product to another; manually integrating these offerings; and managing governance, cost, and usage independently. With Microsoft Fabric, a data team can leverage everything—data integration, data engineering, data warehousing, data science, real-time analytics, and business intelligence—in a shared workspace, with unified development processes and easy adoption. Because Fabric is built as a SaaS platform, it is easy for users to get started, for teams to collaborate in the product, and for administrators to centrally manage security and governance. Copilot is built into all of the authoring experiences in Fabric, making it easy for users to adopt new skills and build their data solutions faster than ever.

Fabric is built upon an open, data lake–based architecture.

This all starts with OneLake. The goal of OneLake is to make sharing data as easy as sharing files in Microsoft Office. Regardless of where the data is stored—whether directly in OneLake; in an existing data lake in Azure, Amazon Web Services, or Google's Cloud Platform; or in an operational database from your business apps—OneLake allows all data practitioners to work seamlessly with the data they have access to Fabric has adopted open standards—both Delta and

Iceberg formats—allowing customers to land the data once it's in OneLake and leverage that data in any of the engines in Fabric or in external products that have also adopted these formats.

Fabric enables every business user with AI-enabled insights.
It is critical that organizations not only have a strong data platform but also make sure business users have access to the relevant data when and where they need it in order to make better decisions. Power BI, as a core part of Fabric, enables business users to easily explore and visualize data. Deep integration across Microsoft Office applications, including Excel, Teams, and PowerPoint, allows business users to access the data in the context of the tools they already know and love. New Copilot-driven data exploration experiences will further enable the business to ask and answer their own questions.

There is so much opportunity for anyone getting started with Microsoft Fabric to learn new tools, increase efficiency in their data stack, and ready their business for the era of generative AI. If you're reading this book, I am guessing you're excited to get started. This book not only provides a high-level overview of what Microsoft Fabric is but also delves deeply into how to use the product and provides guidance on implementation considerations.

As you dive into this book and the product itself, know that Fabric is changing constantly. The product team strives to listen and learn from users, shipping new features, enhancements, and bug fixes weekly. Another resource, aside from this book, is the Fabric user community. You can visit the Fabric Community (*http://aka.ms/FabricCommunity*) to join, ask questions, attend a user group meeting, and learn about the latest feature releases. The product team is listening and can't wait to hear your feedback.

Kim Manis
Corporate Vice President of Product
Microsoft Fabric and Power BI
New York, March 2025

Preface

Every great collaboration starts with a moment of serendipity. Ours began when Nikola, eager to share his insights with the data community, stepped onto the stage at an event organized by Ben. That first encounter—one between a speaker and an organizer—sparked conversations that went far beyond the session itself. Over time, we discovered that while our perspectives and strengths on data and analytics were different, they were also complementary.

When Microsoft introduced Fabric, we immediately recognized an opportunity. This new, unified platform brought together the best of data engineering, data science, business intelligence, and real-time analytics. More importantly, it merged the very domains that defined our respective expertise.

Fundamentals of Microsoft Fabric is the product of that collaboration. This book is designed to be a practical, hands-on guide for data professionals, engineers, analysts, and business users who want to understand and leverage Microsoft Fabric effectively. Whether you're coming from the world of SQL-based data warehousing, Power BI modeling, or real-time analytics, this book will help you navigate Fabric's architecture, capabilities, and use cases.

Our goal is to demystify Fabric: you'll find explanations, best practices, and real-world examples that bridge the gap between theory and application. While Fabric is still evolving, the fundamentals remain the same, and this book serves as a reliable starting point on your journey.

We are excited to share our combined knowledge and passion with you. Writing this book has been an adventure, and we hope reading it will be just as rewarding and fun. Welcome to *Fundamentals of Microsoft Fabric*—let's build something great together!

Who Should Read This Book

This book is designed for professionals working with Microsoft Fabric, including data engineers, analytics engineers, data analysts, data scientists, and data architects. Microsoft Fabric is a persona-oriented SaaS (software as a service) solution, and this book follows a similar structure, allowing readers to consume deep dives based on their specific roles.

Rather than covering fundamental concepts in depth (such as "What is a data warehouse?"), this book assumes readers already have a solid background in their respective fields. It focuses on the specifics of Fabric, making it ideal for those looking to deepen their understanding of Microsoft Fabric and its ecosystem.

Navigating This Book

This book is organized into three parts.

In Part I, "The Foundation of Fabric", we talk about what Fabric is in general, what its components are, and how to get started. We also introduce OneLake, the key feature that every feature and experience in Fabric is built on.

In Part II, "The Features: A Deep Dive", we walk through all the *experiences* (which is what features are called in Fabric) and explain their use cases and how they work. We provide step-by-step guidance and real-world examples.

Finally, in Part III, "Putting Fabric into Production", we make sure you understand not only the individual bits and pieces of Fabric but also what else is needed to put it into production as your analytics platform. Here we answer questions on pricing and security, and we hope to clear up any confusion on when to use what, given that many challenges can be approached from multiple angles or using multiple experiences in Fabric.

Conventions Used in This Book

The following typographical conventions are used in this book:

Italic
: Indicates new terms, URLs, email addresses, filenames, and file extensions.

`Constant width`
: Used for program listings, as well as within paragraphs to refer to program elements such as variable or function names, databases, data types, environment variables, statements, and keywords.

This element signifies a tip or suggestion.

 This element signifies a general note.

 This element indicates a warning or caution.

O'Reilly Online Learning

 For more than 40 years, *O'Reilly Media* has provided technology and business training, knowledge, and insight to help companies succeed.

Our unique network of experts and innovators share their knowledge and expertise through books, articles, and our online learning platform. O'Reilly's online learning platform gives you on-demand access to live training courses, in-depth learning paths, interactive coding environments, and a vast collection of text and video from O'Reilly and 200+ other publishers. For more information, visit *https://oreilly.com*.

How to Contact Us

Please address comments and questions concerning this book to the publisher:

O'Reilly Media, Inc.
1005 Gravenstein Highway North
Sebastopol, CA 95472
800-889-8969 (in the United States or Canada)
707-827-7019 (international or local)
707-829-0104 (fax)
support@oreilly.com
https://oreilly.com/about/contact.html

We have a web page for this book, where we list errata, examples, and any additional information. You can access this page at *https://oreil.ly/fundamentals-of-microsoft-fabric-1e*.

For news and information about our books and courses, visit *https://oreilly.com*.

Find us on LinkedIn: *https://linkedin.com/company/oreilly-media*.

Watch us on YouTube: *https://youtube.com/oreillymedia*.

Acknowledgments

We want to start by thanking everyone who helped us make this book a reality. Our friends at the Microsoft Product Group (special shoutout to Kim Manis for her foreword!), our amazing tech reviewers Meagan Longoria, Emilie Rønning, Shabnam Watson, Olivier van Steenlandt, and Wolfgang Strasser, as well as our fabulous team at O'Reilly, Michelle Smith, Ashley Stussy, Penelope Perkins, Shira Evans, Paula L. Fleming, and Ellen Troutman-Zaig. We couldn't have done this without you, and we appreciate you all so much!

And speaking of those that we couldn't have done this without and who are always supporting us: *thank you* to our families for always supporting us in our endeavors! We love you!

## PART I

The Foundation of Fabric

In this section, we'll cover the core aspects of Microsoft Fabric, starting with what it is, how it works, and why it plays a major role in modern data management. You will learn about its key components, how they fit together, and how to get started with the platform. Each part of Fabric has a specific purpose, and understanding how they connect will help you make the most of its capabilities.

One of the most important components of Fabric is OneLake. This is not just another storage option—it is the backbone of the entire platform. Every tool, feature, and experience within Fabric relies on OneLake for storing, managing, and organizing data. Because of this, knowing how OneLake functions is essential. It provides a unified way to work with data, making it easier to access and use across different workloads.

By the time you finish this section, you will have a clear understanding of what Fabric is, what its main components do, and why OneLake is so important. This knowledge will set the stage for working with Fabric effectively and unlocking its full potential.

## CHAPTER 1

What Is Microsoft Fabric?

Let's start with one important question, What is Microsoft Fabric? Or, more specifically, Why do we need such an offering? In short, Fabric is the answer to a (if not *the*) challenge of our times as data professionals.

The Why and the What of Microsoft Fabric

All organizations have data: it surfaces in different formats, is constantly growing, and needs to be consumed by users to drive decisions and generate insights. Those insights need to run through different workloads, from real-time queries to analytical workloads, reporting, or AI-driven applications, as you see in Figure 1-1.

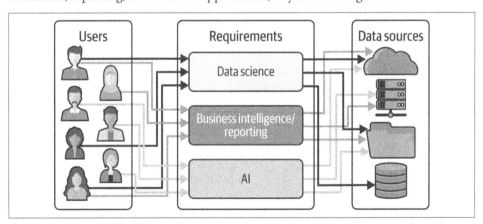

Figure 1-1. Requirements across an organization

Those users or personas usually have vastly different skill sets when it comes to working with data. They may not have any coding skills at all, or they may be using different languages like Python on a Spark cluster or SQL across multiple teams in an organization, as illustrated in Figure 1-2.

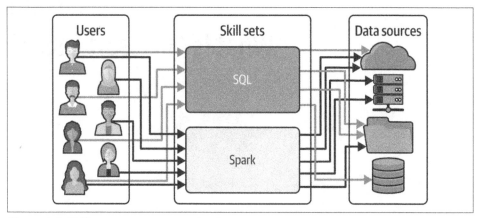

Figure 1-2. Skill sets across an organization

This means that to cope with new challenges and tasks, like responding to unprecedented amounts of data in real time in our data-driven world, users need to produce solutions in different ways. Organizations need to allow different users to use different tools that match their skills and needs, as well as organize their data in a way that works for them. This can be raw source data, a data lake, a data warehouse, or a data mart.

Microsoft Fabric—which we'll also refer to as "Fabric"—aims to solve all these problems in a single offering!

The Big Picture

Fabric addresses each of these complexities, challenges, and needs with a single solution, as you see in Figure 1-3.

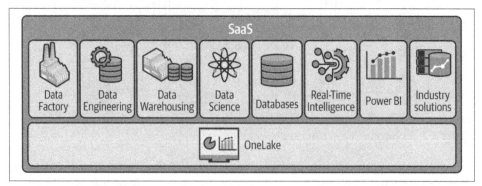

Figure 1-3. Fabric overview

Fabric includes features, services, and tools for every need along the way, from ETL (extract, transform, load; data movement and transformation) to building a data lake or warehouse, performing real-time analytics, and developing visualizations. Fabric even provides artificial intelligence and copilots along the way to support your entire journey. Each of these features within Fabric is called an *experience*.

While we will talk about the concepts, components, and offerings in Fabric in more detail in Chapter 4, let us give you a 30,000-foot overview of what they are and how they contribute to the Fabric ecosystem.

Workspaces and Domains

Your main organizational units in Fabric are called *workspaces*, and your workspaces can be grouped into *domains*.

Domains and workspaces are the overarching organizational concepts for both your data in OneLake and your lakehouses, notebooks, warehouses, pipelines, and all your other items. You work with data in workspaces and can tag a workspace or multiple workspaces to a domain. Your workspaces are also what will be connected to your CI/CD (continuous integration, continuous deployment) repository. All Fabric workspaces support Power BI premium features.

We'll talk more about the details of workspaces and domains in Chapter 3.

OneLake

Fabric uses one shared storage layer called OneLake as its foundation to house all your data. OneLake is often referred to as "the OneDrive for data." Figure 1-4 shows the general overview of OneLake, including its main components and APIs.

OneLake uses the Azure Data Lake Storage (ADLS) Gen2 (Microsoft's data lake solution for big data analytics) technology to manage all your data and items across your domains and workspaces. In addition to storing data, which can be ingested in a multitude of ways (more on that in Chapter 3), it comes with a data virtualization concept called *shortcuts*, which allow you to access in real time data that is sitting in other storage accounts like an AWS S3 bucket or Dataverse.

Data in OneLake is natively stored in Delta format, an open source data storage format that builds on Parquet, adding ACID transactions (atomicity, consistency, isolation, and durability—properties that ensure reliable and consistent database transactions even in the event of failures), schema evolution, and time travel capabilities to ensure reliability, consistency, and efficient data management across analytical workloads. Additionally, OneLake supports access to storage accounts that use the Apache Iceberg format, an open source table format.

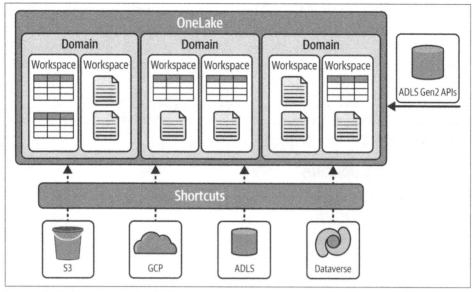

Figure 1-4. Overview of OneLake

All Fabric engines can read and write Delta; since other third-party tools can read the data with APIs, this means your data is not vendor locked.

Data Factory

Microsoft Fabric's Data Factory is designed to offer cloud-scale data movement and transformation services, simplifying the management of complex data integration and ETL processes. It provides a user-friendly, robust, and enterprise-grade experience for data management. As the successor to Azure Data Factory, this service has evolved to incorporate cloud-scale capabilities, addressing the most intricate ETL challenges. Data Factory delivers a modern data integration experience, enabling users to ingest and transform data from various sources, including databases, data warehouses, lakehouses, and real-time data streams.

Data Engineering

Data Engineering in Microsoft Fabric is a comprehensive suite tailored for data engineers to efficiently manage and transform large volumes of data using Apache Spark (plus other engines for Python and T-SQL notebooks, for example), facilitating the creation of lakehouse architectures. A lakehouse integrates the scalable storage of a data lake with the management capabilities of a data warehouse, providing a unified platform for data ingestion, transformation, and sharing. This architecture supports SQL queries, analytics, machine learning, and other advanced techniques on both structured and unstructured data. Microsoft Fabric enables users to create and manage lakehouses, design data movement pipelines, and utilize Spark job definitions for batch or streaming jobs. Additionally, notebooks are available for writing code related to data ingestion, preparation, and transformation. One key aspect about notebooks is that you can use multiple languages not only across notebooks but also within the same notebook, allowing developers to use the language they are most comfortable with.

Data Warehouse

Data Warehouse in Microsoft Fabric streamlines data insights while ensuring robust data security and governance through T-SQL constructs. It utilizes a distributed engine to deliver high performance and scalability. Data stored in Parquet format supports ACID transactions and interoperability across platforms, eliminating the need to duplicate data. Unlike the SQL analytics endpoint of a lakehouse, which can be used only for read-only queries, the Data Warehouse provides full transactional support, accommodating various data ingestion methods. This dual offering caters to diverse user needs, from data engineering to complex SQL operations.

Data Science

Microsoft Fabric's Data Science provides a robust platform for data scientists, supporting an end-to-end workflow for building, deploying, and operationalizing machine learning models. Key features include the use of R and Python in notebooks for data exploration, Data Wrangler for simplified analysis, and MLflow for tracking and comparing model experiments. Users can efficiently perform batch scoring at scale with Predict (a built-in function in Fabric that applies trained machine learning models to new data for generating predictions), benefiting from deep integration across Fabric's stack. This integration enables seamless data scoring in lakehouses, writing back predictions, and visualizing data in reports.

Real-Time Intelligence

Real-Time Intelligence is a fully managed big data analytics offering tailored in Fabric for streaming and time series data. It simplifies data integration, allowing organizations to scale their analytics solutions and make data accessible to various users, from citizen data scientists to advanced data engineers. The platform includes features specifically designed for real-time analytics, such as automatic data streaming, indexing, and partitioning for any data source or format, along with on-demand query generation and visualizations. This enables organizations to quickly access data insights with minimal effort and high efficiency.

Part of Real-Time Intelligence is Data Activator. Data Activator in Microsoft Fabric is a no-code tool designed to automate actions based on patterns or conditions detected in changing data. It allows users to monitor data within Power BI reports and event streams, triggering actions when specified thresholds or patterns are met. This tool streamlines the process of responding to data changes, enabling users to efficiently manage data-driven actions without the need for coding.

Power BI

You probably know this one, but if not: Power BI is a business analytics tool that enables users to visualize data and share insights across their organization or embed them in an application or website. It provides interactive visualizations and business intelligence capabilities with an interface simple enough for end users to create their own reports and dashboards.

 Business intelligence (BI) involves the use of data analysis and visualization tools to turn raw information into strategic insights. It empowers organizations to make data-driven decisions, enhance efficiency, and identify growth opportunities.

Power BI is now part of Microsoft Fabric, enhancing its integration and scalability within the broader ecosystem of Microsoft's cloud services. This integration allows users to seamlessly connect Power BI with other Fabric features, streamlining the process of data analysis and visualization within a unified analytics solution.

Power BI accesses data in Fabric through a *semantic model*. A semantic model is a structured representation of data that defines relationships, calculations, and business logic to simplify analysis and reporting. In Microsoft Fabric, it acts as an abstraction layer, enabling intuitive data interaction without requiring knowledge of the underlying database. Many items are deployed with a default semantic model. We'll explain more about those and semantic models in general in Chapter 9.

Databases

The newest addition to the Fabric experiences is databases—or, for now, only SQL databases. They basically give you the functionality of an Azure SQL Database in Fabric. While this may seem counterintuitive, given that all other experiences cater to analytical workloads, databases do fill a gap for use cases like OLTP workloads, as well as for example metadata repositories.

SQL databases in Microsoft Fabric integrate Azure SQL Database into a scalable platform that simplifies data management and application development. They offer automation, built-in governance, and AI-driven capabilities while connecting directly to OneLake, reducing the need for traditional ETL processes. Developers can use familiar SQL tools alongside features like vector data types for advanced search and analytics. The platform also includes Copilot to assist with database tasks and built-in AI support for applications such as recommendation systems and semantic search.

Security features like encryption, automated backups, and compliance tools help ensure data protection and reliability.

Fabric's SQL databases support modern DevOps workflows with CI/CD integration, source control, and autoscaling. A built-in GraphQL interface allows for flexible querying, making it easier to use SQL in different application architectures. With real-time data replication and direct Power BI connectivity, these databases can handle both operational and analytical workloads.

As you've seen so far, the experiences within Fabric overlap with the features and services available to users, and that's intentional. By enabling different data roles to use the same features and services, Fabric helps bridge knowledge gaps and enhances transparency across the tech stack.

Industry Solutions

Microsoft Fabric delivers specialized data solutions tailored to the unique needs of various industries, enhancing data management, analytics, and decision making. For the manufacturing sector, Microsoft Fabric and Azure AI's Copilot template drive digital transformation by consolidating data foundations, aligning data with industry standards, and providing conversational insights. In retail, these solutions enable the integration of data from multiple sources and facilitate real-time analytics for better decision making, supporting tasks like inventory management, sales forecasting, and fraud prevention. Sustainability-focused solutions streamline ESG (environment, social, and governance) data processing with prebuilt pipelines and models, aiding organizations in fulfilling reporting obligations. Health care solutions simplify complex data transformations, enable large-scale analytics, and leverage generative AI, boosting patient care and operational efficiency.

These industry-focused solutions empower businesses to unify and enhance their data assets, harness advanced analytics, and make swift, informed decisions. By addressing specific industry challenges, Microsoft Fabric helps organizations optimize operations, drive innovation, and increase productivity while achieving sustainability and performance goals.

Copilots

As we mentioned, Fabric offers a variety of AI and Copilot support along the way. There is not a single Copilot in Fabric but a multitude of them, each serving a different purpose. They need to be enabled for your environment. We talk more about this later, and you'll find more information in the documentation (*https://oreil.ly/U8arV*).

The Fabric Roadmap

Microsoft continuously works on improving existing Fabric capabilities and adding new ones. Some of the features and options discussed in this book will probably have already been enhanced in one way or another by the time you play with Fabric.

The Fabric public preview was announced at Microsoft Build in May 2023. It went to GA (general availability) at Microsoft Ignite in November 2023. Another huge wave of features was announced at the Microsoft Fabric Community Conference in the US and Europe in 2024 as well as at Build and Ignite in 2024. Figure 1-5 gives an overview of the initial and post-launch feature waves of Fabric.

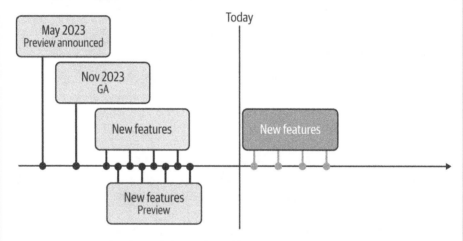

Figure 1-5. Microsoft Fabric release cycle and history

And since then, again, a huge list of new features has been provided, some of them still in preview.

Since Fabric constantly gets new features and capabilities, we're going to see them popping up in the future on very short cadences. No matter how fast we publish this book or an update to it, the actual roadmap will always be out-of-date by the time of publication.

So check out the Fabric roadmap (*https://oreil.ly/eqQG4*) for an always up-to-date list of features that are currently in the works or in preview.

The Fabric Pricing Model

Another interesting thing about Fabric is the licensing, or rather the pricing. Rather than sizing, deploying, and paying for a variety of individual services and offerings, you basically pay for one single product.

Fabric pricing consists of three components: storage, compute, and user licenses, as you see in Figure 1-6.

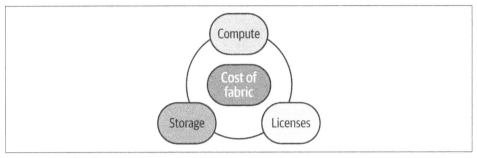

Figure 1-6. The three components of Fabric pricing

Microsoft Fabric pricing is structured around compute (capacities), storage, and user licenses. Compute is measured in capacities, available in Fabric (pay-as-you-go), Fabric Reserved (discounted commitment), and Fabric Trial (free for 60 days). Capacities range from F2 to F2048, with capacity units (CUs) determining compute time rather than raw performance. Fabric and Fabric Reserved capacities are identical, but reserved capacities require a commitment and are billed continually, whereas pay-as-you-go plans are charged only when running. Pausing capacities only benefits pay-as-you-go users, as reserved capacities incur charges regardless.

Storage in OneLake is billed separately per gigabyte, independent of compute usage. Even if compute is paused, storage costs remain.

User licenses are only relevant for Power BI. For capacities smaller than F64, every Power BI user needs a Pro license, while larger capacities require Pro licenses only for report creators. Other Fabric workloads do not need paid user licenses.

Networking charges are expected but not yet implemented. Regional pricing differences can be significant, and users should consider cost, data residency, and feature availability (e.g., OpenAI-powered Copilots may be unavailable in some regions) when selecting a deployment location. We'll explain the details of pricing in Chapter 14.

Summary

Let's wrap up this first chapter. Fabric is an end-to-end SaaS offering, meaning you only provision a single Azure resource type, including a single bill, despite potentially using a variety of different workloads.

Fabric is lake-centric which means that all its data is stored in OneLake. With OneLake on one side and capacities on the other side, Fabric gives you full separation of storage and compute.

Copilots enhance the entire experience to get you to your results even quicker. Fabric is organized through workspaces backed by capacities, which are all premium workspaces so users can share their data as well as their items.

While we have not yet looked at those aspects, Fabric is, of course, a governed platform that includes security, monitoring and role concepts. We will get into that in Chapters 15 and 16. Our next chapter, "Getting Started with Microsoft Fabric," will bring the theoretical concepts from this chapter together in a hands-on experience.

## CHAPTER 2

Getting Started with Microsoft Fabric

In Chapter 1, we gave you an overview of what Microsoft Fabric is. In this chapter, we give you a step-by-step guide on how to get started with Fabric and the Fabric portal. If you've had initial experiences with Fabric, feel free to skip this chapter. Otherwise, while we may be skipping a few details in this chapter to provide you with a big picture (don't worry if you feel like you're missing some pieces here and there), these first steps will hopefully be helpful when it comes to handling and navigating the Fabric features coming up in Part II.

Creating an Azure Account

The very first requirement to get started with Fabric is to set up a Microsoft Azure account. If you already have an account, you can use that. Otherwise, navigate to the Microsoft Azure Portal (*https://oreil.ly/s7s4e*), where you will be greeted by a login form that provides the option to create a new account.

Enabling Fabric

To get started with Microsoft Fabric, navigate to Power BI (*https://oreil.ly/6saf1*) or Microsoft Fabric (*https://oreil.ly/CjhkK*), where you will again be greeted by a sign-in screen (see Figure 2-1).

Figure 2-1. Fabric portal login screen

 The sign-in screen asking for your email may look slightly different depending on whether you already have an Azure account as well as other factors.

Log in with your Azure account, and the system will take you to the home page of either Power BI or Fabric, depending on the URL you chose. For this exercise, both will work and do the same thing.

On this landing page, find the settings as highlighted in Figure 2-2 and select "Admin portal."

Figure 2-2. Settings in the Fabric portal

To see the Admin portal, you will also need to be a member of the Administrator role. We'll talk more about permissions and security in Chapter 16.

While there are all kinds of settings and metrics to be found here (see Figure 2-3), we'll focus on the crucial parts to get started quickly.

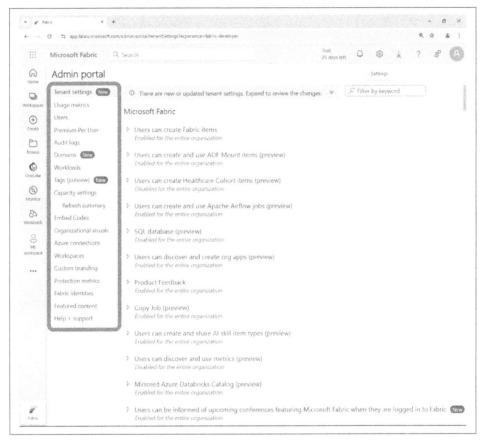

Figure 2-3. Fabric Admin settings

In Tenant settings, find the Microsoft Fabric section highlighted in Figure 2-4, and make sure that users can create Fabric items—either the entire organization or the specific users that you want to be able to use Fabric.

If these settings are grayed out (inaccessible), they are probably controlled by your organization's Fabric administrators. You'll need to reach out to them to get access.

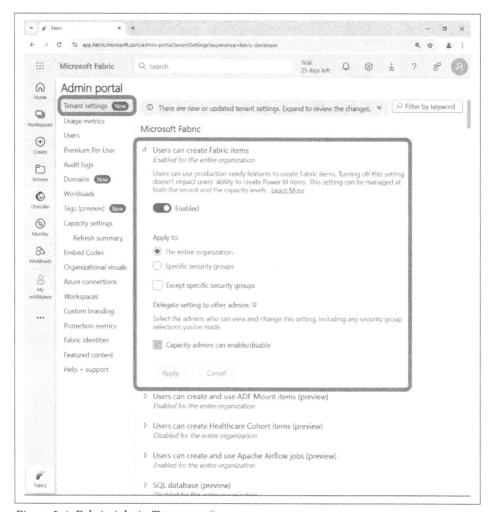

Figure 2-4. Fabric Admin Tenant settings

Once Fabric is enabled, the other thing you'll need is at least one capacity. Navigate to "Capacity settings," as shown in Figure 2-5.

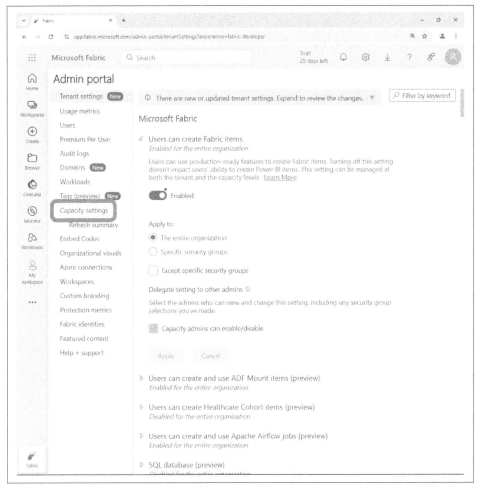

Figure 2-5. Fabric Admin capacity settings

Here, you can purchase and manage one or multiple capacities.

Click Purchase (Figure 2-6); you'll be routed to the Azure portal using a deep link that takes you directly to the creation of a new capacity.

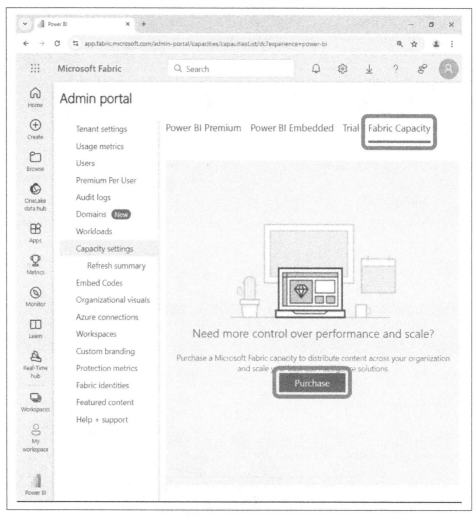

Figure 2-6. Fabric Admin capacity purchase

Provide your subscription, resource group, a name, a region, and—most importantly—the size (Figure 2-7).

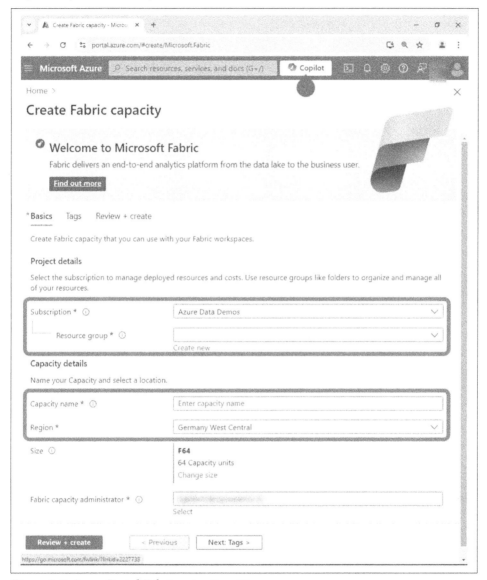

Figure 2-7. Azure Portal Fabric capacity settings

Select "Change size" (Figure 2-7) to display a list of the available sizes in your region and for your subscription, including their prices (see Figure 2-8).

Select the resource size

SKU	Capacity Units	COST (ESTIMATED/MONTH)
F2	2	€300.66
F4	4	€601.32
F8	8	€1,202.65
F16	16	€2,405.30
F32	32	€4,810.59
F64	64	€9,621.19
F128	128	€19,242.38
F256	256	€38,484.76

Figure 2-8. Azure Portal Fabric capacity sizes and costs in your home tenant's currency

We won't make a selection here because we'll tell you to do something even better! We'll use a trial capacity to explore the capabilities of Fabric at no cost for up to two months. A trial gives you the equivalent of an F64 capacity with the exception of very few features (unfortunately, Copilots are one of those).

 Capacity pricing varies by region and is subject to change. Differences in pricing between regions can be significant!

To enable a trial, go back to the Fabric portal, select your account on the upper right of the screen, and click "Free trial" as highlighted in Figure 2-9.

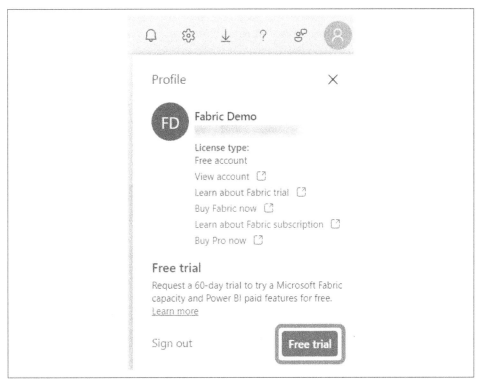

Figure 2-9. Fabric capacity trial start

You'll be asked to confirm that you want to upgrade to a free Fabric trial capacity, which you can confirm by selecting Activate (see Figure 2-10).

Figure 2-10. Fabric capacity trial activation

A message (see Figure 2-11) confirms that your capacity was upgraded and you can choose between being redirected to the Fabric home page or staying on the current page.

Figure 2-11. Fabric capacity trial confirmation

 The number of trials per tenant is limited with the free trial. Also, don't start developing things you intend to use for production while you're in a trial capacity, because moving your trial workspace to another capacity set in a specific region can cause severe problems.

Selecting Fabric Home Page will get you back to the home page of Fabric while still enabling your trial. When you elect to stay on the current page, everything gets refreshed, and you can see the number of days remaining in your trial in the top bar (see Figure 2-12).

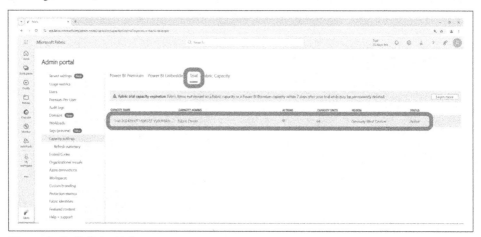

Figure 2-12. Fabric trial capacity overview

In "Capacity settings" (see Figure 2-12) on the Trial tab, our trial capacity shows up (just as regular capacities would on the other tabs if we had bought any).

Our Fabric environment is now ready for use!

If you want to share this environment with other users, you'll need to add them to the appropriate roles, which we'll elaborate on in Chapter 16.

First Steps with Fabric

Now that you have a capacity in place, navigate back to Microsoft Fabric (*https://oreil.ly/RPjVK*) (in this case it *does* matter which page you pick because Power BI (*https://oreil.ly/NuDei*) won't give you the same experience), and you'll get the entire overview of all the experiences or features Fabric has to offer (see Figure 2-13). For this example, we've chosen to work with the Data Engineering experience.

Figure 2-13. Fabric portal overview

We'll walk you through some of those capabilities and their functionalities and features in the next section to give you an idea of handling and navigation.

Creating a Workspace

While you do have a personal workspace to begin with, let's create a new workspace and connect it to our trial capacity. (Of course, if you already have a paid capacity, you can use that instead.) Select "New workspace," provide a name, set "License mode" to Trial, and click Apply as shown in Figure 2-14.

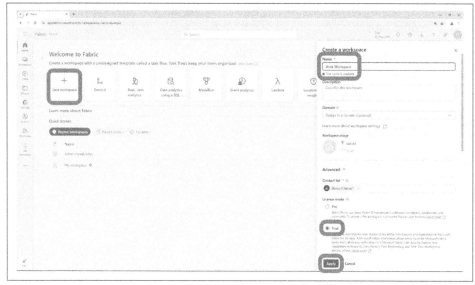

Figure 2-14. Creating a workspace

Building a Lakehouse

We will start by building a lakehouse, which is part of Data Engineering. Select Create (Figure 2-15) and click on the Lakehouse item, which is right on top.

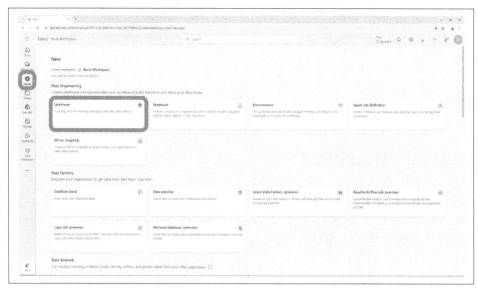

Figure 2-15. Creating a lakehouse

If you don't see the Create button, select the "..." to access it. You can pin it from there to customize your experience.

After selecting Lakehouse, you'll be prompted for a name. Give it the name Book-House, check the box to enable Lakehouse schemas, and click Create (Figure 2-16).

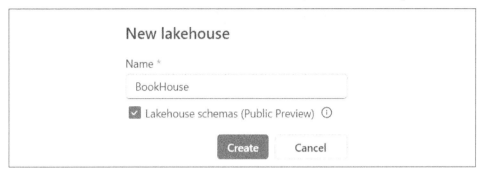

Figure 2-16. Naming the lakehouse

The lakehouse is now created, but as you can see in Figure 2-17, it is, of course, empty.

Figure 2-17. New lakehouse after creation

As you also see highlighted in Figure 2-17, even though the lakehouse is ready, the SQL analytics endpoint and the default Power BI semantic model are still being created (this takes a few minutes and will report as finished once completed). Whenever you create a lakehouse, it will automatically get a SQL analytics endpoint to make it accessible through SQL-based client tools. Although this is still being created, we can start working on the lakehouse.

From the landing page of our (empty) lakehouse, we could go ahead and upload files to it (Figure 2-18), which is what you'd do if you were working with your own data.

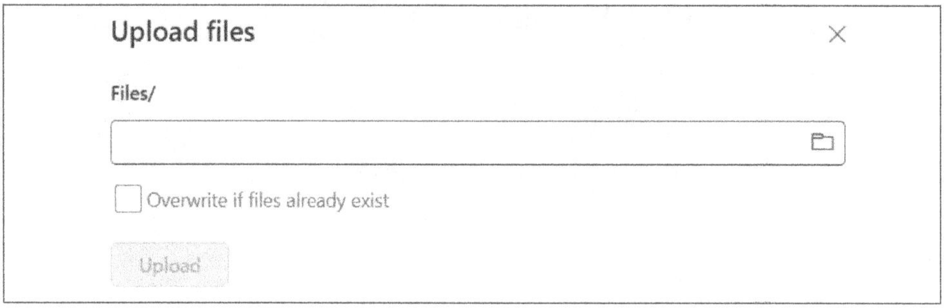

Figure 2-18. Uploading files to a lakehouse

From the same screen where we selected "Upload files," we also have the option to create a new data flow or data pipeline, or create a *shortcut*, which is a data virtualization concept specific to Fabric that allows you to access data from different locations without moving it. We'll explore this in Chapter 3 when discussing OneLake (Figure 2-19).

Figure 2-19. Creating a shortcut

To keep things simple for our first experience, let's start with sample data rather than your own data, which means that this lake will get populated with a few sample files and tables that we can work with. Simply selecting "Start with sample data" (Figure 2-20) on the Data Engineering landing page will trigger this process, which will take a few moments.

Figure 2-20. Starting with sample data

Data in a lakehouse is categorized as either tables or files, and the sample data process generates both for us. In our example, it has generated a table called publicholidays, which you can display by expanding the tables of the lakehouse in the left navigation pane. You can then explore its data by simply selecting it (Figure 2-21).

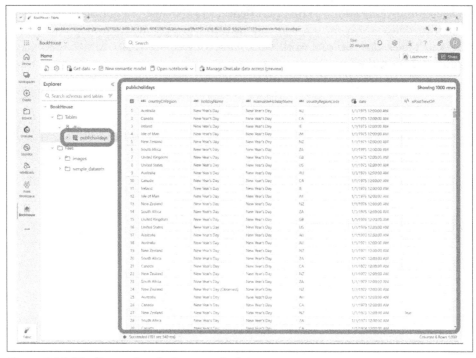

Figure 2-21. Finding and exploring sample data

The first time you access the table, it takes a really long time to display because the Spark pools, etc. in the background need to be initiated. Once that is done, all subsequent reads should be much faster.

If you navigate to the files of the sample dataset, you'll find a couple of CSV and Parquet files (see Figure 2-22). Of course, we could always add additional data by just selecting "Get data" in the top menu.

To explore the data in those files, just select, for example, the us_population_county_area CSV file, right/secondary click it, and select "Load to Tables" and "New table" as shown in Figure 2-23. The "Load to Tables" option is available for CSV and Parquet files.

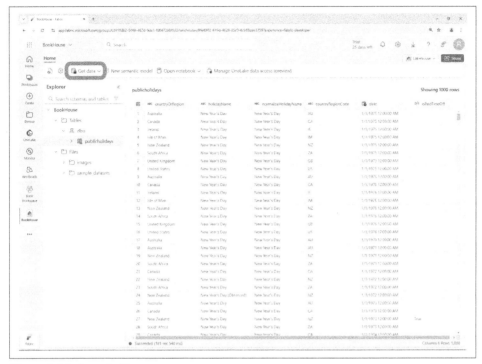

Figure 2-22. Sample files

Figure 2-23. Loading a CSV file to a table

As shown in Figure 2-24, since it's a CSV file that we selected, we can define a column header and specify which separator to use, and this will be loaded into our lakehouse in a table.

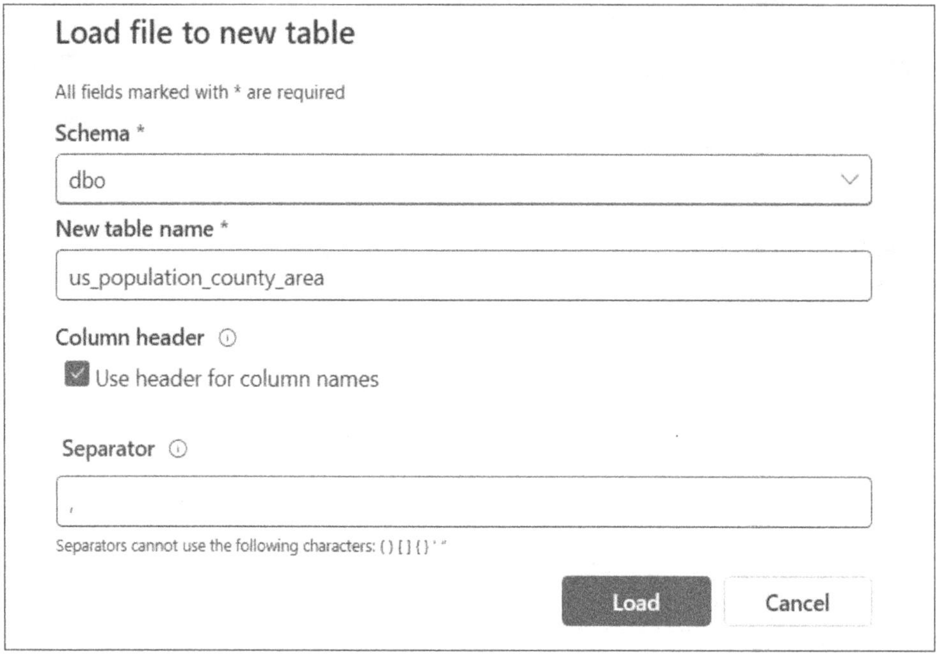

Load file to new table

All fields marked with * are required

Schema *

dbo

New table name *

us_population_county_area

Column header ⓘ

☑ Use header for column names

Separator ⓘ

Separators cannot use the following characters: ( ) [ ] { } ' "

[Load]   [Cancel]

Figure 2-24. Loading a CSV file to a table (settings)

This will make the data available in a table that could then be exposed through the SQL endpoint of our lakehouse.

If we want to explore or transform data, rather than just select a table, we can open the publicholidays table in a new notebook by selecting "Open notebook" and "New notebook" (Figure 2-25).

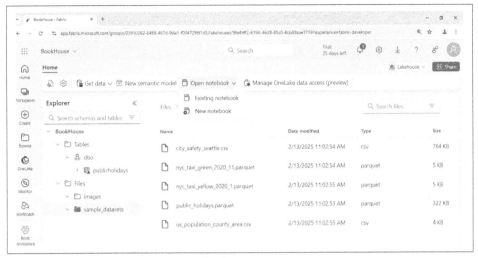

Figure 2-25. Exploring data in a notebook

This will create a new notebook, where we can add code snippets to read that table from our lakehouse. First, expand your lakehouse (Figure 2-26).

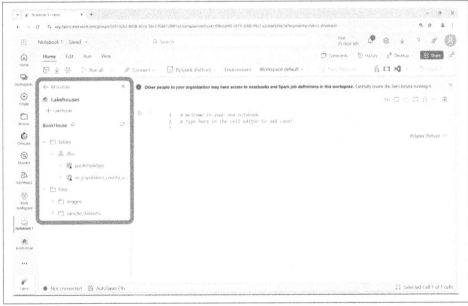

Figure 2-26. Exploring data in a notebook—tables in lakehouse

Right/secondary-click one of your tables and select "Load data" and Spark (Figure 2-27) to add the table to your notebook.

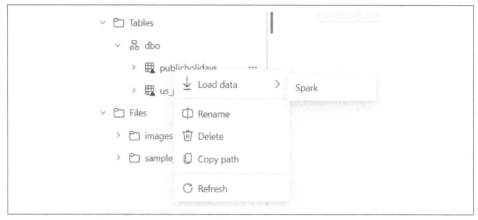

Figure 2-27. Adding a table to a notebook

By selecting the little play button next to the added code, you'll add your table's data to the notebook using Spark (Figure 2-28).

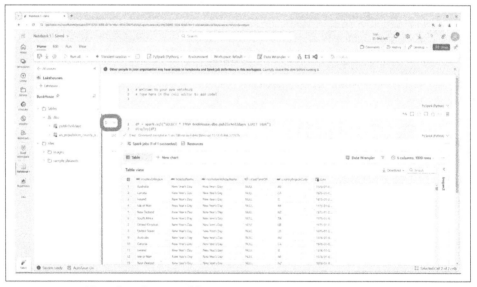

Figure 2-28. Adding data from a table

You could, of course, write more complex queries, create views, insert data into new tables, organize your lakehouse into schemas, build a medallion architecture…but all this is outside the scope of this chapter. We'll dive deeper into lakehouses and their structure in Chapter 5.

Building a Warehouse

In this section, we'll build a warehouse, which may be more familiar to you than a lakehouse if you're coming from a data-warehousing background.

To do that, we go back to the homepage that is now optimized for the Data Engineering experience.

To change our currently selected experience, we go to the lower left and select the Data Warehouse experience. We could also pick Power BI, Data Factory, Real-Time Analytics, etc.

 This is the easiest way to check if a user has access to a Fabric capacity. If only Power BI shows up, then the user is not connected to a paid or trial capacity.

To create a warehouse, we select Create again and this time find and select the Warehouse item, which is part of the Data Warehouse experience. You'll find this a bit further down (see Figure 2-29).

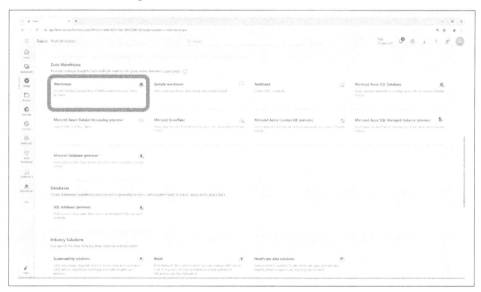

Figure 2-29. Creating a new warehouse

Name your new warehouse "Book Warehouse" and select the Create button as pictured in Figure 2-30.

Figure 2-30. Naming the warehouse

Just as with the lakehouse, we could select "Get data" to import additional data into our warehouse, but we also have the opportunity to just use sample data again, which is what we'll do (Figure 2-31).

Figure 2-31. Adding sample data to the warehouse

When we select "Sample data," a couple of tables are created and sample data is loaded into those tables. Some views as well as a couple of stored procedures are added on top of that, and all of them can be found in their respective subfolders of the default schema (dbo) as shown in Figure 2-32. We will talk more about organizing your warehouse through schemas in Chapter 6.

Figure 2-32. Sample data in the warehouse

By just selecting one of the tables or views, we see a preview of the data inside it.

Visualizing Fabric Data in Power BI

One very crucial part of the end-to-end analytics experience in Microsoft Fabric is not just the storing of data but also the visualization of this data. One way to visualize data—which also shows how seamlessly the components of Fabric are integrated—is directly from the previous screen, which has "New report" on top to create a report based on the data in this warehouse (see Figure 2-33).

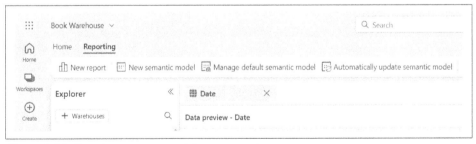

Figure 2-33. Creating a new report from a warehouse

Selecting the "New report" button will start up Power BI. As you can see in Figure 2-34, Power BI already knows about all the tables from the warehouse because they have automatically been added to a semantic model, the default semantic model. (This would also be available through a lakehouse.)

 The default semantic model will always be in Direct Lake mode. We'll learn more about semantic models, which were previously known as datasets, or Direct Lake mode, in Chapter 9.

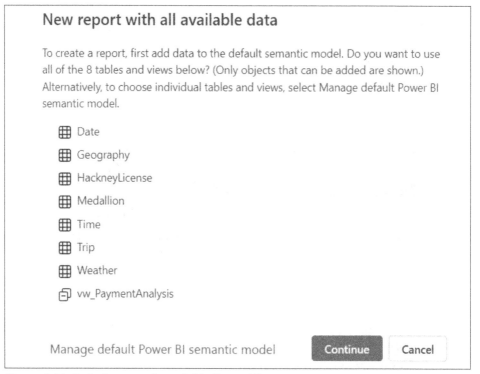

Figure 2-34. Default semantic model in Power BI

In this report, we can, for example, add the total amount from the taxi trips table by just expanding the Trip table and selecting TotalAmount (see Figure 2-35).

Figure 2-35. Adding a first value to a report in Power BI

This results in a single bar (which is the default visualization). We could then, for example, group it by payment type by again simply selecting "Payment type," and our bar chart will adjust accordingly (Figure 2-36).

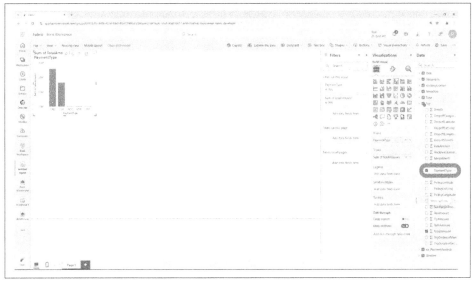

Figure 2-36. Grouped bar chart in Power BI

We can now go ahead and change the visualization type, color palette, add more data and visuals, etc., but that's beyond what we are trying to showcase in this chapter. Our point is simply to show how easy it is to create a simple visual report based on data that was added to Fabric just a few moments before, without setting up any additional manual data sources, gateways, firewall rules, etc.

Summary

With just a few clicks, we've created a new lakehouse and warehouse, loaded data into them, and finished up by creating a simple report. While of course only touching the surface, we hope that this chapter showcased a bit of the power of Microsoft Fabric, from loading to processing to visualizing and analyzing data. The beauty of this is that all the experiences and components are connected to make them work together; you need little to no configuration efforts.

Before we dive into all the different experiences and features, Chapter 3 will walk you through the concept of OneLake, the unified storage layer of Microsoft Fabric.

All Roads Lead to OneLake

One of Fabric's key characteristics is that it is lake-centric. All of its data is stored in a data lake—OneLake. This chapter will walk you through the basics of data lakes and the specifics of OneLake.

Overview of Data Lakes

A *data lake* is a centralized repository that allows for the storage of structured, semi-structured, and unstructured data at any scale. Unlike traditional data warehouses that store data in predefined schemas, data lakes are designed to hold vast amounts of raw data in its native format until it is needed. This flexibility supports diverse data types including text, images, videos, and social media streams, making data lakes an integral part of modern big data architectures.

The primary purpose of a data lake is to provide a scalable and cost-effective solution for storing large volumes of data. This data can be processed and analyzed to extract valuable insights, facilitate real-time analytics, and support data science and machine learning applications. The structure of a data lake allows businesses to store all their data in one place, enabling comprehensive analysis and integration across different data sources.

Evolution of Data Storage Solutions

Data storage solutions have evolved significantly over the years, reflecting the growing complexity and scale of data management needs.

Figure 3-1 shows how data storage solutions have developed over time.

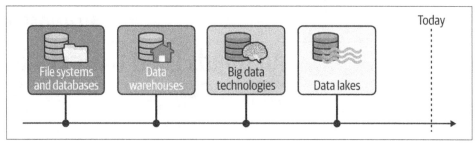

Figure 3-1. The evolution of data storage systems

The journey began with simple file systems and databases, progressed through data warehouses, and has now arrived at data lakes and beyond.

File systems and databases
> In the early days of computing, data was primarily stored in basic file systems and relational databases. These systems were adequate for managing small to moderate volumes of structured data but struggled with unstructured data and scalability.

Data warehouses
> The emergence of data warehouses marked a significant advancement in data storage. These systems are optimized for read-heavy operations and designed to support business intelligence activities. Data warehouses store structured data in a predefined schema, facilitating efficient querying and reporting. However, they are less flexible in handling unstructured or semi-structured data.

Big data technologies
> With the explosion of data from various sources like social media, sensors, and mobile devices, traditional data storage systems began to show limitations. Big data technologies such as Hadoop introduced the concept of distributed storage and processing, enabling the handling of massive datasets across clusters of commodity hardware.

Data lakes
> Building on big data principles, data lakes emerged as a more flexible and scalable solution. They can store data in its raw form, support a variety of data types, and provide a foundation for advanced analytics. Data lakes integrate with modern data-processing frameworks, allowing organizations to derive insights from their data more effectively.

Traditional data storage, such as relational databases, organizes data in structured tables with predefined schemas, making it ideal for transactional systems and structured queries. It requires data to be cleaned and formatted before storage, ensuring consistency and reliability.

A data lake, on the other hand, is designed to store vast amounts of raw, unstructured, and semi-structured data in an open format, preserving its original structure before any transformation. This flexibility supports diverse formats, including text, images, and log files, making it ideal for big data analytics and machine learning. By enabling schema-on-read, data lakes allow data scientists to explore and process information without rigid schema constraints, often leveraging optimized storage formats like Parquet for efficient querying and analysis.

The Importance of Data Lakes

In today's data-driven world, businesses rely heavily on data to drive decisions, innovate, and maintain a competitive edge. Data lakes play a crucial role in this environment for several reasons:

Scalability
> Data lakes are designed to handle large volumes of data, accommodating the growing influx of data from various sources without compromising performance.

Flexibility
> Unlike traditional data warehouses, data lakes support a wide range of data types and formats. This flexibility allows businesses to store everything from transaction logs to multimedia files, enabling comprehensive data analysis.

Cost-effectiveness
> Data lakes utilize cost-effective storage solutions, often leveraging cloud storage services. This makes it feasible for organizations to store large datasets without incurring prohibitive costs.

Advanced analytics
> *Advanced analytics* refers to a set of high-level data analysis techniques, including machine learning, predictive modeling, and AI, used to uncover deeper insights and trends beyond traditional reporting. By storing data in its raw form, data lakes provide a rich resource for data scientists and analysts.

Data integration
> Data lakes enable the integration of data from multiple sources, creating a unified view that supports more informed decision making. This integration is essential for applications like customer 360° views (a comprehensive, unified profile of a customer that consolidates data from multiple sources to provide a holistic understanding of their interactions, behaviors, and preferences), personalized marketing, and operational optimization.

Real-time processing
> Modern data lakes support real-time data processing, allowing businesses to react quickly to changing conditions and make timely decisions. This capability is critical for applications such as fraud detection, supply chain management, and dynamic pricing.

Governance and compliance
> Data lakes can incorporate robust data governance frameworks, ensuring data quality, security, and compliance with regulations. This is increasingly important as businesses navigate complex regulatory environments.

To sum things up, data lakes represent a significant advancement in data storage and management, addressing the limitations of previous systems and providing a scalable, flexible, and cost-effective solution for modern businesses. By enabling the storage of diverse data and file types—and, subsequently, processing of the data via tools that access the lake—data lakes empower organizations to harness the full potential of their data, driving innovation and maintaining a competitive edge in a data-driven world. As the volume and variety of data continue to grow, the role of data lakes in the enterprise ecosystem will become even more critical, supporting the next generation of data-driven applications and insights.

Introduction to OneLake

OneLake is a modern data lake solution developed by Microsoft, designed to streamline data management and analytics in the cloud. As part of Microsoft's suite of cloud-based data services, OneLake integrates seamlessly with various Azure offerings, providing a unified platform for storing, processing, and analyzing data at scale. The development of OneLake reflects Microsoft's commitment to empowering businesses with robust, scalable, and flexible data solutions, addressing the growing need for efficient data management in an increasingly data-driven world.

Figure 3-2 gives you a first look at the structure of OneLake.

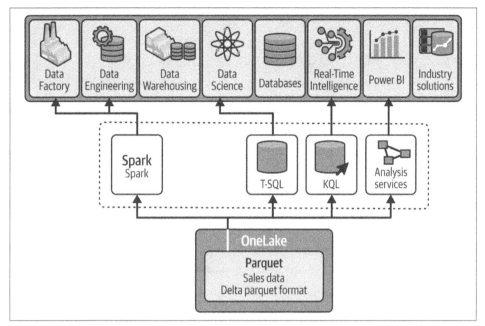

Figure 3-2. OneLake—the big picture

Separation of Compute and Storage

OneLake leverages the architectural principle of separating compute and storage, a significant evolution in data lake design. This separation allows businesses to scale storage and compute resources independently, optimizing costs and performance. By decoupling these components, OneLake ensures that data storage can be scaled without the need to simultaneously scale computing resources, and vice versa. This flexibility is crucial for managing variable workloads and achieving cost efficiency.

File Explorer

OneLake includes a user-friendly file explorer interface, simplifying data navigation and management. The file explorer enables users to browse, upload, download, and manage their data files within the lake, providing an intuitive way to interact with stored data. This feature is particularly useful for users who may not be familiar with command-line interfaces or complex data management tools, making OneLake accessible to a broader range of users.

What Makes OneLake Unique

OneLake offers several features that set it apart from other data lake solutions, enhancing its appeal and functionality.

Shortcuts

One of the most remarkable features of OneLake is its robust support for shortcuts, a transformative tool that greatly enhances data management and accessibility within Microsoft Fabric. The shortcuts feature empowers users to create both *internal shortcuts*, which are references to data stored in various locations within OneLake, and *external shortcuts*, which are references to external storage systems like Azure Data Lake Storage or Amazon S3. This feature is particularly advantageous for large organizations where data is typically dispersed across multiple departments, projects, or geographical regions. Instead of duplicating data across different workspaces or domains, an approach that can lead to increased storage costs and complex data governance issues, shortcuts enable teams to seamlessly reference existing datasets.

Shortcuts follow the "one copy" approach, meaning that your data is only physically stored in one place rather than having multiple redundant and potentially out-of-sync copies of your data in multiple locations.

For example, consider a scenario where a company's marketing team maintains a customer behavior dataset in its workspace. The finance team can create a shortcut to this dataset within its own workspace without physically copying the data. This approach not only conserves storage space but also ensures that both teams are working with the most up-to-date information. Furthermore, these shortcuts preserve the security and access controls of the original data, ensuring that sensitive information remains protected and accessible only to authorized users, regardless of how many workspaces are referencing it. Also, an update to the original table does not require any ETL or similar processes to be run in order for the updated data to be visible to consumers.

Shortcuts also simplify data integration and collaboration across different departments. Analysts and data engineers can incorporate data from various sources into their workflows without the need to repeatedly move or transform the data. This reduces the complexity of data pipelines and ensures consistency across reports and dashboards. As organizations increasingly adopt a data mesh architecture, shortcuts become even more invaluable. They enable each domain to manage and expose its data as a product, while other domains can quickly and easily integrate this data into their own analytics, all without disrupting the original datasets.

Moreover, shortcuts can be created for data stored in external systems, significantly expanding the range of accessible data within OneLake. For instance, if an organization has historical data archived in an Amazon S3 bucket, a shortcut can be established to this data, making it immediately available for analysis in Microsoft Fabric without the need to transfer it to OneLake. This capability supports hybrid and multi-cloud strategies, allowing organizations to maximize their existing data investments while also benefiting from the integrated analytics capabilities of Microsoft Fabric.

In summary, the use of shortcuts in OneLake greatly reduces redundancy, optimizes storage utilization, and simplifies data governance by centralizing data access while preserving the autonomy of individual teams and workspaces. This feature is closely aligned with modern data management principles, where agility, scalability, and security are of utmost importance. It enables organizations to derive insights more quickly and efficiently, enhancing their overall data strategy.

Integration with the Microsoft ecosystem

OneLake's seamless integration with Microsoft's suite of tools and services provides a significant advantage, offering a cohesive and comprehensive data management and analytics platform. This integration ensures that users can leverage familiar tools and workflows, enhancing productivity and reducing the learning curve.

Scalability and flexibility

By separating compute and storage, OneLake provides unparalleled scalability and flexibility. Businesses can scale their storage capacity to accommodate growing data volumes while independently managing compute resources based on workload demands, optimizing both performance and cost.

Advanced security and compliance

OneLake incorporates robust security features and compliance frameworks, ensuring that data is protected and managed in accordance with industry standards and regulations. This focus on security and compliance is critical for businesses operating in regulated industries or handling sensitive data.

Cost efficiency

The architectural design of OneLake, along with its integration capabilities and support for shortcuts, contributes to significant cost efficiencies. Businesses can minimize storage costs, avoid unnecessary data duplication, and optimize resource utilization, resulting in a more cost-effective data management solution. Part of that cost efficiency is also driven by the fact that shortcuts don't consume any actual storage in OneLake. In addition, *mirroring*, a data ingestion method we'll discuss later in this chapter and in detail in Chapter 11, comes with free storage.

As you can see in Figure 3-3, OneLake differentiates itself from traditional lakes while keeping their key characteristics.

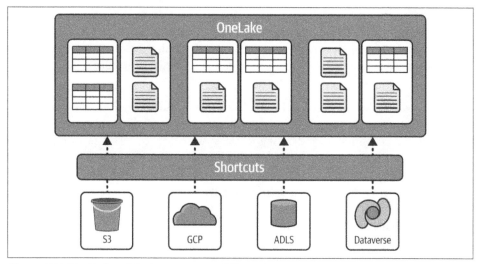

Figure 3-3. OneLake with shortcuts as a differentiator

In a nutshell, OneLake represents a significant advancement in data lake technology, offering a powerful, scalable, and flexible solution for modern data management and analytics. Developed by Microsoft, OneLake leverages the company's extensive expertise in cloud computing and data services, providing a robust platform that integrates seamlessly with a wide range of tools and services. Its unique features, such as the separation of compute and storage, user-friendly file explorer, and innovative shortcuts, differentiate it from other data lake solutions, making it an attractive choice for businesses looking to harness the full potential of their data. As data volumes continue to grow and analytics become increasingly complex, OneLake stands out as a critical tool for driving data-driven decision making and innovation.

The Foundation of OneLake

The foundation of OneLake is built on unified storage, advanced data formats, interoperability, and a focus on scalability and performance. These elements combine to create a robust, flexible, and high-performing data lake solution that meets the diverse needs of modern enterprises.

At the core of OneLake's architecture is the concept of *unified storage*. This approach ensures that all types of data—structured, semi-structured, and unstructured—are stored in a single, cohesive repository. Unified storage eliminates data silos, enabling seamless access and analysis across various data types. This centralization simplifies data management, reduces redundancy, and ensures consistency across the enterprise. By supporting unified storage, OneLake eliminates data silos and ensures consistency across data types. Unified storage also supports the diverse needs of modern data-driven businesses. Whether dealing with transactional data, log files, multimedia content, or real-time streaming data, OneLake provides a flexible and scalable environment that can accommodate the full spectrum of data requirements. This foundation is essential for enabling comprehensive analytics and insights.

The use of Delta and Iceberg formats enhances data reliability and performance, while interoperability with ADLS Gen2 APIs ensures seamless integration with existing tools and systems.

Finally, OneLake's scalability and performance capabilities enable organizations to handle massive datasets efficiently, driving faster insights and facilitating data-driven innovation. As a result, OneLake stands out as a foundational component of a comprehensive data management and analytics strategy.

Delta and Iceberg Formats

OneLake supports the advanced data formats Delta and Apache Iceberg, which are pivotal for managing big data efficiently:

Delta Lake format
Delta Lake is an open source storage layer that brings ACID transactions to big data workloads. Delta format enhances reliability and performance by enabling scalable and reliable data engineering pipelines. It supports features such as time travel (data versioning), schema enforcement, and the ability to handle both batch and streaming data efficiently. By using the Delta format, OneLake ensures data integrity and enables complex data processing operations with ease.

Iceberg format
Apache Iceberg is another open source table format designed for large analytic datasets. It is built to manage petabyte-scale tables while providing fast read and write operations. Iceberg's support for schema evolution, hidden partitioning, and robust metadata handling makes it ideal for modern data lake architectures. OneLake's support for Iceberg ensures compatibility with various analytics engines and improves query performance by optimizing data layout and minimizing data scans.

Interoperability

OneLake's design emphasizes interoperability with a wide range of tools and systems. This capability is crucial for organizations that use diverse technologies and need to integrate their data lake with existing workflows and applications.

OneLake is fully compatible with Azure Data Lake Storage Gen2 APIs, which provide hierarchical namespace support, enhanced security features, and optimized performance. This compatibility enables OneLake to integrate with applications and services that already use ADLS Gen2, ensuring a smooth transition and consistent experience. By leveraging these APIs, OneLake offers robust access control, simplified management, and high-performance data processing capabilities.

Scalability and Performance

Scalability and performance are foundational aspects of OneLake, designed to meet the demands of large-scale data environments:

Scalability
> OneLake is built to scale horizontally, allowing organizations to expand their storage capacity as their data grows. This scalability ensures that OneLake can handle massive datasets, from terabytes to petabytes, without compromising performance. By leveraging cloud-based infrastructure, OneLake provides virtually unlimited storage capacity, enabling businesses to store and analyze ever-increasing volumes of data.

Performance
> OneLake is optimized for high performance, supporting fast data ingestion, processing, and querying. The use of the advanced data formats Delta and Iceberg contributes to improved read and write speeds, efficient data compression, and minimized latency. Additionally, the separation of compute and storage resources ensures that performance can be tuned and scaled independently, optimizing resource utilization based on workload demands. This design allows for rapid data access and real-time analytics, empowering organizations to derive insights quickly and make data-driven decisions.

Data Stored in OneLake

OneLake is designed to store a wide variety of data types to meet the diverse needs of modern enterprises. The majority of data stored in OneLake is obviously primary data—you might even call it your actual or real data—and there are multiple types of operational data in OneLake and in general.

OneLake's flexible and scalable architecture allows it to store a wide variety of data types, making it an essential component of a comprehensive data management strategy. By accommodating structured, semi-structured, and unstructured data, as well as supporting real-time and big data, OneLake provides a unified platform for storing and analyzing diverse data sets. This capability ensures that organizations can leverage all their data assets to drive insights, innovation, and competitive advantage.

Metadata, including technical, operational, business, and security information as well as items, is an integral part of OneLake. The platform supports the storage and management of various metadata types, as well as analytical items like notebooks and scripts. This comprehensive metadata management enhances data discovery, governance, quality, and collaboration, making OneLake a powerful and efficient data lake solution.

Figure 3-4 shows the variety of data and formats that get stored in OneLake.

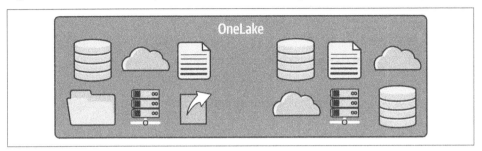

Figure 3-4. The variety of data stored in OneLake

Structured data

Structured data is highly organized and formatted to fit into traditional databases or spreadsheets. It follows a consistent schema and is typically stored in rows and columns.

Structured data originates from relational database management systems (RDBMSs) such as SQL Server, Oracle, MySQL, and PostgreSQL, and it can be ingested into OneLake. It includes tables, indexes, and views. In terms of content, it is often referred to as *transaction data* and *operational data*. Transaction data is generated from business transactions such as sales records, financial transactions, and order processing. Operational data is produced by day-to-day business operations and includes inventory levels, human resources records, and customer relationship management (CRM) system data.

Besides raw data originating from other systems and sources, another typical example of structured data is *derived data*. Derived data is raw data that has been processed and transformed to provide insights and analytics, such as *aggregated data* (summarized data from various sources, such as monthly sales totals, average customer ratings, and summary statistics) and *analytical data* (processed data ready for analysis, including data cubes, dashboards, and reports).

Semi-structured data

Semi-structured data does not follow a rigid schema but contains tags or markers to separate data elements, making it more flexible than structured data. Typical examples of semi-structured data are:

JSON and XML files
    Data formatted in JSON (JavaScript Object Notation) and XML, often used for web applications and APIs.

Log files

System and application logs generated by servers, applications, and network devices. These files often contain valuable insights for monitoring and troubleshooting.

Sensor data

Data from Internet of Things (IoT) devices, including temperature readings, humidity levels, and other environmental sensors.

Email

Content and metadata from email communications.

Unstructured data

Unstructured data lacks a predefined format, making it the most challenging type of data to store and analyze. OneLake can handle vast amounts of unstructured data efficiently. Unstructured data can usually be found in:

Multimedia files

Images, videos, and audio files used in media production, marketing, and communications.

Documents

Text documents, PDFs, presentations, and other file types used in business operations and communications.

Social media data

Data from social media platforms such as posts, comments, likes, and shares.

Web data

Content scraped from websites, including HTML, CSS, and JavaScript files.

Metadata

Metadata plays a crucial role in managing and understanding the data stored within the lake. It provides context, facilitates data discovery, and ensures that data is used appropriately. In Fabric, that metadata is also stored in OneLake.

Metadata can be grouped into a number of types, each containing different kinds of information:

Technical metadata

Technical metadata includes:

Schema information

Details about the structure of data, such as table definitions, column types, and data formats

Data lineage
> Information about the origin of data, how it has moved through various stages of processing, and any transformations applied

Storage details
> File paths, locations within the data lake, and storage formats

Operational metadata
> Operational metadata includes:

Data quality metrics
> Information on data accuracy, completeness, consistency, and validity

Usage statistics
> Data on how often datasets are accessed, modified, or queried

Processing logs
> Records of data ingestion processes, ETL jobs, and data transformation steps

Business metadata
> Business metadata includes:

Data catalogs
> Descriptions of datasets, business terminology, and data classifications

Tags and annotations
> Keywords, labels, and notes added to datasets to facilitate search and discovery

Security metadata
> Security metadata includes:

Access control information
> Permissions and roles associated with different datasets and users

Audit logs
> Records of who accessed or modified data and when

Notebooks and analytical items

In addition to traditional metadata, OneLake can also store analytical items such as:

Notebooks
> Interactive documents that contain live code, equations, visualizations, and narrative text. These are commonly used for data analysis, exploration, and machine learning tasks.

Scripts and code
Scripts and code written in Python, R, Scala, and other programming languages used for data processing and analysis.

Machine learning models
Trained models, along with their configurations and performance metrics.

Dashboards and reports
Visualizations and reports created using Power BI.

Organizing Data in OneLake

To organize and group or partition your data in OneLake, you'll need to understand two coexisting concepts: *domains* and *workspaces*.

Domains

Domains are logical partitions within OneLake, designed to organize and manage data according to specific business units, departments, or other organizational criteria. Each domain can be seen as a separate, secure data space with its own set of permissions, governance policies, and data structures.

Domains align with the organizational structure of a business, making it easier to manage data relevant to specific business units or departments. Domains allow for precise control over data access and governance, ensuring that only authorized users can access sensitive information. They provide a framework for managing data lifecycle, quality, and consistency within specific organizational contexts.

Domains in OneLake serve as foundational elements that enhance data governance, security, organization, collaboration, scalability, and integration. They are essential for managing data effectively within large organizations, ensuring that data is accessible, secure, and well organized to support business objectives.

A domain can stretch across multiple capacities!

Workspaces

Workspaces are collaborative environments within OneLake where users can create, manage, and share semantic models, reports, dashboards, and other analytical items such as lakehouses or pipelines. Each workspace acts as a container for these resources, facilitating teamwork and project management.

Workspaces are designed to enable teams to work together on data-related projects, sharing insights and resources effectively. They help in organizing projects and resources in a logical manner, making it easier to manage and navigate. Workspaces allow for setting permissions and access controls, ensuring that only authorized users can view or edit the contents.

Key Differences Between Domains and Workspaces

Both domains and workspaces both play crucial, but different, roles in OneLake. Domains provide a structured and secure environment aligned with the organizational hierarchy, while workspaces offer flexible, collaborative environments for managing projects and team efforts. Together, they ensure that data is well organized, secure, and accessible to those who need it within the organization.

Every Fabric item has to be assigned to a workspace. But not every workspace requires a domain. Domains are an additional, but optional, grouping layer, so a domain without a workspace would make no sense as it couldn't contain any items. Figure 3-5 shows the relationship between domains, workspaces, and shortcuts in OneLake.

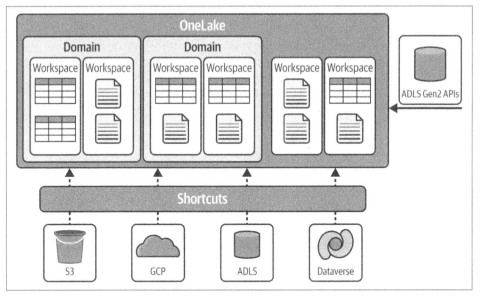

Figure 3-5. Differences between domains and workspaces in OneLake

Let's look at some key differences between domains and workspaces.

Scope and purpose

Domains focus on organizing data across the entire organization according to business units, departments, or any other structure that fits your needs, ensuring data governance, security, and organizational alignment.

Workspaces, on the other hand, focus on facilitating collaboration and project management within specific teams or projects, centralizing resources and enabling efficient teamwork.

Imagine a large tech company that decides to implement a data mesh approach to better manage its diverse and distributed data landscape. In this context, the domains in Microsoft Fabric collectively represent the entire company, serving as the overarching structure that contains all the data, resources, and users across the organization. Domains could be sales, HR, IT, marketing, or others departments. Within each domain, workspaces function as a specific data product or business unit, like a self-contained project team responsible for its own data, reports, and analytics. For example, the international sales team and the domestic sales team could each have their own workspace, while both belong to the sales domain. This setup aligns with data mesh principles by empowering each team to manage its data while ensuring governance and connectivity across the organization.

> A *data mesh* is a modern approach to data management that decentralizes control, distributing data ownership to domain-oriented teams that handle their datasets as independent products. It leverages self-service infrastructure, enabling teams to efficiently access, process, and share data while following governance and quality standards. By eliminating centralized bottlenecks and promoting interoperability, data mesh supports scalable, business-driven data management across an organization.

Security and governance

Domains implement organization-wide security and governance policies, managing access to data based on business unit or departmental needs. Workspaces implement project-specific or team-specific access controls, managing permissions for collaborative work on semantic models, reports, and other resources.

Organization

While domains organize data at a higher level, often aligning with the organizational structure, workspaces organize resources at a project or team level, focusing on the needs of specific collaborative efforts.

Ingesting Data to and Integrating Data with OneLake

Data ingestion and integration are critical processes that ensure data from various sources is efficiently and effectively brought into OneLake. OneLake supports a variety of data ingestion methods and integration mechanisms, making it a versatile platform for managing complex data environments.

Methods of Data Ingestion

There are many ways to ingest data into OneLake, as shown in Figure 3-6. We will discuss them in more detail in Part II of this book, but here's a quick overview.

You can either use a shortcut, which is not really ingesting data but only making it available in your lake, or you can use Spark, Dataflows, data factory activities, pipelines, streams, T-SQL, or mirroring. While you may have heard of the others, let me elaborate a bit more on mirroring. *Mirroring* in Microsoft Fabric is a feature designed to simplify data integration and enhance analytics experiences by creating a real-time, read-only replica of data in the open Delta format, without the need for ETL processes. It is basically a smart way of replicating your data from other sources into one lake in almost real time without the need to manually load the data. We will dive deeper into mirroring in Chapter 11.

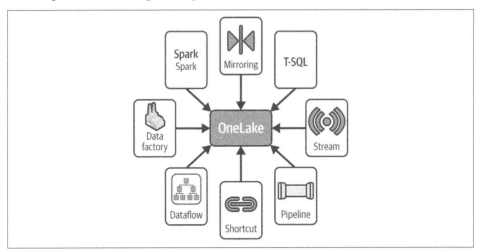

Figure 3-6. Data ingestion into OneLake

Integration Mechanisms

OneLake integrates seamlessly with a wide range of services, enabling a cohesive data management and analytics ecosystem.

Microsoft services

First and foremost, Fabric and OneLake obviously integrate very well with other Microsoft services such as the following:

Power BI

Power BI can connect directly to OneLake, enabling users to create interactive reports and dashboards from their data stored in the lake. This integration supports advanced data visualization and business intelligence. Given the full and native integration of Power BI and OneLake, utilizing OneLake as your data source allows you to use both services to their full potential. We'll talk more about this in Chapter 9.

Azure Machine Learning

Data scientists can use Azure Machine Learning to build, train, and deploy machine learning models using data stored in OneLake. This integration facilitates the development of predictive analytics and AI solutions.

Microsoft Dynamics 365

Integration with Dynamics 365 enables businesses to combine operational data from their CRM and ERP (enterprise resource planning) systems with other data sources in OneLake for comprehensive analytics. This is typically done using a feature called Fabric Link, which automatically generates shortcuts.

Azure Databricks

Microsoft Fabric integrates with Databricks by providing a unified environment where users can access Databricks' advanced analytics and machine learning capabilities alongside Fabric's comprehensive data management tools. This integration allows for seamless data sharing and collaboration, enabling users to perform complex data processing and analysis within Databricks and leverage Fabric's data visualization and reporting features. The collaboration streamlines workflows and enhances data-driven insights through a cohesive and efficient platform.

Third-party tools

OneLake's open architecture also allows it to integrate with a variety of third-party data-processing and analytics tools. While there is no way to come up with a comprehensive list, a few popular choices and tools include:

Apache Spark

Microsoft Fabric integrates with Apache Spark by enabling users to leverage Spark's powerful distributed computing capabilities for big data processing directly within the Fabric environment. This integration allows for efficient execution of complex analytics, machine learning, and data processing tasks using Spark, while benefiting from Fabric's seamless data connectivity and visualization tools. The combination facilitates robust data workflows and accelerates insights through scalable and high-performance data processing.

Tableau

Microsoft Fabric integrates with Tableau by allowing users to connect, visualize, and analyze data stored in Microsoft Fabric directly within Tableau's powerful visualization platform. This integration ensures seamless data flow and consistency, enabling users to create interactive and insightful dashboards that draw from Fabric's comprehensive data management and analytics capabilities. It enhances data-driven decision making by combining Tableau's intuitive visualizations with Fabric's robust data infrastructure.

Snowflake

Microsoft Fabric integrates with Snowflake by providing a seamless connection that allows users to access, analyze, and visualize Snowflake data directly within the Microsoft Fabric environment. This integration leverages Snowflake's data-warehousing capabilities and Fabric's analytics tools, enabling efficient data management and comprehensive insights through a unified interface. The collaboration enhances data-driven decision-making processes by streamlining workflows and ensuring data consistency across platforms.

Amazon S3

Microsoft Fabric integrates with Amazon S3 by enabling users to connect and manage their S3 data directly within the Fabric environment. This integration allows for seamless data access, transfer, and analysis, leveraging Fabric's robust data management and analytics tools. Users can efficiently incorporate S3 data into their workflows, enhancing data driven decision making through Fabric's comprehensive visualization and reporting capabilities.

API-based and endpoint integration

OneLake supports API-based integration, allowing developers to build custom applications and services that interact with the data lake. For organizations operating in hybrid environments, OneLake can also integrate with on-premises data sources, providing a seamless data management experience.

OneLake provides REST APIs for programmatically accessing and managing data. These APIs can be used to automate data ingestion, retrieval, and management tasks. By supporting ADLS Gen2 APIs, OneLake ensures compatibility with a wide range of existing applications and tools that already use these APIs for data operations. SSIS (SQL Server Integration Services) and other ETL tools can be used to create data integration workflows that move data between on-premises systems and OneLake, facilitating hybrid data management, mostly using Fabric's SQL endpoints.

To sum up, all of these features show how OneLake offers a comprehensive and flexible platform for data ingestion and integration, supporting a wide range of methods and tools to bring data from various sources into the lake. Whether through batch or real-time ingestion, migration tools, or integration with Microsoft and third-party services, OneLake ensures that businesses can efficiently manage their data. Its support for API-based integration, data virtualization, and hybrid data environments further enhances its versatility, making it an essential component of modern data architectures. As organizations continue to embrace data-driven strategies, the robust ingestion and integration capabilities of OneLake will be crucial in unlocking the full potential of their data assets.

Figure 3-7 illustrates the variety of ways Fabric can interact with other tools and vice versa.

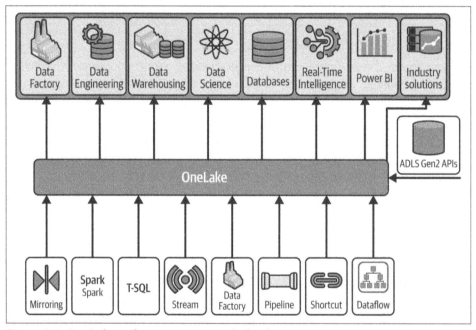

Figure 3-7. OneLake and its interaction with the data ecosystem

OneLake Catalog

The OneLake catalog serves as a centralized hub where you can discover, explore, and manage the Fabric items you need, as well as govern your data. It includes two tabs, Explore and Govern.

The Explore tab offers a list of items, along with an in-context item detail view, allowing you to browse and explore items while maintaining your list context. It also provides filters and selectors to help refine and focus the list, making it easier to find what you're looking for. By default, the OneLake catalog opens to the Explore tab.

The Govern tab gives you insights into the governance status of all the data you own in Fabric and provides actionable recommendations to improve its governance posture.

To access the OneLake catalog, click the OneLake icon in the Fabric navigation pane. If the desired tab is not displayed by default, select it as shown in Figure 3-8.

Figure 3-8. OneLake catalog

OneLake Explorer

Since OneLake is often referred to as the OneDrive for data, there is, of course, also an application to view items in OneLake on your computer without going through the portal. The OneLake file explorer (shown in Figure 3-9) integrates OneLake directly with Windows File Explorer, allowing you to easily access all OneLake items you have permission to view within the Windows File Explorer interface. Data in OneLake Explorer can also be synced back to Fabric. You can download OneLake file explorer from the official download page (*https://oreil.ly/Mi8D9*).

Figure 3-9. OneLake file explorer

In our case, OneLake explorer shows you the workspace we created in Chapter 2. We can navigate down to the individual files, as we have seen in our lakehouse (see Figure 3-10).

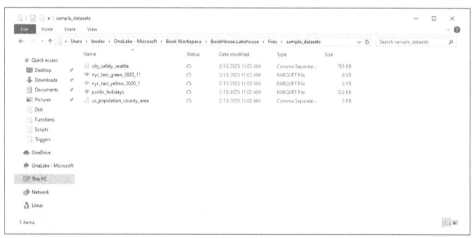

Figure 3-10. Item level in OneLake file explorer

In addition, we can see the Parquet files backing our warehouse (see Figure 3-11).

Figure 3-11. Parquet files backing a warehouse table in OneLake file explorer

Summary

OneLake stands out as a modern and robust data lake solution, integral to Microsoft Fabric, designed to meet the complex data management and analytics needs of today's businesses. By storing all data in a centralized lake, OneLake leverages unified storage to eliminate data silos and support diverse data types, from structured to unstructured. It incorporates the advanced data formats Delta and Iceberg for efficient data handling, and the separation of compute and storage enhances scalability and cost-effectiveness. OneLake's seamless integration with Microsoft's suite of tools and third-party services, coupled with its advanced security and compliance features, makes it a versatile and powerful platform. This flexibility ensures that businesses can drive innovation, gain comprehensive insights, and maintain a competitive edge in an increasingly data-driven world.

In the next part of this book, we will deep dive into the different experiences—or features—and capabilities of Fabric!

PART II
The Features: A Deep Dive

In this section, we'll go through all the *experiences* in Microsoft Fabric—Fabric's core features—explaining what each one does and how it works.

We'll break down each experience with step-by-step guidance and real-world examples, showing you how to apply it effectively. This will help not only in understanding the experiences' technical workings but also in seeing their practical value for solving data challenges. The key experiences we will explore include:

Data Factory
  The orchestration and data movement engine of Fabric, enabling pipelines and ETL/ELT processes

Data Engineering
  A powerful environment for working with large-scale data processing, optimized for Spark workloads

Data Warehousing
  A fully managed, scalable solution for building structured, analytical data stores

Data Science
  Tools and workflows designed for machine learning, model training, and AI-powered analytics

Real-Time Intelligence
  A framework for processing streaming data, enabling immediate insights and decision making

Power BI

The analytics and visualization powerhouse of Fabric, allowing interactive reporting and dashboards

SQL Databases

Fabric's answer to bridging the gap between analytical and OLTP workloads

Mirroring

A capability for syncing and managing external data sources within Fabric without complex data movement

GraphQL

An API layer for querying and interacting with data in a flexible and efficient way

AI and Copilots

AI-driven assistants that enhance productivity by automating tasks and generating insights

This deep dive will provide detailed explanations, practical steps, and real-world use cases for each experience, helping you understand not just how they work but how they can be applied effectively in different data scenarios.

## CHAPTER 4

Data Factory

This chapter kicks off Part II of this book, where we will dive into all the different features and experiences that Microsoft Fabric has to offer. The first feature we'll explore is Data Factory. This chapter can be considered a stepping-stone to Chapter 5, where we'll show you how Data Factory and Data Engineering work together.

Microsoft Fabric Data Factory is a cloud-based data integration service designed to make ETL and ELT (extract, load, transform) processes as smooth as possible. It is the go-to service for orchestrating your ETL. One of its standout features is the ability to cater to users across a spectrum of technical expertise. For those seeking a no-code or low-code experience, Data Factory provides an intuitive drag-and-drop interface that allows users to design, orchestrate, and manage data pipelines visually. This makes it ideal for business analysts or data professionals who want to focus on workflows without diving into the complexities of coding.

For example, a marketing team might need to automate the process of aggregating data from a web analytics platform, a CRM, and an ad platform. Using Data Factory's no-code interface, team members can create a pipeline that extracts data from all three sources, performs basic transformations like filtering and joining, and loads the results into a central data warehouse—all without writing a single line of code. This simplicity empowers nontechnical users to build effective data solutions independently.

However, Data Factory doesn't stop at no-code solutions. For data engineers or advanced users who need greater control and flexibility, the platform integrates code-heavy options such as notebooks. These notebooks, which will be explored in depth in Chapter 5, enable users to implement custom transformations, perform advanced analytics, or handle specialized use cases using multiple languages such as PySpark and Spark SQL. For example, a data engineering team working on fraud detection might use notebooks to apply machine learning models to transaction data as part of their pipeline.

This dual functionality makes Microsoft Fabric Data Factory a versatile tool, bridging the gap between no-code simplicity and the power of advanced, code-driven customization. It ensures that organizations can scale their data operations while catering to the needs of diverse roles, from business analysts to data scientists and engineers.

In the next section, we'll take a closer look at pipelines and how they facilitate data movement and orchestration in Data Factory.

 Data Factory in Fabric is not the same thing as Azure Data Factory, which you may have worked with before. While it may feel the same in some cases, it is a different product; this means that you cannot simply "copy and paste" your Azure Data Factory workloads into Fabric Data Factory.

Pipelines

In Microsoft Fabric Data Factory, pipelines play a vital role in organizing and automating data workflows, from ingestion and transformation to delivery. A *pipeline* serves as a logical framework, grouping together activities that allow users to manage and automate tasks such as moving, preparing, and transforming data across multiple sources and destinations. Pipelines enable the creation of comprehensive data flows that connect diverse systems, apply necessary transformations, and deliver data to various storage environments like data lakes and warehouses.

Each pipeline is composed of one or more activities, each representing a distinct operation. These activities range from basic copy tasks, which handle data movement between sources and destinations, to data flow tasks, which carry out complex transformations. Pipelines allow users to create workflows that link these tasks, manage dependencies, and set up execution triggers, such as scheduled runs or event-based actions. Additionally, control activities like loops, conditionals, and error handling help ensure pipelines are both dynamic and resilient.

In Data Factory, pipelines are tightly integrated with the wider Microsoft Fabric ecosystem, making it easier to connect with services such as Fabric Lakehouse, Data Warehouse, and real-time analytics. This integration enables businesses to efficiently move, process, and manage their data within a unified platform, reducing the need for extensive configurations to make all components in your solution work together. Fabric Data Factory aims to streamline the creation of data workflows with no-code or low-code interfaces, while still providing the flexibility to support more complex use cases.

A Step-by-Step Guide to a Data Pipeline

You created your Fabric capacity and workspace in Part I, so let's create a data pipeline in Data Factory.

Given that your data estate will look different from ours, we do not expect you to follow along "hands on" for every step. The goal for our step-by-step guides is not for you to entirely replicate the result but to give you a solid understanding of processes and flows.

We will start by selecting Create and selecting the Data pipeline item (see Figure 4-1).

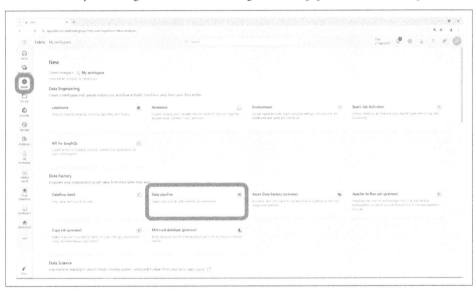

Figure 4-1. Creating a new pipeline

Just like with previous items, you'll need to provide a name. We'll name this one "Book Pipeline" as shown in Figure 4-2.

Figure 4-2. Naming the pipeline

By default, your pipelines will be named "pipeline" followed by a number pipeline1, pipeline2, etc. Make sure to establish and adhere to a proper naming convention!

This is the space where you will build your data pipeline. The designer features a central canvas for organizing activities and a toolbox on the left that offers a range of activities to choose from. You can see a few of them showcased in Figure 4-3.

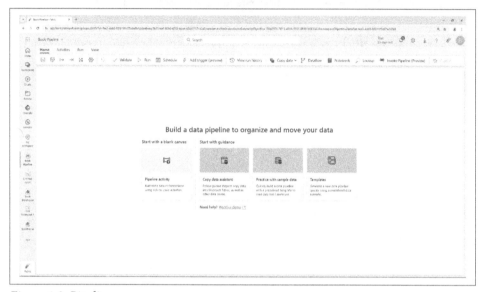

Figure 4-3. Pipeline canvas

You now have created your first pipeline, but it doesn't contain any activities yet. In the next sections of this chapter, we'll explore how to move and transform data as well as how to orchestrate and execute those tasks.

Moving and Transforming Data

The most important part of Data Factory is certainly data movement. We can also modify and transform our data further down the road, but those tasks require you to get the data into Fabric first. Data Factory offers three main ways to move data, differing in features and complexity: *Copy activity*, *Dataflow Gen 2*, and *Copy job*.

Copy activity

The Copy activity is a critical task within a Data Factory pipeline, designed to handle data movement between various sources and destinations. Rather than being a stand-alone item, it serves as part of a larger orchestration process, working alongside other activities in the pipeline to automate data workflows. The Copy activity allows data transfer between on-premises systems and cloud environments, supporting scenarios where businesses need to move large amounts of data from legacy systems to modern cloud infrastructures or between various cloud services. This flexibility makes it a powerful tool for enterprises undergoing digital transformation.

One of the key advantages of the Copy activity is its ability to work across diverse environments, enabling smooth data transfers from on-premises data centers to cloud-based systems like ADLS or Amazon S3. With built-in connectors for databases, file systems, SaaS applications, and cloud storage, it supports a wide array of data sources, making it versatile enough for any data integration scenario. Whether you're dealing with relational databases like SQL Server or Oracle or working with cloud storage systems, the Copy activity ensures that data can be read and written across multiple platforms.

To optimize performance, the Copy activity allows for customization of throughput and parallelism, which influence how quickly data is transferred and how many tasks can be processed simultaneously. These settings are crucial for improving data transfer speeds, particularly when handling large datasets or working across cloud environments where bandwidth and processing power are variable. By tuning throughput and parallelism, you can ensure that your pipeline makes the most efficient use of resources, balancing data transfer speed with system load.

The Copy activity provides several strategies to handle large-scale data transfers, including staging, partitioning, and compression. *Staging* helps manage data transfers by temporarily storing the data in an intermediary location before delivering it to its final destination. *Partitioning* splits large datasets into smaller chunks for parallel processing to speed up transfers, while *compression* reduces the size of the data being transferred, saving bandwidth and time, especially in cloud-to-cloud or cross-region data transfers.

Data Factory supports an extensive list of data sources, making the Copy activity adaptable to various scenarios. Supported sources include the on-premises databases SQL Server, Oracle, and MySQL, as well as cloud storage options Azure Blob Storage, Amazon S3, and Google Cloud Storage. Additionally, SaaS platforms including Salesforce and Google Analytics can be integrated, allowing you to pull data from numerous enterprise systems into a unified pipeline.

To finish this section up, let's walk through the steps required to add a Copy activity to our previously created pipeline.

In the pipeline designer, select Copy activity and select "Add to canvas" (see Figure 4-4). This will be the core task in your pipeline, handling the movement of data.

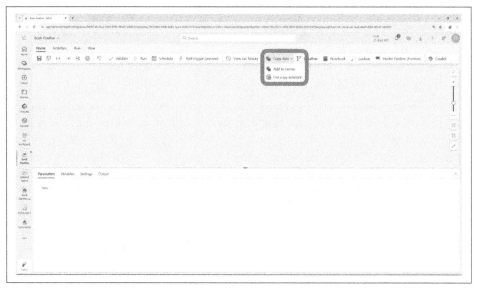

Figure 4-4. Adding a Copy activity

When you add a Copy activity, the General settings tab displays the name, description, and whether it is activated (see Figure 4-5).

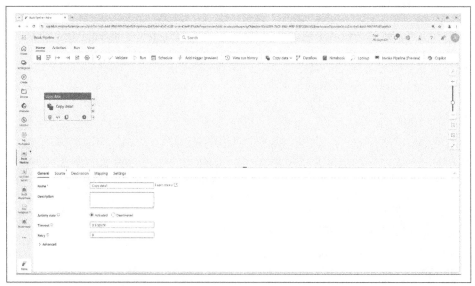

Figure 4-5. Copy activity General tab

To move data, we first need to configure the source. Click on the Source tab and create a new reference to your source by selecting the appropriate data source (e.g.,

SQL Server, Azure Blob Storage) and entering the necessary connection details, such as file paths, database names, and credentials (shown in Figure 4-6).

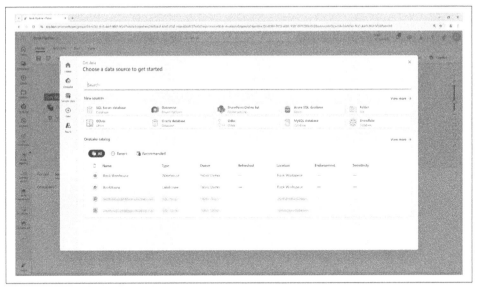

Figure 4-6. Selecting the source for the Copy activity

Accessing data from a source requires that the source either have a *public endpoint* and be accessible to Fabric or have a *gateway* set up. By default, a connection will be made under the context of your user.

A public endpoint is an internet-accessible address that allows direct connections to a data source, enabling external applications to retrieve data without needing additional network configurations, typically relying on authentication and firewall rules for security.

The on-premises data gateway (*https://oreil.ly/SGbU_*) is a bridge that securely connects Microsoft cloud services to on-premises data sources. It allows users to run queries and refresh data without exposing their internal network by encrypting traffic and relaying requests through a secure outbound connection.

After setting up the source, move to the Destination tab to define the data destination. Create a new dataset for the destination, select the target destination (e.g., Azure Data Lake, SQL database, Amazon S3), and configure the connection details for the destination system (shown in Figure 4-7). When moving data into Fabric, your destination will typically be either be a lakehouse or a warehouse.

Figure 4-7. Copy activity Destination tab

In the Mapping tab, you can define how the fields from the source map to the destination. This step allows manual field mapping if the data structures differ between the source and destination, or you can opt for automatic mapping if the fields match by name and data type (shown in Figure 4-8). This means that the entire Mapping tab is optional.

Figure 4-8. Copy activity Mapping tab

The final tab, Settings, allows you to manage parallelism and other settings like logging and fault tolerance. To get started, you can leave all of those at their defaults (shown in Figure 4-9).

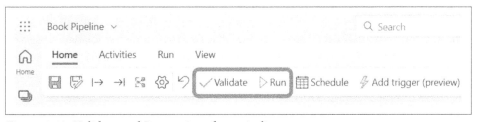

| General | Source | Destination | Mapping | **Settings** |

Intelligent throughput optimization ⓘ   Auto ⌄

☐ Use custom value

Degree of copy parallelism ⓘ   Auto ⌄

Fault tolerance ⓘ   ⌄

Enable logging ⓘ   ☐

Enable staging ⓘ   ☐

Figure 4-9. Copy activity Settings tab

By following these steps, you've successfully created your first Copy activity within a pipeline.

To make sure all the required settings have been specified, you can either validate or run the pipeline (not the individual task, but the entire pipeline!) using the buttons highlighted in Figure 4-10.

Validating a pipeline checks whether the required settings exist and look plausible. It does not run a full simulation, so any issues with the source, such as conversion errors, would not be found at this point but only when running the pipeline.

Book Pipeline ⌄   Q Search

Home   Activities   Run   View

Home

💾 📝 ⊢→ →⊣ ⚙ ↺   ✓ Validate   ▷ Run   ⊞ Schedule   ⚡ Add trigger (preview)

Figure 4-10. Validate and Run options for a pipeline

Dataflow Gen 2

Unlike the Copy activity, a Dataflow Gen 2 is not necessarily part of a pipeline, but a pipeline has the capability to execute a Dataflow. A Dataflow is, by default, a standalone Fabric item that *can* be added as a pipeline activity. Since we're already working with a pipeline, we'll stay in that pipeline and add a new Dataflow to it by selecting the Dataflow button (see Figure 4-11).

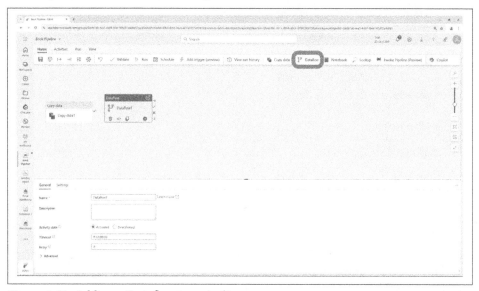

Figure 4-11. Adding a Dataflow to a pipeline

Dataflow Gen 2 in Microsoft Fabric marks a significant advancement in the platform's data transformation capabilities. It introduces more powerful, scalable, and flexible data flows that are optimized to handle complex and large-scale data scenarios through a no-code/low-code solution. Unlike previous iterations, Dataflow Gen 2 is deeply integrated with the Microsoft Fabric ecosystem, allowing for data transformations directly within data lakes, warehouses, and other storage solutions. One of its core benefits is the ability to manage massive data volumes and advanced transformations without requiring data movement across systems.

The most notable enhancement in Dataflow Gen 2 is its focus on scalability and performance. Leveraging cloud native distributed compute and storage infrastructure, it can process data at petabyte scale without sacrificing efficiency. The incorporation of in-memory processing accelerates transformations by minimizing the time spent on I/O operations, ensuring that even complex Dataflows are executed swiftly. This enables organizations to manage their data operations cost-effectively, while fully utilizing the power of cloud computing to handle growing data workloads.

As stated previously, another major advantage of Dataflow Gen 2 is its no-code and low-code interface, which enables users to build complex data transformations visually by selecting preconfigured complex transformations and linking datasets, without writing code. It is particularly beneficial for data professionals who may lack coding expertise but still need to carry out intricate operations such as joins, aggregations, filters, and data cleaning. Dataflow Gen 2 supports a variety of transformations, from basic row-level changes to advanced operations like processing unstructured data and working with nested structures, making it adaptable to a wide range of use cases.

Additionally, Dataflow Gen 2 integrates with the Microsoft Fabric environment, making it easy for users to access and transform data from other Fabric services including Fabric Lakehouse, Real-Time Analytics, and Data Warehouse. This integration eliminates the need for custom connectors or manual data migration, facilitating a smoother data flow across environments and data estates. The built-in monitoring and debugging tools also ensure that users can track and optimize performance in real time, ensuring that their data transformations are both efficient and error-free.

Our previous step only added a link to a Dataflow in our pipeline. We can now either go back to the Create menu or simply select New in the Settings of the Dataflow in the pipeline (see Figure 4-12).

Figure 4-12. New Dataflow from pipeline

As with the Copy activity, we'll start by adding a source (see Figure 4-13). This can be done right from the canvas or with the "Get Data" icon on the upper left.

Figure 4-13. Dataflow canvas

Select "Get data from another source" to get a full overview of supported data sources.

If you select New, you will see a full list that ranges from manually uploading files over Microsoft offerings to directly accessing third-party databases and software through hundreds of connectors (see Figure 4-14).

Let's shorten that list by filtering on Fabric items and selecting a lakehouse as our source (see Figure 4-15).

The wizard will walk you through connecting to your lakehouse and selecting the data you want to load, even providing a preview.

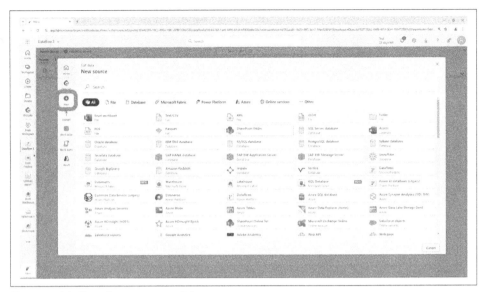

Figure 4-14. Dataflow-supported data sources

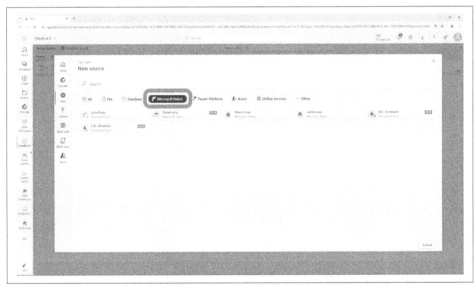

Figure 4-15. Dataflow Fabric sources

You can finalize this step by selecting the Create button (illustrated in Figure 4-16).

Figure 4-16. Data preview for Dataflow Fabric source

In the Dataflow that you just got created, you now have the option to add all kinds of transformations to your data (see the Transform tab in Figure 4-17).

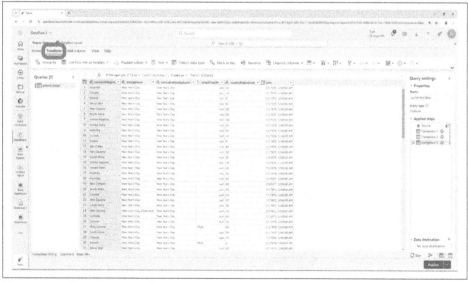

Figure 4-17. Dataflow transformations

Transformations enable you to change data types, add calculated columns, remove or rename columns, filter your data, and much more.

Once you've applied all your transformations, pick a destination for your data and publish your Dataflow (both steps shown in Figure 4-18).

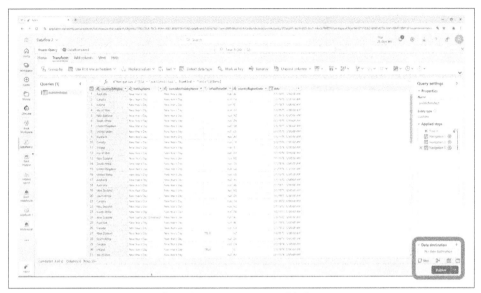

Figure 4-18. Selecting a Dataflow destination and publishing

Copy job

The Fabric Copy job is a powerful item for managing and automating data ingestion, functioning independently like Dataflows. This independence allows users to create, manage, and run Copy jobs outside of broader workflows, providing flexibility in how data is ingested and moved between systems. The Copy job simplifies the complexities of large-scale data ingestion, making it easier to transfer vast amounts of data without extensive coding or manual effort.

One of the standout features of the Fabric Copy job is its ability to manage incremental data loads, which is particularly beneficial for large datasets. Instead of reloading entire datasets, the Copy job transfers only the data that has changed by tracking modifications through a watermark column—typically a datetime or integer field —that helps identify previously copied records. This approach not only improves efficiency and reduces the load on source systems but also accelerates data ingestion. Additionally, performance optimization is a key aspect of the Copy job; it runs distributed queries while ensuring that only data within the specified watermark range is transferred, minimizing unnecessary data movement. This method significantly enhances ingestion speed compared to a single-threaded full load, making the Copy job ideal for large datasets and complex workflows that require scalability and high performance.

The Fabric Copy job is a simple way to automate data ingestion. Its ability to handle incremental loads, schedule automated refreshes, and optimize performance through distributed querying makes it a versatile solution for various data scenarios. While the majority of use cases can be handled effectively by the Copy job, more complex data environments may require more advanced techniques, such as the ability to identify modified records. Nonetheless, for most organizations, the Copy job provides a streamlined and efficient way to ensure that data pipelines remain up-to-date and fully optimized.

Like the Dataflow, a Copy job is a separate item, so it must be created from the Data Factory section of the Create page. Unlike a Dataflow, at the time of writing, it cannot be created from a Pipeline canvas.

To create a new Copy job, navigate to the Create Page and select Copy job as shown in Figure 4-19.

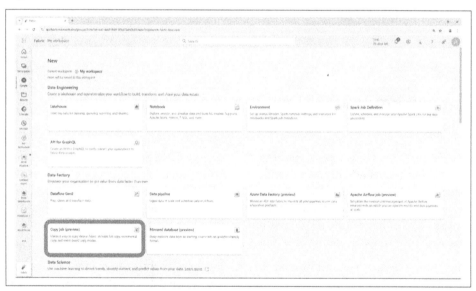

Figure 4-19. Creating a new Copy job

After providing a name for the job, a wizard will display (shown in Figure 4-20) and walk you through the setup.

First, you'll enter the source and destination information, just like for the other data movement mechanisms.

On the Settings dialog, however (Figure 4-21), you can choose between a full load and an incremental load. The latter requires a numeric or date column to detect changes and will base its load patterns on that column.

Figure 4-20. Copy job wizard

Figure 4-21. Copy job wizard Settings dialog

Depending on your source, you may also be able to pick a streaming copy of your data.

Comparing Data Movement Functions

When comparing Copy activity, Dataflow, and Copy job in Microsoft Fabric, key differences emerge:

Execution context
> Copy activity is always embedded within a pipeline. It cannot exist independently, meaning its scheduling and orchestration depend on the broader pipeline workflow. Dataflow and Copy job, however, are standalone items. This independence allows them to be created, configured, and executed separately from specific pipelines, providing more flexibility for individual or recurring tasks.

Primary function
> The main purpose of both Copy activity and Copy job is data movement. They focus on transferring data from one location to another, without performing transformations along the way. Dataflow, on the other hand, specializes in data transformation. While it also moves data, its strength lies in applying complex transformations (like joins, aggregations, or filtering) to the data during the process. Copy activity and Copy job do not provide this advanced level of transformation natively.

Data transformation capabilities
> Dataflow is designed with rich transformation capabilities, including a no-code/low-code interface that allows users to perform advanced transformations visually. It's ideal when you need to modify or enrich data as it moves between systems.

Scheduling and automation
> Copy jobs and Dataflows can be scheduled to run independently of a pipeline. This makes them highly suitable for automated, recurring workflows, especially when regular updates or transformations are required. Copy activity, being a part of a pipeline, relies on the pipeline's triggers and cannot be scheduled independently. It depends on pipeline execution logic for automation.

Use cases
> Copy activity is best suited for simple data movement within a larger pipeline where it complements other tasks, such as data validation or notification. Copy job is ideal for large-scale, recurring data ingestion, particularly when you need an independent, automated solution for copying data across systems. Dataflow is the tool of choice when the task involves not just moving but also transforming data, such as when applying complex business rules or cleaning up datasets before storing them in a destination.

Which method you choose may come down to personal preference. Often we see Dataflows as the "almost default" among citizen data engineers who heavily rely on Power Query and its interface.

Extending Data Orchestration

While data movement is certainly the most important part of Data Factory, as mentioned above, there are many other activities that allow for the creation of feature rich pipelines and orchestrations.

The movement tasks that we already covered as well as all other activities can be found on the Activities tab. Click the ellipses ("…") for a complete, searchable list of all supported activities (see Figure 4-22).

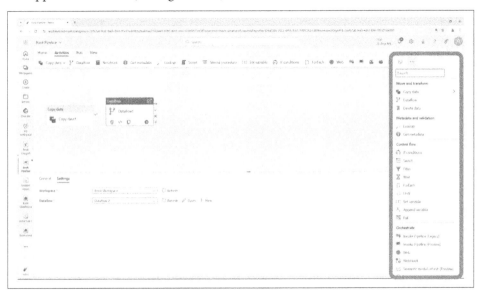

Figure 4-22. Pipeline activities

These activities are grouped into the following categories:

Move and transform
    These are the activities used to move data that we discussed in the previous sections. The only additional activity here is "Delete data," which you'd use for deleting data from supported data stores, by removing files, entire folders, or specific rows based on defined conditions.

Metadata and validation
    This group enables you to query for a single value (e.g., to later use in a variable) or for an entire metadata table from different sources, either of which can then be used in your pipeline. For example, they could be used to parameterize your

pipeline, or they could help automate your Copy activities by using a central repository that controls which tables to load rather than creating a manual Copy activity for each table.

Control flow

In this group, you'll find tools to control your pipeline with loops, variables, and conditions. It also contains additional activities to wait for other activities that finish or to throw an error.

Orchestrate

This group allows you to run other activities such as other pipelines, notebooks, calling web endpoints, Azure Functions, and more. These activities' sole purpose is to call and control other activities, so they do not perform any movements or transformations themselves.

Notifications

The activities in this group allow you to send out notifications through either email (using an Outlook 365 connection) or Teams, which can be useful to let your users know when a specific pipeline has completed or failed.

Transform

These activities allow you to transform your data in your language and method-ology of choice through stored procedures, notebooks, Spark jobs, scripts, or KQL.

Machine learning

There's only one activity in this group, which allows you to run Azure Machine Learning jobs, meaning you can reference and execute an existing job in Azure ML from a pipeline.

Take a look at Figure 4-23 for an example of a full pipeline, that brings all these pieces together.

This showcases again how Data Factory allows for a no-code approach to orchestrate your data movement and transformation, making it the go-to solution for such needs in Fabric.

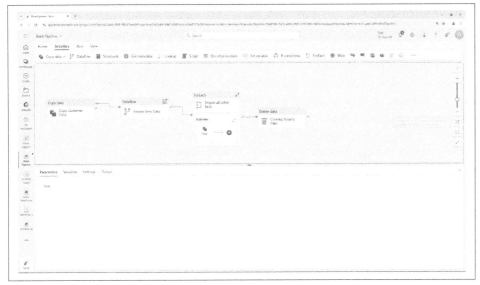

Figure 4-23. Full orchestration pipeline example

Schedules and Triggers

We already looked into running a pipeline or task manually, which is great for ad hoc requests and testing. But running manually isn't a great option for jobs that run every hour or in the middle of the night.

This is where schedules and triggers come into play; both can be found right next to the Run button (see Figure 4-24).

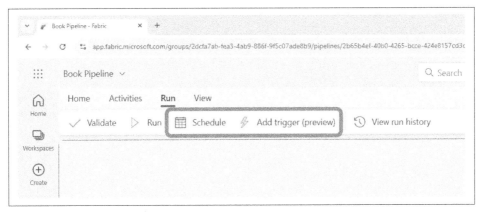

Figure 4-24. Schedule and trigger options

Schedules

In Data Factory, schedules are a powerful feature used to automate the execution of pipelines at predefined intervals, ensuring that data workflows are consistently and reliably run without manual intervention. A schedule-based trigger allows users to specify when a pipeline should start—such as hourly, daily, weekly, or monthly—or even with more customized intervals. This is particularly useful for recurring tasks like nightly ETL processes, regular data refreshes, or periodic data backups. This scheduling flexibility means you can set the exact time and frequency of execution, making it easy to align data processes with business needs.

Schedules also offer time zone and recurrence options, enabling users to adjust pipeline execution based on regional or global requirements. You can configure the trigger to account for specific time ranges, ensuring that pipelines run only within a designated window (for example, between 9 A.M. and 5 P.M. in a specific time zone). Moreover, scheduling options can include start and end dates, allowing for temporary data workflows that run only during a specific project period. By using schedule-based triggers, users ensure that data pipelines are executed consistently, which is vital for maintaining up-to-date and synchronized data across different systems.

To add a schedule, simply select the Schedule button shown in Figure 4-24 and then configure the timing and frequency of the pipeline's execution, as shown in Figure 4-25. Make sure to activate the schedule for it to be executed.

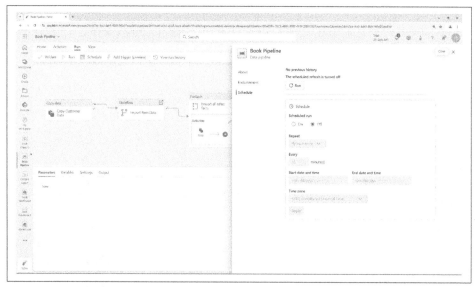

Figure 4-25. Schedule settings

Triggers

Unlike schedules, which run your pipeline at a certain time, triggers fire up your pipeline based on external events. To add a trigger, first select the "Add trigger" button. The most important setting is which events the trigger should react to. (See the Source field in Figure 4-26.)

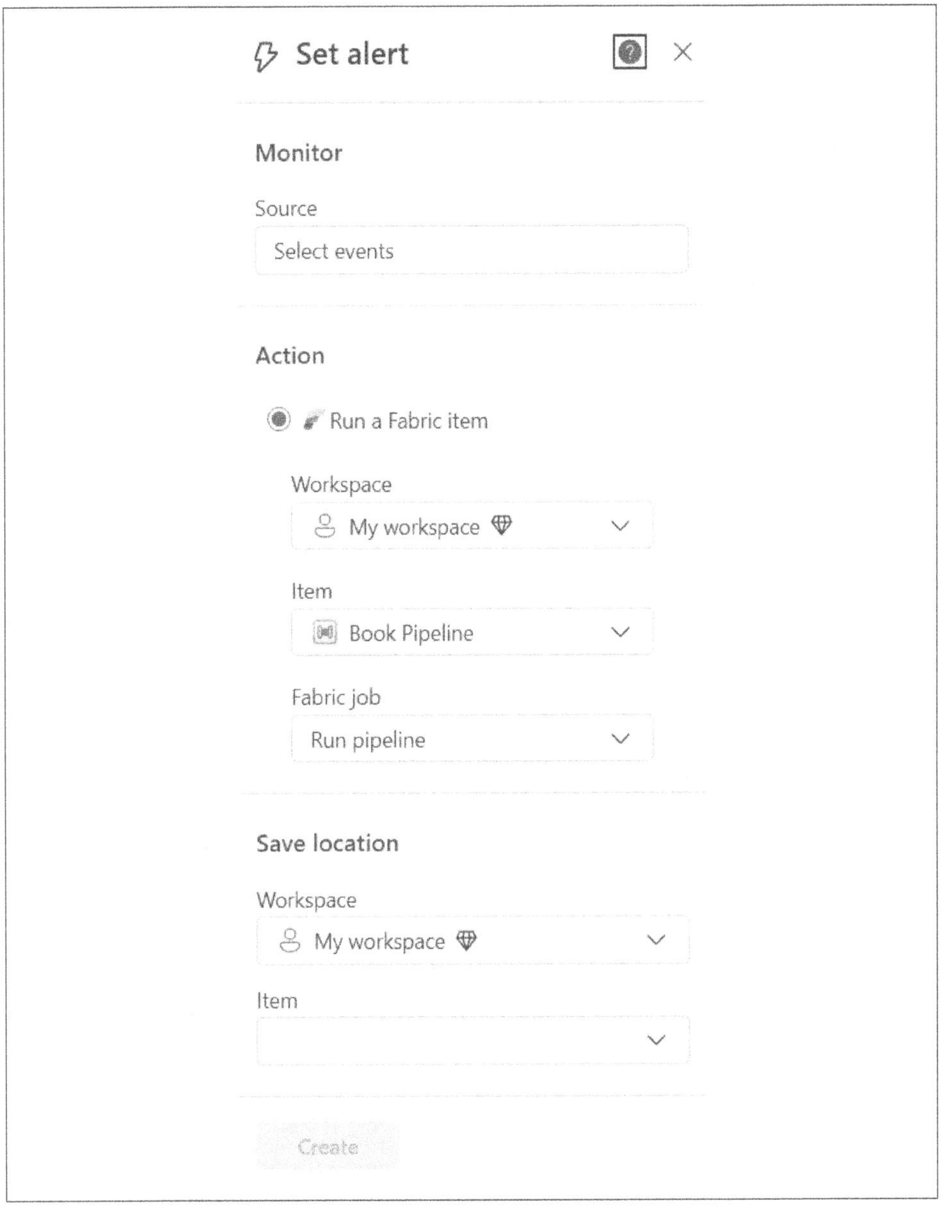

Figure 4-26. Trigger basic settings

Select "Select events" and select a data source. At the time of writing, Azure Blob Storage is the only option (see Figure 4-27)

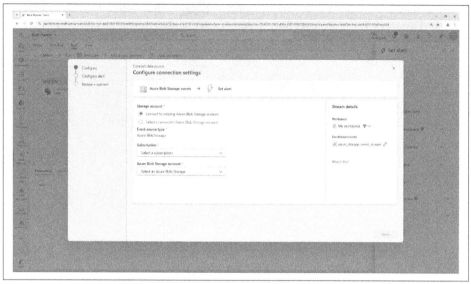

Figure 4-27. Selecting a data source for Triggers

By monitoring your items on a blob container for changes, you can run your ETL pipeline as soon as a new file has been added.

Apache Airflow

In addition to pipelines, Data Factory supports using Apache Airflow for orchestration. While we will not deep dive into Airflow—that would be a book in itself—let's at least give you a high-level overview. Apache Airflow is an open source platform used to programmatically schedule and monitor workflows. It enables you to define, schedule, and manage complex data workflows or pipelines through *directed acyclic graphs* (DAGs). A DAG is essentially a collection of tasks with defined dependencies that ensure the tasks are executed in a specific order.

Airflow is commonly used in data engineering and data science for automating tasks like ETL processes, data migration, and other workflows that require careful scheduling and dependency management. It provides the ability to schedule tasks to run at specific intervals, automating recurring processes without manual intervention. Task dependencies can also be defined, ensuring that tasks are executed in the correct sequence.

Airflow is highly extensible, with a broad range of prebuilt integrations to work with various databases, cloud platforms, and services. Users can also create custom integrations to meet specific needs. Airflow comes with a user-friendly interface for monitoring the status of workflows and tasks, along with detailed logging to help with troubleshooting. It's also designed to be scalable, handling larger workflows and data volumes as the need for more complex automation grows.

Summary

Microsoft Fabric Data Factory is a cloud native service for managing, processing, and orchestrating data workflows. It handles tasks from extracting raw data to transforming and loading it into target systems for analysis. Data Factory seamlessly integrates data across cloud, on-premises, and hybrid environments.

Supporting both ETL and ELT processes, it offers flexibility in cleaning and transforming data either before or after loading. Data Factory automates workflows through scheduling and triggers, and its no-code/low-code interface makes it accessible to both technical and nontechnical users. Integration with other Microsoft Fabric services ensures smooth data flows across your organization's architecture.

In short, Microsoft Fabric Data Factory simplifies and scales modern data engineering workflows.

In Chapter 5, we'll look into the Data Engineering experience in Microsoft Fabric.

Data Engineering

In Chapter 4, we looked into how we can use the tools and mechanisms in Data Factory to load data into Fabric; in this chapter, we'll focus on the Data Engineering experience.

Data engineering involves creating the technical infrastructure required to capture, store, and process significant volumes of data. This field includes designing pipelines to extract data from multiple sources, transforming it to ensure high quality and uniformity, and storing it in databases or storage solutions where it can be analyzed. Data engineers use a variety of technologies to keep these systems reliable, efficient, and scalable. Their work ensures that data is readily available and usable, forming the backbone of data analytics and supporting informed, data-driven decisions within businesses.

A real-world example of data engineering in action can be seen in an ecommerce company that processes millions of transactions daily. Using Microsoft Fabric, data engineers design pipelines that extract raw sales data from various sources, such as web logs, customer databases, and third-party payment processors. Spark jobs running in notebooks clean and aggregate this data—removing duplicates, handling missing values, and standardizing formats—before storing it in a lakehouse for further analysis. Orchestration tools ensure that these processes run seamlessly at scheduled intervals, enabling real-time inventory updates and dynamic pricing strategies. This end-to-end workflow allows business analysts and data scientists to access high-quality, structured data for sales forecasting, customer segmentation, and personalized marketing campaigns, showcasing the critical role of data engineering in driving data-driven decision making.

In data engineering, data processing, transformation, and orchestration are vital roles that convert raw data into actionable insights, often through tools like Spark, notebooks, pipelines, and jobs. Data processing entails cleaning, aggregating, and structuring raw data from multiple sources, leveraging Spark's capacity to handle large datasets efficiently and at scale. Transformation refines this data to meet analytical and business requirements. Using notebooks, data engineers can iteratively transform, visualize, and verify data, fostering collaboration and precision. Orchestration then automates and schedules these workflows, ensuring each stage operates reliably and sequentially. Pipelines and jobs empower data engineers to design, track, and manage these workflows, allowing control over dependencies, triggers, and scheduling. Together, these functions enable a cohesive process that prepares high-quality, timely data for analytics and machine learning, supporting a seamless journey from data ingestion to insightful results.

This also implies that certain tasks from Chapter 4—for example, pipelines—are part of a data engineer's role. In Microsoft Fabric, within the Data Engineering experience, data is organized and stored in lakehouses.

Fundamentals of a Lakehouse

A *lakehouse* is a modern data architecture that blends the strengths of a data lake with advanced data management features into a unified platform. At its core, a lakehouse enables organizations to manage all types of data—structured, semi-structured, and unstructured—within a single environment. The primary advantage of a lakehouse is its ability to store raw data in its native format, such as JSON, images, videos, or logs, while also allowing for more complex processing and analytics on that data, including real-time insights and machine learning applications. Unlike traditional storage systems, which often require separate environments for different data formats, the lakehouse brings everything together into a cohesive platform that is both scalable and flexible.

Lakehouses also provide robust data management capabilities, such as enforcement of schema definitions, data versioning, and ACID transactions.

> *ACID transactions* are a set of properties that ensure reliable database processing: atomicity (all-or-nothing execution), consistency (preservation of data integrity), isolation (independent operation of transactions), and durability (permanent changes once a transaction is complete). These properties ensure reliable transaction processing and maintain data accuracy.

These characteristics ensure data integrity and consistency across various processes, making it easier for organizations to manage, query, and analyze large datasets. A key feature of the lakehouse architecture is its support for advanced analytics workloads, enabling machine learning, artificial intelligence, and big data processing all from the same platform. Additionally, a lakehouse can handle massive volumes of data, scaling easily to accommodate growing data needs without compromising performance.

By supporting multiple data formats and use cases, lakehouses create a streamlined environment for data teams to collaborate, reducing the need for multiple platforms or complex data pipelines. This flexibility allows organizations to ingest, process, and analyze data at scale while keeping the complexity of infrastructure low, making lakehouses a popular choice for modern, data-driven enterprises seeking to unlock the full value of their data.

Lakehouses Versus Data Lakes

You may be thinking, Isn't a lakehouse the same as a data lake?

In fact, a data lake and a lakehouse represent two distinct approaches to data storage and processing, each designed to meet different needs. As we discussed in Chapter 3, a *data lake* is a large, scalable repository that stores massive amounts of raw, unstructured, or semi-structured data in its original format, supporting a wide range of data types, including text, images, video, audio, and structured datasets from databases. This flexibility makes data lakes ideal for handling "big data" and for analytics, machine learning, and data science use cases. However, without careful management and governance, data lakes can become disorganized and challenging to query, sometimes leading to what's known as a "data swamp."

In contrast, a *lakehouse* blends the flexibility of a data lake with the structure and management capabilities of a data warehouse. It provides schema enforcement, data versioning, and transaction support, enabling more efficient data querying and analytics. By supporting both structured and unstructured data, a lakehouse enables organizations to perform SQL-based analytics directly on large datasets without needing to move data into a separate data warehouse. This hybrid architecture makes lakehouses an attractive option for companies looking to streamline their data infrastructure, uniting storage and analytics in a single, more manageable platform (see Figure 5-1). The data of a lakehouse is usually stored in a data lake (in the case of Fabric, it's stored in OneLake), so it's more of a value-added approach, rather than an entirely different concept.

If you're already familiar with the concept of data warehousing, your next question might be, What's the difference between a lakehouse and a warehouse then? We'll get to that in Chapter 6!

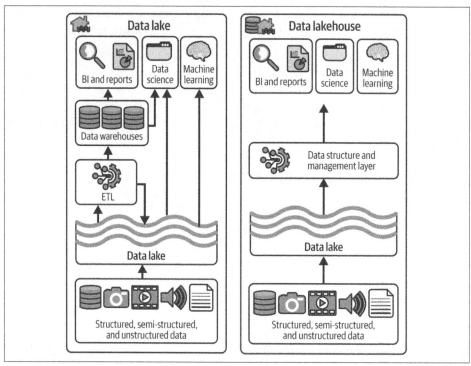

Figure 5-1. Data lake versus data lakehouse

The Medallion Architecture

Data in a lakehouse is often organized using what's called *medallion architecture*. Medallion architecture is a structured approach to lakehouse design that organizes data across distinct layers, enhancing data quality, accessibility, and utility. Data is segmented into three stages—bronze, silver, and gold—each representing a step in the data's journey from raw intake to business-ready output. This naming is purely a suggestion: you can name your layers and stages however you see fit, and, in theory, you could keep all your data in one layer.

Bronze layer—raw data

The bronze layer serves as the initial storage for raw data from diverse sources, where data is often retained in its original form. This layer acts as a historical record, preserving unprocessed data for potential reprocessing or analysis. The data here is only minimally organized, with basic metadata applied to support accessibility.

Silver layer—cleaned and enriched data

The silver layer refines data further. Data undergoes processes to clean, enrich, and standardize formats; remove duplicates; and address missing values. Data engineers use this layer to provide a structured view that is consistent and reliable, ideal for foundational analytics and deeper business insights.

Gold layer—business-ready data

The gold layer is the culmination, where data is fully processed, aggregated, and tailored to meet specific business needs. This layer offers a "single source of truth" for reporting, dashboards, and high-performance analytics, aligning data to specific use cases with high-quality standards for decision making. This is where you'd build out your fact and dimensional tables, which will then be used by your report developers.

This organized layering in the medallion architecture supports data governance, reliability, and accessibility, ensuring that organizations can manage data at scale and convert it effectively from raw information into valuable, actionable insights (see Figure 5-2).

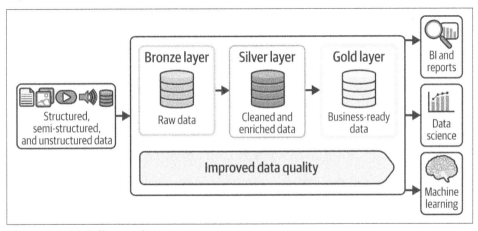

Figure 5-2. Medallion architecture

While the medallion architecture is not the only way to organize your lakehouse, it is one of the most popular ways and has become the de facto standard used by most data engineers. Just like the naming of the layers, the number of layers is entirely up to you. While most organizations manage fine with three layers, we've also seen cases where additional layers (e.g., a platinum layer) have been added.

Lakehouses in Microsoft Fabric

Although *lakehouse* is a generic term, there are some specifics to the way a lakehouse is implemented in Fabric.

Lakehouse Schemas

In Microsoft Fabric, a *lakehouse schema* defines the structure and organization of data within the lakehouse, combining elements of both a data lake and a data warehouse to support analytics and data management in a single unified environment. The lakehouse schema is designed to allow both structured and unstructured data to coexist and be accessed using various analytics tools, bridging the gap between raw data storage and structured, query-optimized data for analytics and reporting. Lakehouse schemas are also a very elegant way to build your medallion architecture. So rather than separating your layers across multiple lakehouses, you can simply put your tables into different schemas (we'll elaborate more on this later in this chapter).

Integrating Data into a Lakehouse

You have several options to move data into your lakehouse. We discussed the Data Factory in Chapter 4, as well as shortcuts in Chapter 3, but there are two more ways to get data into a lakehouse: streaming (which we'll cover in Chapter 8) and directly updating data in OneLake, such as through OneLake file explorer.

You may remember from Chapter 3 that, under the hood, OneLake offers the same APIs as any other ADSL Gen 2. This means you can simply copy files to it and then consume those files because a lakehouse natively supports accessing data stored in files rather than tables.

Querying and Working with Data in Your Lakehouse

One very popular and easy way to access your lakehouse is with the SQL analytics endpoint that gets created automatically when you deploy a lakehouse, as we saw in Chapter 2. The SQL endpoint is a valid way to query your lakehouse if SQL is the your language of choice.

For a lakehouse, the SQL endpoint is read-only!

Many engineers have different preferences—or additional requirements—that SQL can't (easily) satisfy. This is where the other—probably more popular—approach comes into play: notebooks.

Notebooks play a vital role in data engineering, offering a cohesive environment that supports interactive development, rapid iteration, and data exploration. They allow data engineers to break down code into smaller, testable segments, enabling them to execute and visualize results immediately, experiment with different approaches, and refine their methods in real time. This iterative workflow fosters faster development cycles and effective problem-solving, making it easy for engineers to transform, analyze, and clean data. Notebooks also enhance collaboration, as engineers can document their steps, share code, and present visualizations, creating a transparent workflow that keeps team members and stakeholders aligned.

A major strength of notebooks is their flexibility in integrating multiple languages and frameworks—such as Spark, SQL, and Python—within a single interface and a single notebook, allowing for comprehensive, end-to-end data workflows. Data engineers can harness Spark's distributed processing capabilities for handling large datasets; use SQL for structured data manipulation; and tap into Python's extensive libraries for transformation, visualization, or machine learning, all within one notebook. This seamless integration eliminates the need to shift between separate tools, streamlining workflows and boosting productivity. Notebooks enable data engineers to build dynamic pipelines, visualize intermediate results, and fine-tune models in a single, unified environment, simplifying complex data engineering tasks.

In Fabric, notebooks further enable real-time data exploration, helping engineers delve into datasets to uncover patterns before implementing transformations. By combining code, narrative text, and visualizations, notebooks provide an effective means of documenting data lineage and transformation logic. This approach enhances reproducibility and traceability, while also facilitating the onboarding of new team members and reinforcing best practices in data engineering. Acting as both a development and communication tool, notebooks bridge the gap between raw code and meaningful insights, forming an indispensable component of the modern data engineering toolkit.

All your notebooks and their dependencies can be part of your orchestration pipelines, as mentioned in Chapter 4.

To enhance the functionality of notebooks, you can use libraries. A *library* is a collection of prebuilt or custom code packages that extend your functionality, providing additional features for data processing or machine learning or integrations with external systems. Fabric has many common libraries already built in, but you can also add your own.

Leveraging Spark for Data Engineering

Apache Spark is a powerful, open source analytics engine designed for large-scale data processing, enabling data engineers to efficiently transform and analyze vast datasets. Its distributed, in-memory processing architecture enables Spark to handle big data tasks with remarkable speed, making it ideal for diverse data workflows such as ETL pipelines, machine learning, and real-time analytics. Spark supports multiple languages, including Python, Scala, and SQL, offering flexibility for data engineers to leverage their preferred tools. In Microsoft Fabric, Spark integrates seamlessly, providing a robust framework for scaling data engineering tasks.

Data engineers can use Spark pools to handle ETL operations, data transformations, and interactive data exploration, while optimizing cost and performance according to specific requirements.

 A *Spark pool* is a scalable cluster of Apache Spark resources used to run big data and machine learning workloads in parallel.

To perform data transformations at scale, data engineers can write Spark applications in languages like PySpark (Python for Spark) or Scala and submit them to Spark pools. This setup supports complex ETL pipelines, allowing engineers to extract data from multiple sources, transform and clean it, and load it into structured storage for further analysis. Spark's distributed architecture ensures efficient data processing, even with massive datasets, and facilitates scalable, automated data workflows, making it an essential component for handling data at scale in Fabric.

Another concept or term that you may come across is *Spark jobs*. Spark jobs are units of work executed within a Spark session, leveraging the distributed computing power of Apache Spark for tasks like data processing, ETL, and machine learning. Besides running code through interactive notebooks, Fabric provides job scheduling capabilities, allowing users to execute batch processing, streaming analytics, and AI workloads efficiently. With automatic scaling and built-in optimization features, Spark jobs in Fabric enable users to handle large-scale data workloads with minimal management overhead.

Spark in notebooks enhances flexibility by enabling interactive transformations with PySpark, allowing data engineers to tackle complex tasks in a single, cohesive interface. Engineers can leverage advanced Spark functions—like `filter`, `groupBy`, and map—within notebooks to transform and analyze data interactively. This environment is ideal for prototyping, where engineers can iteratively develop and visualize their data workflows, making real-time adjustments and optimizations. For example, a notebook can be used to load a large dataset, remove duplicates with `dropDupli cates`, handle missing values with `fillna`, and aggregate data using `groupBy` and `agg`, providing a streamlined process for data cleansing and transformation.

By combining Spark transformations with Python's extensive data libraries, engineers can achieve a cohesive workflow within a single environment. This setup not only enhances data accessibility but also promotes collaboration and reproducibility, enabling data engineers to explore, document, and refine their data processes effectively. As a result, leveraging Spark in notebooks forms an essential part of the modern data engineering toolkit, bridging the gap between data exploration and production-ready workflows.

A Step-by-Step Example: Building an ETL Pipeline in a Notebook

To get started, we will create a new lakehouse called LakehouseChapter5 and add sample data to it. Not sure how to get started? Please refer to Chapter 2, where we built our first lakehouse.

We'll start by creating our medallion layers: right/secondary click the Tables section in your lakehouse to display the option to create a new schema (see Figure 5-3). We will use this to create a new schema for all our layers—a bronze, a silver and a gold schema.

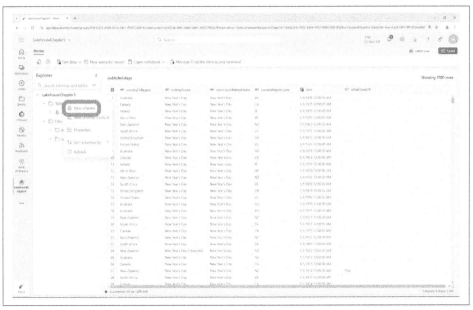

Figure 5-3. Adding schemas to a lakehouse

Your final result should look like the illustration in Figure 5-4.

Figure 5-4. Medallion architecture through schemas

As our last step of preparation, we'll load the New York Taxi Yellow dataset from Files to a new table in the bronze layer. While we could do all of that from our notebook, let's keep things simple for now.

Navigate to the file and select "Load to Tables" and "New table" as shown in Figure 5-5.

"Load to Tables" is only available for CSV and Parquet files.

Figure 5-5. Load data to table from file

Select the bronze layer and shorten the name of the table to nyc_taxi_yellow as shown in Figure 5-6.

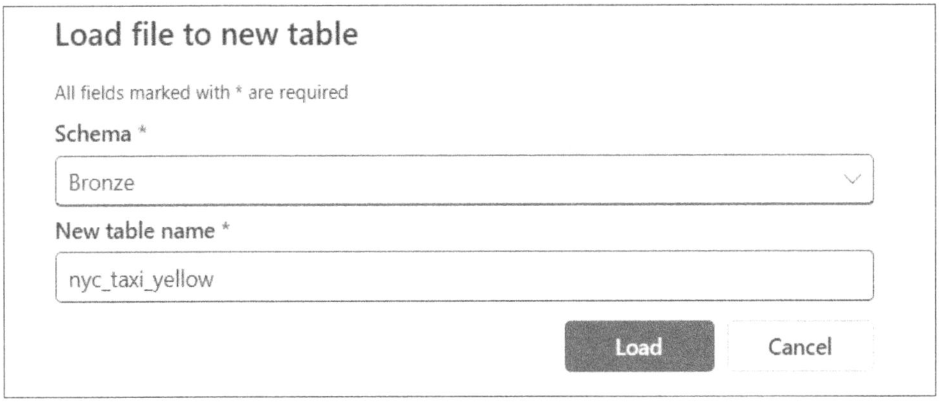

Load file to new table
All fields marked with * are required
Schema *
Bronze
New table name *
nyc_taxi_yellow
Load
Cancel

Figure 5-6. Loading a file to a new table in bronze layer

Now it's time to create our notebook, which you can do from the top menu (see Figure 5-7).

Open notebook
Existing notebook
New notebook

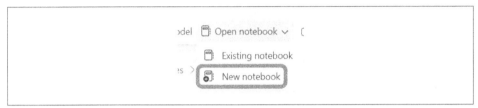

Figure 5-7. New notebook

First, we'll explore the data in our sample file. In your lakehouse, navigate to the corresponding file. Then select "Load data" and "Spark" (see Figure 5-8).

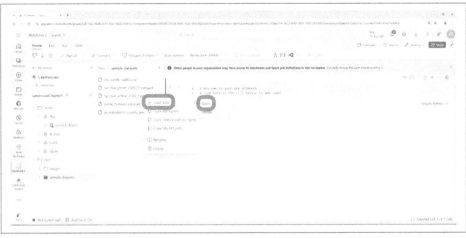

Figure 5-8. Loading a file using Spark

This creates the code to load this file's contents to a dataframe. You can execute the cell using the Play button on the upper left (see Figure 5-9). A DataFrame in PySpark is a distributed collection of data structured into named columns, similar to a table in a relational database or a pandas DataFrame. It is designed for large-scale data processing, capable of handling both structured and semi-structured data, and leverages Spark's parallel processing for efficient data manipulation and analysis.

Figure 5-9. Code to load a file to a dataframe using Spark

This will immediately show us the data, as well as a first overview about it (see Figure 5-10).

Figure 5-10. Output of `display(df)`

As you can see, the file has only one row. If you right/secondary click the table in the bronze layer, you'll get the exact same results.

Now, we need to make sure our data can be easily refreshed from our file to our table.

To achieve that, we will modify the code in our cell to that shown in Example 5-1.

Example 5-1. Updated Spark code

```
df = spark.read.parquet("Files/sample_datasets/nyc_taxi_yellow_2020_1.parquet")
df.write.format("delta") \
.mode("overwrite") \
.saveAsTable(f"LakehouseChapter5.Bronze.nyc_taxi_yellow")
```

The mode overwrite ensures that all contents in the table will be overwritten. If we used append instead, the data would be appended every time we run this cell.

Usually, we'd clean the data first if needed, but for our sample data, we can skip that step.

For our silver layer, we only care about the day of a trip, its distance, and its fare.

> This specific step is mostly happening due to the nature of our test data. In your silver layer, you would usually not drop any data because you don't need it, but would rather keep it then drop it in your gold layer.

We therefore add another cell by selecting the "+ Code" button below our existing cell (see Figure 5-11).

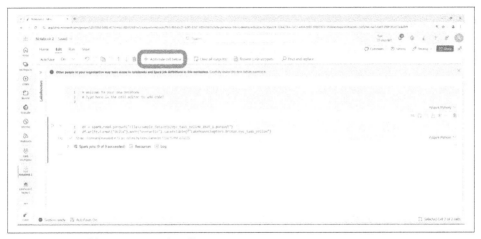

Figure 5-11. Adding a new code cell

In this cell, we add the code to convert our trip's timestamp to a date and add the distance and fare amount as shown in Example 5-2.

Example 5-2. Spark code to clean data to silver layer

```
df = spark.sql(
    "SELECT cast(tpepPickupDateTime as date) DTE, tripDistance, fareAmount "
    "FROM LakehouseChapter5.Bronze.nyc_taxi_yellow"
)

df.write \
  .format("delta") \
```

```
    .mode("overwrite") \
    .saveAsTable(f"LakehouseChapter5.Silver.TaxiTrips")
```

This will automatically create the target table in our silver layer and populate it.

For our business users, we will eventually aggregate that data by month using another code snippet, as shown in Example 5-3.

Example 5-3. Spark code to transfer aggregated data to gold layer

```
df = spark.sql(
    "SELECT last_day(DTE) MT, "
    "sum(tripDistance) Distance, "
    "sum(fareAmount) Amount "
    "FROM LakehouseChapter5.Silver.TaxiTrips "
    "GROUP BY last_day(DTE)"
)

df.write \
  .format("delta") \
  .mode("overwrite") \
  .saveAsTable(f"LakehouseChapter5.Gold.TaxiTrips")
```

To check our result, we'll add one last code cell with the code from Example 5-4.

Example 5-4. SQL code to query the gold layer

```
%%sql
SELECT * FROM LakehouseChapter5.Gold.TaxiTrips
```

In this code cell, you'll see the language changed directly to Spark SQL on the lower right, which allows us to directly write a SQL query as shown in Figure 5-12. Only this specific cell will be executed using the Spark SQL Kernel, while the remainder of the notebook will still be using the default for the notebook.

This language switch happened because of %%sql at the beginning of the cell. In a Fabric notebook, %% at the beginning of a code cell is a magic command that specifies the language or performs a special function.

For example, here are some more magic commands:

%%pyspark
Runs the cell using PySpark.

%%scala
Executes Scala code.

%%sql
Runs SQL queries directly on Spark tables.

%%mssparkutils
Provides access to Microsoft-specific utilities like file handling, secrets, and job control.

Figure 5-12. Spark SQL cell

These magic commands allow users to mix multiple languages in the same notebook while leveraging Spark's distributed processing capabilities.

We have now created a simple notebook that will load a Parquet file, move it to our bronze layer, clean it and store it to our silver layer, aggregate it to our gold layer, and then show the result using SQL.

We could either select "Run all" at the top to execute the entire notebook (see Figure 5-13) or run the cells individually by selecting the triangle/play button next to the active cell.

Figure 5-13. Full notebook

Summary

In this chapter, we looked at data engineering in Microsoft Fabric, focusing on the tools, architectures, and workflows that enable efficient data ingestion, transformation, and orchestration. Building on the foundational data-loading techniques introduced earlier, this chapter examined how data engineers utilize Spark, notebooks, pipelines, and jobs to transform raw data into actionable insights. We introduced key concepts such as lakehouse architecture and medallion architecture, demonstrating how data can be organized across bronze, silver, and gold layers for structured refinement and high-quality output. Through these tools and methods, data engineering in Microsoft Fabric supports scalable, efficient data processing, enabling organizations to manage large datasets, streamline workflows, and derive valuable insights. Data engineering also allows you to build up your entire ETL process using notebooks.

In Chapter 6, we'll look at the counterpart of lakehouses: data warehouses.

Data Warehousing

In Chapter 5, we discussed how the Data Engineering experience, backed by lakehouses, provides a scalable and unified environment for ingesting, transforming, and managing large volumes of structured and unstructured data, enabling seamless integration with analytics, AI, and machine learning workloads within Microsoft Fabric. Microsoft Fabric also provides the ability to create and query data warehouses, which we'll talk about in this chapter.

A real-world example of using data warehouses in Microsoft Fabric can be seen in a global retail company that needs to analyze sales performance across multiple regions. The company ingests transactional data from various store locations into a Fabric data warehouse, where structured schemas ensure consistency and fast querying. Using SQL-based transformations, the data is aggregated to calculate key metrics like total revenue, product demand, and customer purchase patterns. Business intelligence teams can then leverage Power BI to create interactive dashboards that provide executives with real-time insights into regional sales trends, inventory optimization, and marketing effectiveness. This structured and high-performance data warehouse enables the company to make strategic business decisions, such as adjusting product pricing, managing supply chains efficiently, and identifying growth opportunities based on historical and predictive analytics.

Fundamentals of Data Warehousing

A *data warehouse* is a core element of today's data management and analytics systems. It serves as a centralized platform for storing, managing, and analyzing large volumes of structured data from various sources. Data warehouses are specifically organized to support BI functions such as reporting, querying, and analysis. Since they are optimized for read-heavy operations, they are well-suited for tasks like generating dashboards and analytics reports and supporting executive decision making.

The key characteristics of a data warehouse are:

Structured data
Data warehouses primarily handle structured data, meaning it is arranged in predefined formats such as tables, columns, and rows, with established relationships between data points. This structure is typically enforced through ETL processes, ensuring that data entering the warehouse adheres to specific formats and business rules.

Historical data storage
Data warehouses are built to store extensive historical data, often spanning many years. This makes them invaluable for long-term trend analysis, enabling organizations to rely on detailed records for forecasting and strategic planning.

Schema-on-write
The schema, or data structure, must be defined before data is written into the warehouse. This "schema-on-write" approach ensures data consistency and integrity but requires a solid understanding of the business rules and data structure prior to ingestion.

Optimized query performance
Data warehouses are fine-tuned for high query performance, especially when handling complex operations like aggregations, joins, and filtering across large datasets. Performance enhancements are achieved using technologies such as indexing and partitioning.

Warehouses Versus Lakehouses

Data warehouses and data lakehouses differ significantly in their architecture and the types of data they can manage. A data warehouse is built specifically for handling structured data, organized into predefined schemas to optimize fast querying, making it well-suited for tasks like BI and analytics that focus on historical, relational data. On the other hand, a data lakehouse blends the capabilities of both data warehouses and data lakes, enabling it to accommodate both structured and unstructured data with greater flexibility. While data warehouses follow a schema-on-write approach—defining the data structure prior to ingestion—data lakehouses can, in addition, also use schema-on-read, where the structure is applied only when the data is accessed. However, when storing data in a lakehouse in Parquet format, for example, you are still assigning a schema when writing those files. This allows lakehouses to store vast amounts of raw data, making them ideal for big data processing, machine learning, and advanced analytics, while still offering the performance benefits typical of data warehouses.

Due to the type of data lakehouses typically hold, we often see lakehouses being used for the bronze and silver layer, with the gold layer being a data warehouse.

There are some major differences between data engineering, or using lakehouses, and using a data warehouse that are specific to Microsoft Fabric, as you'll see in Table 6-1.

Table 6-1. Key differences between a warehouse and a lakehouse

Data warehouse	Lakehouse
SQL endpoint is writeable	SQL endpoint is read-only
Language is T-SQL only, resulting in faster and cheaper queries	Can use T-SQL, Spark SQL, Python, PySpark, Scala, and R
Support for multi-table transactions	No multi-table transactions
Tables and views	Tables and files

In summary:

SQL endpoint
    The SQL endpoint in a data warehouse is writeable, whereas it is read-only for a lakehouse.

T-SQL vs Python/PySpark
    In a data warehouse, you will use T-SQL as your language, whereas in a lakehouse, you can use SQL but also other languages such as Python. Despite the fact that lakehouses provide a SQL endpoint and the opportunity to wrap a SQL query in Python code, the primary language used will differ between the two.

SQL performance
    Because data warehouses use SQL as their native language, as a rule of thumb, SQL queries will run faster and cheaper than they will in lakehouses.

Files
    Because data warehouses rely on structured data, all information is stored in tables; the concept of reading from files does not apply to the native data warehouse. There are ways, however, to include data from a lakehouse in a data warehouse, which we'll discuss in more depth in "Querying a Warehouse" on page 110.

Warehouses in Microsoft Fabric

Since we already created a warehouse in Chapter 2, let's dive right into how we work with a data warehouse in Fabric.

Integrating Data into a Warehouse

To integrate data directly into your data warehouse, you can either use Data Factory (pipelines, Copy jobs, dataflows…) or you can insert data using the SQL analytics endpoint. To make things slightly more confusing, you can also access data that isn't actually stored in your warehouse, so not all your data needs to be integrated or inserted into your warehouse tables.

You can also directly integrate data from a CSV or Parquet file using the T-SQL COPY command. The COPY command facilitates high-throughput data ingestion from an external Azure storage account, allowing configuration of source file format options, designation of a location for rejected rows, skipping of header rows, and other customizable settings. If you are unfamiliar with this, we recommend the article "Ingest Data into Your Warehouse Using the COPY Statement" (*https://oreil.ly/ka5ef*).

Querying a Warehouse

With SQL being the "language of the data warehouse," the SQL endpoint is the obvious first choice for querying. The SQL endpoint allows querying across multiple warehouses—and also across lakehouses. This means you can send a query to the SQL endpoint that immediately joins a table in your warehouse with data from your lakehouse. This is how data residing in files that are not natively built into the warehouse can be included. To visually bring another warehouse (or lakehouse) into your query editor, select the "+ Warehouses" button. You'll see a popup like the one shown in Figure 6-1.

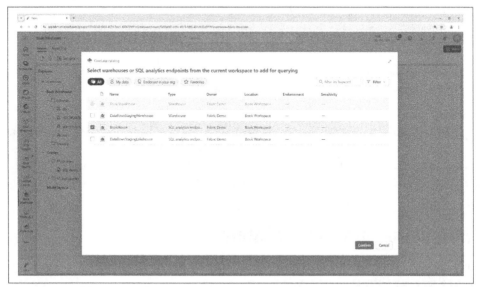

Figure 6-1. Adding a warehouse

Example 6-1 shows how you can cross-query a warehouse and a lakehouse.

Example 6-1. Cross-warehouse SQL query

```
SELECT * FROM BookHouse.dbo.publicholidays a
INNER JOIN [Book Warehouse].dbo.[Date] b on a.date = b.Date
```

To run this query, you can use the built-in query editor in Fabric. Select "New SQL query" as shown in Figure 6-2.

Figure 6-2. New SQL query in Fabric

You can then run the query from there (see Figure 6-3). The editor has full Intellisense and Copilot support; once your query is ready, just select the Run button.

Figure 6-3. Running a SQL query in Fabric

Another way to query your warehouse is to use external tools such as SQL Server Management Studio (SSMS). To connect from an external tool, you must first retrieve the endpoint by selecting the settings for your warehouse, as shown in Figure 6-4.

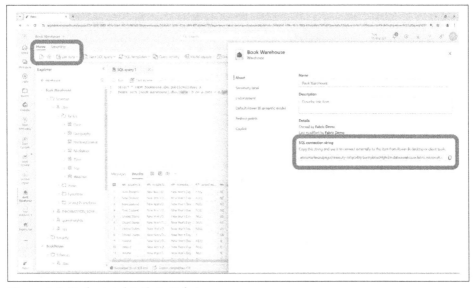

Figure 6-4. Endpoint details in Fabric

You can then connect to this endpoint with the tool of your choice, using Microsoft Entra ID authentication, and run your query. Figure 6-5 shows an example using SSMS.

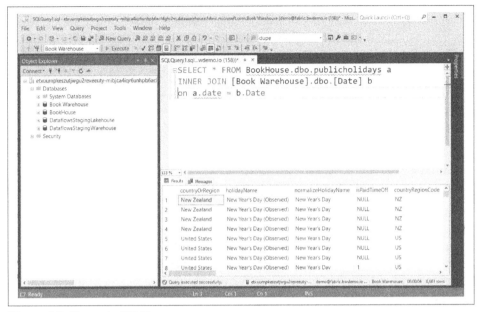

Figure 6-5. Query in SSMS

This provides you the flexibility of using the tools you feel most comfortable with while also providing a rich editor on the portal that does not require any additional tooling.

Elements of a Fabric Data Warehouse

Have you worked with SQL Server, Azure SQL DB, or similar flavors of SQL before? Then all of the elements of a Fabric data warehouse should be very familiar to you:

Schemas

In Microsoft Fabric, *schemas* act as containers that organize database objects like tables, views, stored procedures, and functions within a data warehouse. They serve as a logical framework for categorizing data based on different business domains or departments, providing a clear structure to manage access and permissions. This organization not only enhances data security by controlling access at the schema level but also makes it easier to navigate and maintain the database as it grows, ensuring that related data and resources are grouped together logically.

Tables

The core structures in a data warehouse are *tables*, where data is stored in rows and columns, resembling a spreadsheet. Each table typically represents a specific entity, such as "Sales" or "Customers," and stores records that align with that entity. Tables are designed to handle large volumes of structured data, making them foundational for querying, reporting, and analytics. With the help of indexing and partitioning techniques, tables in Microsoft Fabric are optimized for efficient data retrieval and querying, supporting the high-performance requirements of business intelligence workloads.

Unlike other database systems (e.g., SQL Server, which stores its data in an *.mdf* file), the data of a data warehouse in Fabric is stored in Delta files in OneLake.

Views

Views in Microsoft Fabric are virtual tables created by defining a query that pulls and filters data from one or more tables. Unlike tables, views do not store data themselves; they provide a dynamic way to present specific slices of data based on predefined criteria. Views are particularly useful for simplifying complex queries and abstracting underlying data complexity. By creating views, data engineers can present data in a user-friendly format, improve security by restricting access to specific data, and support business needs by delivering targeted data views for analytics and reporting.

Views affect your available semantic model storage modes, as they will cause Direct Lake queries to fall back to DirectQuery queries! We will talk more about storage modes in Chapter 9.

Stored procedures

Stored procedures are predefined sets of SQL commands stored within the database, allowing for reusable and efficient execution of routine operations. In Microsoft Fabric, stored procedures are widely used to automate repetitive tasks, such as data transformations, validation, and bulk data loading. By encapsulating logic in stored procedures, developers can streamline processes, reduce code duplication, and ensure consistency across data operations. Stored procedures also help in optimizing performance, as SQL code is precompiled and executed within the database, making them a powerful tool for maintaining the efficiency of a data warehouse.

SQL functions

    SQL functions in Microsoft Fabric are specialized SQL routines designed to perform specific calculations or transformations on data, often returning a single value or result. These can be used within SQL statements to simplify and reuse common expressions, making complex queries more manageable and readable. Functions are especially valuable in scenarios that require consistent calculations, such as date conversions, data formatting, or aggregations. By leveraging functions, data engineers can encapsulate logic in reusable components, which enhances code maintainability and promotes standardized data handling across the data warehouse.

Data Warehouses Versus Traditional SQL Engines

Microsoft Fabric data warehouses use a distributed query engine that enhances performance by decomposing queries into smaller tasks and executing them concurrently across multiple compute nodes. This approach ensures efficient query execution, even when dealing with large datasets and complex analytical computations. Additionally, Fabric separates data loading from user queries, preventing ingestion processes from interfering with query performance. This separation allows data to be ingested continuously—whether through batch processing, streaming data, or ELT pipelines—while ensuring that users querying the warehouse do not experience slowdowns or resource contention. By isolating these workloads, Fabric enables a more stable and predictable environment where analysts and business users can retrieve and analyze data without being affected by ongoing data ingestion or transformation activities. This design is particularly beneficial for organizations that require both real-time data updates and consistent query performance, as it eliminates bottlenecks and ensures that analytical workloads remain responsive regardless of the volume or frequency of data-loading operations.

You may be familiar with the engine of traditional offerings like Azure SQL Database. While the SQL endpoint of a warehouse provides a lot of functionality, including the ability to manipulate and insert data, its functionality is not identical to what you are used to. For example, cloned tables and time travel are two capabilities that separate a Fabric warehouse from the traditional SQL engines.

Clone table

Microsoft Fabric enables near-instantaneous, zero-copy table cloning with minimal storage costs, allowing metadata replication while referencing the same data files in OneLake. This approach ensures efficient storage utilization while maintaining the integrity of the original dataset. Table clones support a variety of use cases, including development, testing, consistent reporting, data recovery, historical analysis, and data archiving. They provide an isolated environment in which developers and testers can experiment without impacting production data, ensuring stability while trouble-shooting, validating, or implementing new features.

Clones also facilitate consistent reporting and machine learning model development by enabling the duplication of datasets for analysis without disrupting ongoing ETL processes. Additionally, they serve as a safeguard against accidental data loss or corruption, allowing quick restoration to a previous state. Historical reporting bene-fits from table clones by preserving past data snapshots for auditing or compliance purposes. Clones are created using simple T-SQL commands and can be generated within or across schemas in the same warehouse. However, they remain separate from their source, meaning changes to one do not affect the other. If you want to dive deeper into this, check out the article "Clone Table in Microsoft Fabric" (*https:// oreil.ly/msgWX*).

Time travel

The time travel capability enables users to query historical data as it existed at specific timestamps. This functionality supports stable reporting, historical trend analysis, performance evaluation, auditing, and machine learning model reproduction. Users can retrieve prior data states using the T-SQL `FOR TIMESTAMP AS OF` clause, which applies to entire queries, including all joined tables. The retrieved data is read-only; write operations are not permitted during these queries. The warehouse automati-cally retains data versions for 30 calendar days, allowing queries within this retention period. However, schema modifications, such as adding or removing columns, pre-vent querying data states before the change.

This time travel capability is particularly beneficial for maintaining consistent report-ing during ongoing ETL processes, conducting historical trend analyses, performing audits, and reproducing machine learning results. It's important to note that the `FOR TIMESTAMP AS OF` clause can be specified only once per query and currently supports only the UTC time zone. Additionally, time travel is not supported for the SQL analytics endpoint of the lakehouse. Example 6-2 shows a sample query.

Example 6-2. SQL query using time travel

```
SELECT * FROM [Book Warehouse].dbo.Date
OPTION (FOR TIMESTAMP AS OF '2025-02-13T11:39:35.28')
```

T-SQL Limitations

T-SQL in a Fabric warehouse also comes with a couple of limitations. Some of them, such as not being able to use `CREATE ROLE` or `CREATE USER`, may seem obvious due to the way permissions are handled in Fabric (more details on this in Chapter 16 where we will discuss security), some others may be more surprising. At the time of writing, warehouse tables do not support `IDENTITY` columns, and there is no `MERGE` statement.

Because the list of limitations changes constantly due to new features being added to the warehouse experience, we refer you to the list of T-SQL limitations (*https:// oreil.ly/25UeK*).

Summary

Data warehousing in Microsoft Fabric provides a powerful, structured, high-performance environment tailored to business intelligence and analytics needs. Fabric data warehouses are optimized for handling large volumes of historical, structured data, enabling complex querying and reporting. Unlike lakehouses, which offer schema-on-read flexibility for unstructured data, Fabric data warehouses focus on structured data operations.

Microsoft Fabric's unique integration between data warehouses and lakehouses supports cross-querying and combines T-SQL for warehouse tasks with Python for lakehouse applications. Featuring familiar SQL elements like schemas, tables, views, and stored procedures, Fabric's data warehousing capabilities offer robust support for enterprise-grade analytics and decision making.

In our next chapter, Chapter 7, we will elaborate on Fabric's data science capabilities.

Data Science in Microsoft Fabric

Not so long ago, in 2012, data scientist was branded "the sexiest job of the 21st century" by the *Harvard Business Review* (*https://oreil.ly/4q-Ss*). Obviously, we can argue about the validity of this label more than a decade after it was proclaimed. However, the fact is that individuals "who can coax treasure out of messy, unstructured data" are still in high demand, and Microsoft Fabric doesn't disappoint anyone who considers themselves a data scientist.

Before we dig deep into examining particular data science workloads in Microsoft Fabric, let's first look at Figure 7-1 for an overview of the most common data science process stages from a high-level perspective. Please keep in mind that this process is not exclusively related to Microsoft Fabric—it's more of a generic, tool-agnostic approach.

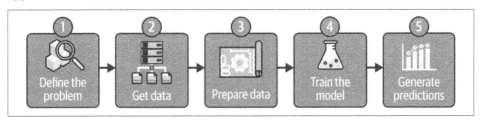

Figure 7-1. The most common data science workflow

In this chapter, we'll discuss four options that Microsoft Fabric provides to support data science workloads: MLflow, SynapseML, AutoML, and Semantic Link. These options include various ready-made solutions that can be seamlessly integrated with other Fabric experiences, as well as some unique features, such as Semantic Link, to support specific Fabric-related use cases.

Let's start by introducing the process of creating machine learning *experiments* (which allow data scientists to log parameters, code versions, and output files when running their code) and examining several important features that play a key role in building machine learning models. The two tools we'll looks at first are MLflow and SynapseML. MLflow is used to streamline machine learning development, including tracking experiments and sharing and deploying machine learning models. In contrast, SynapseML enables a simplified process for creating scalable machine learning pipelines. A machine learning pipeline is a series of interconnected data-processing and data-modeling activities for streamlining the process of working with machine learning models. Figure 7-2 displays a typical workflow in this phase.

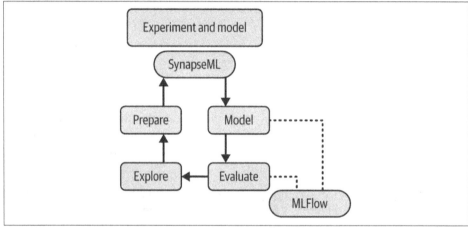

Figure 7-2. MLflow and SynapseML used in synergy for ML workloads

MLflow

MLflow is a free and open source library for the complete machine learning lifecycle, including experimentation, reproducibility, and deployment. There are numerous benefits to using MLflow, so let's focus on the most important ones. First, it enables data scientists to manage their machine learning projects more systematically, by tracking experiments. In addition, it can be used to facilitate deployment in various environments, and it supports a wide range of machine learning frameworks and tools. Thus, it is a suitable choice for use in diverse projects, such as sales forecasting, model deployments, and similar.

The most commonly used component of MLflow is *tracking*. It allows tracking of machine learning models, including information such as parameters, metrics, and artifacts. An experiment is a separate item in Microsoft Fabric, and can be created in two ways:

- From the web UI, as shown in Figure 7-3

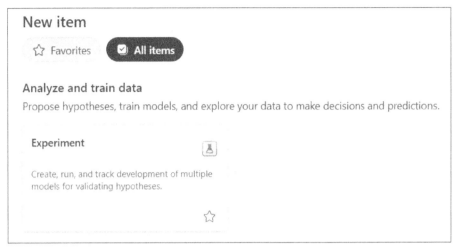

Figure 7-3. Creating an Experiment item in Fabric

- Directly from the authoring experience using the `mlflow.create.experiment()` or `mlflow.set.experiment()` API, as shown in the following code snippet:

```
import mlflow
#Define experiment name
EXPERIMENT_NAME = "customer-churn-experiment"  # MLflow experiment name
```

Each time you train the model, it's tracked as an experiment run.

As well as experiment tracking, MLflow provides additional features for enhancing data science workloads in Microsoft Fabric. For example, you can leverage a *model registry*, a centralized model repository that allows the storing and versioning of machine learning models, thus making it easier to manage model lifecycle and deployments.

MLflow also supports packaging models into a format that can be deployed across multiple platforms, and it enables model deployment by using REST APIs.

Due to its versatility, MLflow can be implemented in dozens of real-life scenarios. Let's examine a few of them.

Experimentation Tracking for Sales Forecasting

A global retailer plans to create a machine learning model to forecast future sales based not only on historical data but also on additional factors, such as promotions, holidays, and weather. The company's data science team leverages different algorithms and applies various hyperparameters to tune the model. *Hyperparameters* in machine learning are external configuration variables that data scientists use to manage machine learning model training. By using MLflow's experiment-tracking capabilities, they log each run and record parameters, metrics, and model artifacts. After running 50 experiments with different hyperparameters, the data science team can easily review logs in MLflow, visualize performance metrics, and finally choose the optimal model configuration.

Deploying Models as REST APIs to Support Nontechnical Teams

Similarly, a telecommunication company creates a machine learning model to predict customer churn. After the model is trained, MLflow is used to package and deploy it into the production environment as a REST API on Microsoft Fabric. This allows various teams to access the API in real time, assign scores to customers, and predict which customers are likely to leave. In this way, nontechnical users can integrate churn prediction analysis without needing to understand the underlying machine learning model.

Managing Model Versions

A large logistics company relies on a machine learning model to predict demand for its transportation services. However, ever-changing market conditions require constant updates and retraining of the model. MLflow's model registry feature allows easy version control, keeping track of which model version is in production and which model version is in development. This enables the data science team to register multiple versions of its demand forecasting model in MLflow. Then, for example, the team can mark version 1.0 as a production version, while at the same time experimenting with version 1.1. This ensures that the production environment always runs the most reliable model.

SynapseML

Data scientists and developers may leverage SynapseML to build complex machine learning pipelines at scale, making it ideal for enterprises dealing with large datasets and diverse machine learning requirements.

In a nutshell, SynapseML is an open source library built on top of Apache Spark and integrated into the Microsoft Fabric platform. It's best for dealing with big data scenarios because it enables data scientists to perform myriad tasks, such as distributed training or deep learning. In addition, it integrates with widely adopted machine learning frameworks like PyTorch, TensorFlow, and ONNX.

Since SynapseML supports various programming languages, including Python, Scala, and Java, it is a suitable choice for different types of data science solutions. Data scientists can use prebuilt machine learning models to perform tasks like text processing, anomaly detection, and image recognition. Finally, SynapseML integrates with other Microsoft services, such as Azure AI services, enabling data scientists and developers to integrate AI features like translation and computer vision in their applications.

There is a wide range of use cases for SynapseML. Here, we'll single out a few:

Sentiment analysis for social media data
Social media posts generate a vast amount of data. Let's imagine that the marketing team wants to analyze customer sentiment from this data. They can leverage SynapseML to load a large dataset that contains social media post data into Spark; perform various text-processing operations; and use pretrained models to classify sentiment as either positive, negative, or neutral. The best thing is that SynapseML supports distributed workloads and data processing, so different developers may process the data in parallel.

Anomaly detection of IoT data
Real-time sensors from IoT devices are another huge producer of data. Let's say that a manufacturing company collects this data and needs to process it. Using SynapseML's anomaly detection capabilities, data scientists may process vast amounts of data in a Spark cluster and identify unusual patterns or, even more important, potential equipment failures. This helps implement predictive maintenance scenarios and reduce downtime and repair costs.

Speech-to-text for call center analytics
Nowadays, almost every company relies on an efficient customer service department. Let's imagine that a customer service department plans to transcribe and analyze recordings of phone calls to improve customer satisfaction. They can integrate SynapseML with Azure AI services and use distributed processing to perform speech-to-text conversions on hundreds or even thousands of call recordings. These transcriptions can then be analyzed, keywords or customer sentiment can be searched for, and, finally, actionable insights can be provided to enhance the service quality.

Image recognition
SynapseML can also be used to create an image recognition model that inspects products and flags defects. By labeling images of both defective and nondefective products within the dataset, SynapseML can train a machine learning model on Spark and automate the detection process, providing high-quality outputs with minimal manual intervention.

Recommendation system for ecommerce business
Building a recommendation system is probably a key requirement for any online retailer. Data scientists at these companies can leverage SynapseML to build a robust recommendation system based on customer behavior and

customer purchase history. In addition, SynapseML can apply advanced filtering techniques to recommend products, boosting sales and improving the customer experience.

AutoML

AutoML is a feature that was introduced to automate machine learning model building in Microsoft Fabric; it can be used by those without in-depth data science knowledge and skills. AutoML utilizes machine learning techniques to automatically choose algorithms, tune hyperparameters of the dataset, and generate a model based on the input dataset.

Let's examine the key features of AutoML:

Automated model selection
  Based on the provided data, AutoML applies an auto selection of the best-fit algorithm for that data.

Feature engineering
  AutoML can identify and transform relevant features from data, improving model performance.

Hyperparameter tuning
  AutoML will automatically optimize the tuning of model parameters to improve accuracy.

Model explanation
  AutoML provides interpretable features that help users understand the factors leading to a prediction.

Deployment and management
  Users can deploy the generated models directly within Microsoft Fabric and manage them through the platform.

Data scientists may leverage AutoML in various real-life scenarios. Here are some of the most common use cases where AutoML can help build and train machine learning models:

Customer churn prediction
  An ecommerce business wants to predict which customers are going to discontinue their subscriptions by taking into account features such as purchase history, engagement, and support interactions. Using AutoML in Microsoft Fabric, the company can present historical customer data, and an ML model will be created automatically, able to detect repeatable patterns of churn. It will also be able to predict who those customers are so that the company can take action before they walk out the door.

Demand forecasting for inventory management

An ecommerce platform needs to forecast product demand. Using historical sales data as input, AutoML trains a time series forecasting model. This model will predict future sales trends, allowing the company to optimize stock levels and minimize overstock or out-of-stock situations.

Fraud detection in financial transactions

A financial institution needs to be able to recognize fraudulent transactions in real time. With AutoML, the company can upload a transaction dataset that is already labeled as either fraudulent or regular based on historical data. AutoML can evaluate the data, figure out which classification algorithms have the best potential to accurately identify a fraudulent transaction, tune them all together, and spit out a single model that can be implemented to detect suspicious transactions automatically. This helps the company significantly tighten security while reducing losses.

Image classification in health care

AutoML can be used to classify medical images such as X-rays and MRIs at a hospital for diagnostics. Once image datasets with labeling are uploaded, AutoML can automatically create and optimize a deep learning model to detect anomalies such as tumors, enabling medical professionals to make a faster and more accurate diagnosis.

Semantic Link

Since Microsoft Fabric was publicly unveiled in May 2023, there have been an ocean of announcements about the new platform. In all honesty, plenty of those were just a marketing or rebranding of the features and services that had already existed before Fabric. In this ocean of announcements, some features flew under the radar, with their true power still somehow hidden behind the glamour of their "noisy neighbors."

Semantic Link is probably one of the best examples of these hidden Fabric gems.

 Despite all of the aforementioned data science and machine learning tools and features, we consider Semantic Link one of the most revolutionary features in the entire Microsoft Fabric realm because it opens a whole new world of possibilities when creating a unified view of data across multiple disparate sources.

If you look at the official documentation (*https://oreil.ly/7hdjH*), you'll learn that "Semantic link is a feature that allows you to establish a connection between semantic models and Synapse Data Science in Microsoft Fabric." Doesn't sound too exciting, right?

But, what if we tell you that you can leverage this feature to optimize your Power BI semantic models quickly? Or to visualize all dependencies among tables, columns, and measures in the semantic model? How about running the DAX code from the Fabric notebook? (DAX stands for Data Analysis Expressions and represents the programming language for creating calculations in tabular models, including Power BI.) These are only some of the Semantic Link use cases. And this is just for starters.

In this section, we'll examine some handy implementations of the Semantic Link feature in real-life scenarios. First, however, let's take a short ride through the evolution of collaborative work between a data scientist and a BI developer—if something like that even existed in the past.

In Figure 7-4, you may notice that these two personas were totally isolated in the pre-Fabric era.

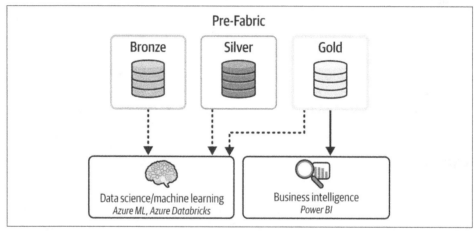

Figure 7-4. No integration between data science and BI workloads

As you read in Chapter 1, Microsoft Fabric was introduced as an end-to-end analytics platform, where all data personas can seamlessly collaborate and access the "one copy" of the data stored in OneLake. Figure 7-5 depicts how Fabric provided a unified location for all data professionals in the form of the Fabric workspace.

However, regardless of how big a step this was in the direction of unification, these workloads were still isolated and seen as separate solutions. There was no way to unify data science workloads with BI reporting and vice versa. Well, not before Semantic Link entered the picture. Figure 7-6 shows how Semantic Link creates a bridge between data science and business intelligence by providing the possibility of leveraging semantic model data in data science using a familiar set of tools: notebooks, Python, and Spark, to name a few of the most popular.

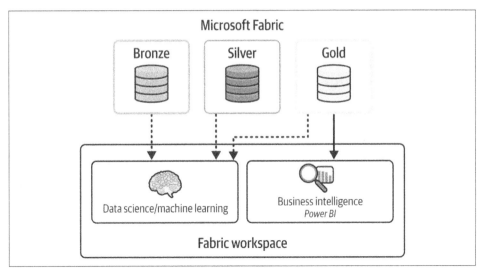

Figure 7-5. Fabric workspace as a unified container for various items

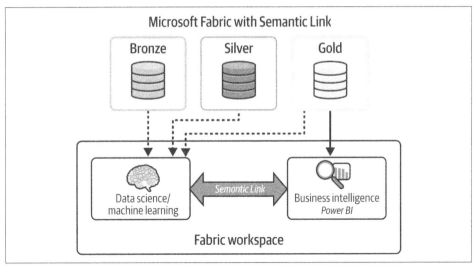

Figure 7-6. Semantic Link as a bridge between data science and BI

Semantic Link relies on a special Python library called SemPy. This library enables connecting to any Power BI semantic model and accessing all the information about the model including, but not limited to, relationships, measures, and calculated columns.

What's even more powerful is that if "Read Write" is enabled for XMLA Endpoint in the Admin portal, you can also apply changes to existing semantic models directly from the Fabric notebook! This opens a whole new world of possibilities because previously, writing via XMLA Endpoint was the exclusive privilege of various external tools such as Tabular Editor, VS Code, and similar.

Let's now examine five real-life scenarios where Semantic Link may be used to enhance the development process.

Writing Python code is not something you would expect from every data professional. Hence, the credit for the ease of use of various Semantic Link implementations goes to Michael Kovalsky. Michael works at Microsoft, and he created and maintains an entire library called Semantic Link Labs (*https://oreil.ly/FrTXM*). This library extends the generic SemPy library, consisting of ready-made functions you can use out of the box to leverage the Semantic Link feature in Microsoft Fabric.

Visualize Dependencies in the Semantic Model

How many times have you had to deal with monster semantic models—you know, those models consisting of tens or even hundreds of tables, with spaghetti relationships all over the place, and hundreds of measures and calculated columns implemented to enrich the model with additional business logic? Yes, I know, we've all been there.

Wouldn't it be great if we could somehow visualize all dependencies among the various structures in the model?

Figure 7-7 illustrates a dependency tree of the FactInternetSales table from the sample AdventureWorks database, which can be downloaded for free from the Microsoft website (*https://oreil.ly/PyHtZ*).

We were able to plot the dependency tree by executing exactly six lines of Python code in the Fabric notebook:

```
import sempy.fabric as fabric
from sempy.dependencies import plot_dependency_metadata
dataset = "S1"
sales = fabric.read_table(dataset, "aw_FactInternetSales")
dependencies = sales.find_dependencies()
plot_dependency_metadata(dependencies)
```

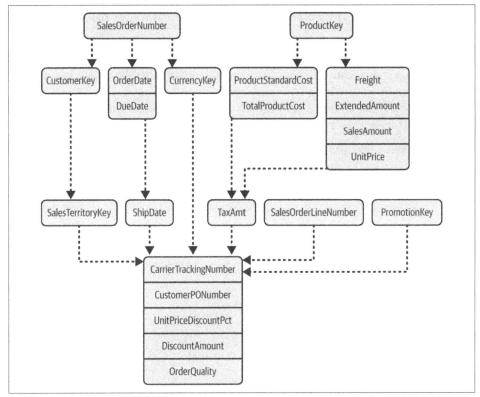

Figure 7-7. Visualizing model dependencies more easily than ever with Semantic Link

Similarly, we could have also visualized measure dependencies, as shown in Figure 7-8.

```
1   import sempy_labs
2
3   sempy_labs.measure_dependency_tree (dataset = 'End-To-End Collisions NYC grey', measure_name='Cyclists Injured')
   ✓  3 sec - Command executed in 2 sec 624 ms by Nikola Ilic on 10:37:59 AM, 9/18/24
∑ [Cyclists Injured]
├── ⊞ 'Collisions'
└── ⊟ 'Collisions'[NUMBER OF CYCLIST INJURED]
```

Figure 7-8. Visualizing measure dependencies

There are also plenty of other built-in functions that enable you to analyze and understand all the details of the semantic model, such as tables, columns, relationships, measures, calculation groups, and row-level and object-level security definitions, to name just a few.

Optimize Semantic Models with Best Practice Analyzer Rules

For all of you who consider yourselves professional Power BI developers, Best Practice Analyzer (BPA) probably sounds familiar. In a nutshell, BPA scans the semantic model and flags any issues found. These might include inappropriate use of data types, bad practices in writing DAX code, and suboptimal relationship types, all the way to alerting if the columns are missing descriptions. Based on the findings, you may decide to apply fixes to the model directly or to ignore the warning.

Before Semantic Link, all these tasks could have been performed only by using BPA with the external tool Tabular Editor. Now, with Semantic Link, the same outcome can be achieved directly from a Fabric notebook.

Figure 7-9 shows the result of the semantic model scan using BPA in the notebook.

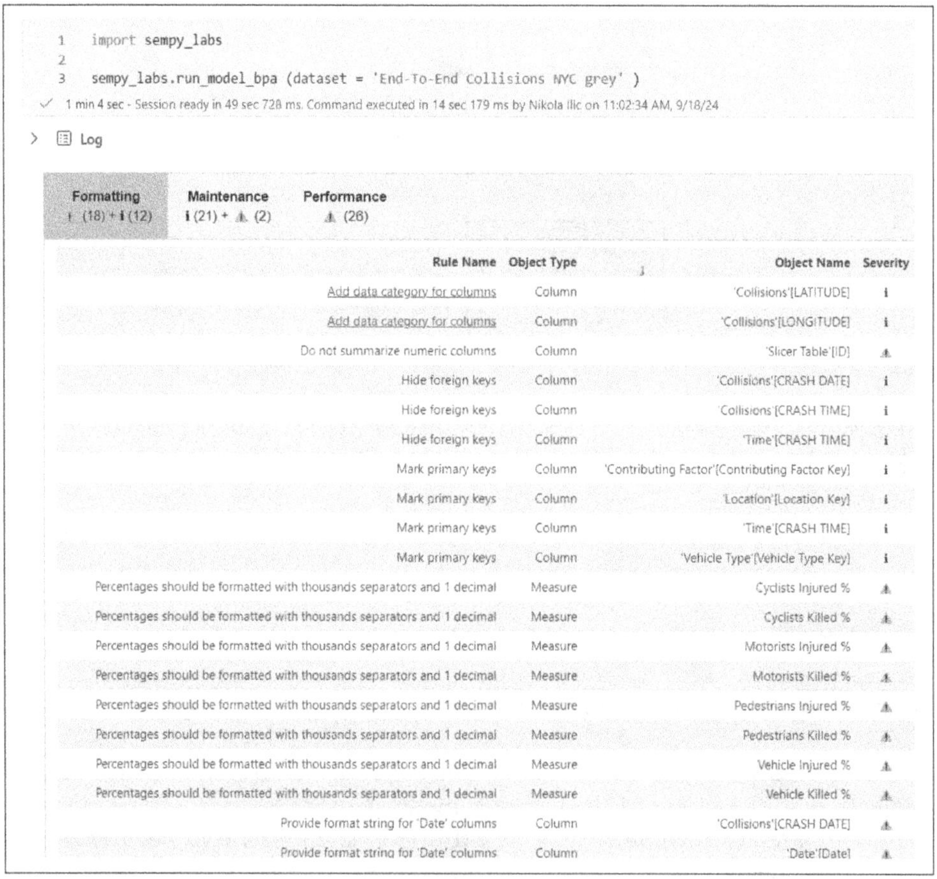

Rule Name	Object Type	Object Name	Severity
Add data category for columns	Column	'Collisions'[LATITUDE]	i
Add data category for columns	Column	'Collisions'[LONGITUDE]	i
Do not summarize numeric columns	Column	'Slicer Table'[ID]	⚠
Hide foreign keys	Column	'Collisions'[CRASH DATE]	i
Hide foreign keys	Column	'Collisions'[CRASH TIME]	i
Hide foreign keys	Column	'Time'[CRASH TIME]	i
Mark primary keys	Column	'Contributing Factor'[Contributing Factor Key]	i
Mark primary keys	Column	'Location'[Location Key]	i
Mark primary keys	Column	'Time'[CRASH TIME]	i
Mark primary keys	Column	'Vehicle Type'[Vehicle Type Key]	i
Percentages should be formatted with thousands separators and 1 decimal	Measure	Cyclists Injured %	⚠
Percentages should be formatted with thousands separators and 1 decimal	Measure	Cyclists Killed %	⚠
Percentages should be formatted with thousands separators and 1 decimal	Measure	Motorists Injured %	⚠
Percentages should be formatted with thousands separators and 1 decimal	Measure	Motorists Killed %	⚠
Percentages should be formatted with thousands separators and 1 decimal	Measure	Pedestrians Injured %	⚠
Percentages should be formatted with thousands separators and 1 decimal	Measure	Pedestrians Killed %	⚠
Percentages should be formatted with thousands separators and 1 decimal	Measure	Vehicle Injured %	⚠
Percentages should be formatted with thousands separators and 1 decimal	Measure	Vehicle Killed %	⚠
Provide format string for 'Date' columns	Column	'Collisions'[CRASH DATE]	⚠
Provide format string for 'Date' columns	Column	'Date'[Date]	⚠

Figure 7-9. Best Practice Analyzer executed from a Fabric notebook

What's even more powerful—and this is one of the huge advantages compared to the "old-fashioned" BPA in Tabular Editor—you can now run BPA rules in bulk! This means, with a single line of code, you can scan all semantic models in a workspace. This was not possible before Semantic Link, because in Tabular Editor, BPA can scan only one model at a time.

Translate Semantic Models

In real life, it's common to have users speak different languages. This is especially relevant in enterprises doing their business in different countries, where each subsidiary prefers to have the data in their local language.

Let's imagine that our company, based in the US, has a subsidiary in Italy, and users in Italy want to see the data in Italian. To achieve this seemingly simple requirement, before Semantic Link, someone who was proficient in both English and Italian had to go through the model and manually translate each object! Many workarounds were introduced over time, but the sad truth was that translating model metadata was a tedious and daunting task.

With Semantic Link, this task requires a single line of code. We know that this sounds *too good to be true*, so please take a look at Figure 7-10, which shows how the model objects can be translated into Italian.

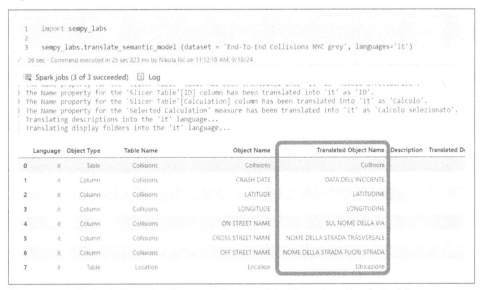

Figure 7-10. A single line of code to translate model objects into the desired language

The only thing you need to do is to provide the model name and the desired language. Semantic Link will take care of all the hard work in the background.

Migrate Existing Semantic Models to Direct Lake

Microsoft introduced plenty of innovative solutions across the Fabric platform. One that particularly stands out is Direct Lake, a groundbreaking feature for Power BI semantic models. We cover Direct Lake in detail in Chapter 9.

Currently, most Power BI semantic models use either Import or DirectQuery storage mode or are built as composite models. Don't worry; we also cover all these options in depth in Chapter 9. However, chances are that with the expected growth in Fabric adoption, more and more Power BI semantic models will be using Direct Lake mode.

While creating a Direct Lake model from scratch is a fairly straightforward process, it would be legitimate to ask, What happens with the thousands of existing Import and DirectQuery models? Do we need to re-create the entire model from scratch, including establishing all relationships, re-creating tens or hundreds of measures, and rebuilding hierarchies and calculation groups?

Fear not, Semantic Link again comes to the rescue! The entire process is documented here (*https://oreil.ly/uo5LO*).

By leveraging various Semantic Link Labs built-in functions, you can extract the entire model structure, including any business logic implemented in the model, and re-create the model to use Direct Lake mode, without any manual intervention or need to rebuild from scratch. Not only that, but you can easily rebind all the existing reports to new Direct Lake models. Do I need to tell you how powerful it is? And, the best thing is that it can be done by running a single line of Python code:

```
import sempy_labs
sempy_labs.report.report_rebind_all (dataset = 'Current semantic model'
,new_dataset = 'New semantic model')
```

This will probably be one of the most common use cases for Semantic Link in the coming months, as many organizations seek the most convenient way to migrate their existing Import and DirectQuery models to Direct Lake.

Augment the Gold Layer

If we agree that the gold layer contains business-reporting-ready data, usually implemented as a star schema data model, and all the necessary, verified business logic (calculations that are checked and verified by domain experts), the common scenario is to use a reporting tool of choice, such as Power BI, to consume the data from this gold layer. There's more information about star schema and its relevance for Power BI models (*https://oreil.ly/QAzDH*) on the Microsoft website.

In real life, we usually create data marts to support individual departments or business groups (e.g., financials, marketing, HR), so we end up having multiple reports (e.g., sales, financial forecast, customer retention) with each connected to a particular semantic model. Now, imagine the following scenario: you get a requirement from a user—and let's pretend that it's a very important user like a CFO—who needs to have both sales and financial forecast data at their disposal. We can either create a dashboard and pin visuals from both reports, or we can design another semantic model, Sales+forecast, to combine information from the existing models. Let's discard the "dashboard option" and focus on the option to merge information from multiple semantic models.

At first glance, this might look like a trivial task—grab tables from here and there, and there you go. But, let's stop for a moment and consider the following:

- This approach requires the serious involvement of someone responsible for creating semantic models, which means there is a dependency on the availability of this individual.

- What about the calculations that were already verified and are part of the existing semantic models? If we create a new semantic model by simply combining tables from the existing ones, calculations need to be defined from scratch. This is fine if you have just a few of them, but what if your semantic model contains hundreds of calculations?

In this case, we want to focus on the following scenario: let's imagine that you have an existing semantic model with a one-billion-row fact table on a day-level of granularity. The semantic model contains more than one hundred verified calculations. Now, a small group of users needs to analyze the data on a monthly level (for budgeting, forecasting, etc.). To satisfy this requirement, you have a few options at your disposal:

Extend the existing semantic model
> You can extend the existing semantic model with the aggregated table to a monthly level. This approach may work very well until the queries hit your aggregated tables. If not, performance will probably suffer. In addition, someone needs to create those aggregated tables, add them to a semantic model, establish relationships, set the proper storage mode for each table, and, finally, manage aggregations from Power BI.

Create a new semantic model
> You can create a new semantic model with a fact table on a monthly level. The performance of this model should definitely be better than that of the previous one, but what happens with the hundred-plus calculations? Yes, you're right: you would have to re-create them in the new semantic model.

Augment the existing data model
> You can augment the existing data model by leveraging Semantic Link. This would be a mix of the previous two approaches: you'll create a new semantic model, assuming that we store the SQL query results in the Delta table, but

this semantic model may also include more than a hundred verified calculations available out of the box.

When run from a Fabric notebook, the following query will change the granularity—we are moving from the individual date to the year/month level—while keeping the existing measures available:

```sql
%%sql
SELECT
    YEAR(`Dates[Date]`) as _Year
    , MONTH(`Dates[Date]`) as _Month
    , CAST(SUM(`Sales Amt`) AS DECIMAL (18,2)) as SalesAmt
    , CAST(SUM(`Sales Qty`) AS DECIMAL (18,2)) as SalesQty
FROM pbi.`S1`.`_Metrics`
GROUP BY YEAR(`Dates[Date]`)
    , MONTH(`Dates[Date]`)
```

If necessary, this code snippet can be run to create a Delta table, which will persist the query results in the lakehouse.

 Leveraging Semantic Link to create a new semantic model as a combination of multiple existing semantic models, although it looks very handy, is far from the best practice, and it should definitely not be your default choice. However, it's good to have the possibility to choose between different options and, based on the specific scenario, decide which one works in the most efficient way in that particular use case.

Summary

Data scientists will definitely feel like first-class citizens in Microsoft Fabric. This comes as no surprise given the numerous capabilities that Fabric provides out of the box. MLflow is the best example, as a built-in feature for managing the complete machine learning lifecycle. On a similar note, the SynapseML Spark library provides scalable machine learning tools, and users can easily streamline their predictions to Power BI. Let's not forget AutoML, which automates the process of building machine learning models in Fabric.

All of these capabilities undoubtedly have their place in regular data science work-loads. However, there is one special ingredient for data science in Microsoft Fabric: the Semantic Link feature is that "X factor," something that gives a whole new dimension to the data science experience and opens an infinite number of use cases. We firmly believe that Semantic Link is the missing link, bridging the gap between data science and business intelligence.

In Chapter 8, we explore scenarios for handling streaming data by using the Real-Time Intelligence workload in Microsoft Fabric.

Real-Time Intelligence

Once upon a time, handling streaming data was considered an avant-garde approach in the data processing world. Since the introduction of relational database management systems in the 1970s and traditional data warehouse systems in the late 1980s, all data workloads began and ended with so-called *batch processing*. Batch processing relies on the concept of collecting numerous tasks in a group (or batch) and processing these tasks in a single operation.

On the flip side, there is a concept of *streaming data*. Although streaming data is still sometimes considered a cutting-edge technology, it already has a solid history. The roots of streaming data processing go as far back as 2002, when Stanford University researchers published a paper called "Models and Issues in Data Stream Systems" (*https://oreil.ly/iEYVz*). However, it wasn't until almost a decade later (2011) that streaming data systems started to reach a wider audience with the release of the open source Apache Kafka platform for storing and processing streaming data. The rest is history, as people say. Nowadays, processing streaming data is considered not a luxury but a necessity.

Microsoft recognized the growing need to process data as soon as it arrives. Microsoft Fabric doesn't disappoint in that regard: Real-Time Intelligence is at the core of the entire Fabric platform and offers a whole range of capabilities to handle streaming data efficiently.

Before we dive deep into explaining each component of Real-Time Intelligence, let's take a step back and for a more tool-agnostic look at stream processing in general.

What Is Stream Processing?

If you enter "what is stream processing" in Google Search, you'll get more than 100,000 results! Therefore, we're sharing the illustration in Figure 8-1, which represents *our* understanding of stream processing.

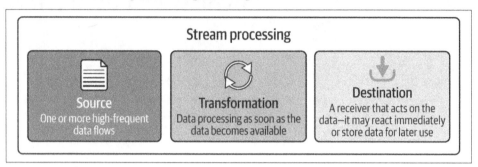

Figure 8-1. The key components of stream processing

We consider any high-frequency data flow as a source. The key ingredients of streaming data systems are the nature of data processing and potential data transformation, which occur at the time the data is created. Various data destinations that may react immediately or store the data for later usage are the final pieces in this jigsaw.

Let's now examine typical use cases for stream processing. Each of the real-life scenarios listed here relies heavily on having the data processed as soon as it's created in the source system:

- Fraud detection
- Real-time stock trades
- Customer activity
- Log monitoring for troubleshooting systems, devices, etc.
- Security information and event management, such as analyzing logs and real-time event data for monitoring and threat detection
- Warehouse inventory
- Rideshare matching
- Machine learning and predictive analytics

As you may have noticed, streaming data has become an integral part of numerous real-life scenarios and is considered vastly superior to traditional batch processing for the aforementioned use cases.

Let's now explore how streaming data processing is performed in Microsoft Fabric and which tools we have at our disposal. Figure 8-2 shows the high-level overview of all Real-Time Intelligence components in Microsoft Fabric.

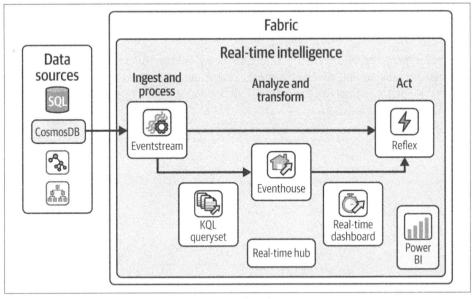

Figure 8-2. Real-Time Intelligence in Microsoft Fabric

In the following sections, we will break down each of these components in more detail. For starters though, let's take a 10,000-foot overview of the entire workflow. We usually start by identifying data sources. An *eventstream* is then created to connect to the specified data source and ingest the streaming data into Fabric. Eventstreams can optionally be leveraged to transform the data on the fly, before sending the transformed data to a destination. A destination can be both an Activator reflex item, which enables immediate action if the specified conditions are met, and an eventhouse, where we can store data for later usage. Once the data is stored in the eventhouse, it can be consumed in numerous ways—for example, it may be queried by leveraging the KQL queryset item or visualized by using Real-Time Dashboards or Power BI reports.

Last, but not least, please keep in mind that every Real-Time Intelligence item can be accessed and managed from a Real-Time hub, a central storage repository for all organizational data, which is an important part of OneLake. (We covered OneLake in depth in Chapter 3.)

Real-Time Hub

Let's kick it off by introducing a Real-Time hub. Every Microsoft Fabric tenant automatically provisions a Real-Time hub. This is a focal point for all *data in motion* across the entire organization. Similar to OneLake, there can be one, and only one, Real-Time hub per tenant; you can't provision or create multiple Real-Time hubs.

The main purpose of the Real-Time hub is to enable quick and easy discovery, ingestion, management, and consumption of streaming data from a wide range of sources. Figure 8-3 shows an overview of all the data streams in the Real-Time hub in Microsoft Fabric.

Figure 8-3. Real-Time hub in Microsoft Fabric

Let's now explore the available options in the Real-Time hub, starting from the top:

All data streams
> The "All data streams" tab displays all the streams and tables you can access. Streams represent the output from Fabric eventstreams, whereas tables come from KQL databases. We'll explore both eventstreams and KQL databases in more detail later in this chapter.

My data streams
> The "My data streams" tab shows all the streams you brought into "My work-space" in Microsoft Fabric.

Data sources
> The "Data sources" tab is at the core of bringing the data into Fabric, both from inside and outside. It enables you to choose among numerous, out-of-the-box provided connectors, such as Kafka, CDC (change data capture) streams for various database systems, external cloud solutions like AWS and GCP (Google Cloud Platform), and many more. Figure 8-4 shows a small fraction of the connectors available in the "Data sources" tab.

Figure 8-4. Connectors in the "Data sources" tab in the Real-Time hub

Microsoft sources

The "Microsoft sources" tab filters the previous set of sources to display Microsoft data sources only.

Fabric events

The "Fabric events" tab displays the list of system events generated in Microsoft Fabric that you can access. Here, you may choose among Job events, OneLake events, and Workspace item events. Let's look at each of these options:

- *Job events* are produced by status changes on Fabric monitor activities, such as job created, succeeded, or failed.

- *OneLake events* are produced by actions on files and folders in OneLake, such as file created, deleted, or renamed.

- *Workspace item events* are produced by actions on workspace items, such as item created, deleted, or renamed.

Azure events

The "Azure events" tab shows the list of system events generated in Azure Blob Storage.

Real-Time hub provides various connectors for ingesting the data into Microsoft Fabric. It also enables the creation of streams for all of the supported sources. After a stream is created, you can process, analyze, and act on it:

Processing

Processing a stream enables you to apply numerous transformations, such as aggregate, filter, and union. The goal is to transform the data before you send the output to a supported destination.

Analyzing

Analyzing a stream enables you to add a KQL database as a destination for the stream, then open the KQL database and execute queries against it.

Acting

Acting on streams refers to setting alerts based on conditions and specifying actions to be taken when certain conditions are met.

Eventstreams

If you're a no-code or low-code data professional and you need to handle streaming data, you'll love eventstreams. In a nutshell, an eventstream allows you to connect to numerous data sources (which we saw in the Real-Time hub section), optionally apply various data transformation steps, and then output results into one or more destinations. Figure 8-5 illustrates a common workflow for ingesting streaming data into three destinations—eventhouse, lakehouse, and Activator.

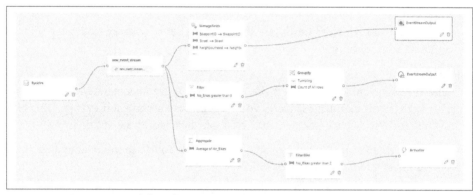

Figure 8-5. Common workflow for ingesting data with eventstream

Eventhouse and Activator are core components of the Real-Time Intelligence workload in Fabric. Hence, we cover them in more detail in the following sections of this chapter. A lakehouse, as we discussed in Chapter 5, may be used for storing unstructured, semi-structured, and structured data in OneLake. It's similar to an eventhouse, but it belongs to a Data Engineering workload.

Within the eventstream settings, you can adjust the retention period for the incoming data. By default, data is retained for one day, and events are automatically removed when the retention period expires.

Aside from that, you may also want to fine-tune the event throughput for incoming and outgoing events, as shown in Figure 8-6. There are three options to choose from: Low (< 1 MB/s), Medium (1–50 MB/s), and High (> 100 MB/s).

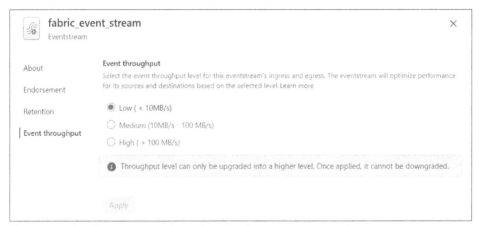

Figure 8-6. Configuring event throughput in the eventstream settings

In the Endorsement tab of the eventstream settings, you can label the eventstream as Promoted (recommended for others to use) or Certified (considered a trusted source), as shown in Figure 8-7.

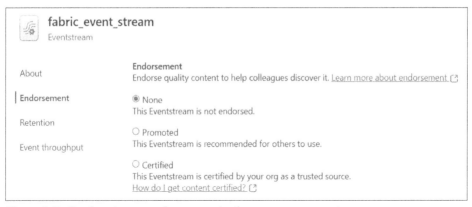

Figure 8-7. Configuring an endorsement in the eventstream settings

Eventstreams can be easily activated and deactivated with the option in the ribbon. This can be done on two different levels:

Deactivate/Activate All
    This will pause/resume all the activities in the eventstream.

Deactivate/Activate toggle switch button
    This will pause/resume all the activities on a particular eventstream node.

Eventhouse and KQL Database

In the previous section, you learned how to connect to various streaming data sources, optionally transform the data, and load it into the final destination. As you might have noticed, one of the available destinations is the eventhouse. In this section, we'll explore two Microsoft Fabric items used to store data within the Real-Time Intelligence workload—an eventhouse and a KQL database.

Eventhouse

An eventhouse is nothing but a container for KQL databases. An eventhouse itself does not store any data; it simply provides the infrastructure within the Fabric workspace for dealing with streaming data. Figure 8-8 displays the System overview page of an eventhouse.

 You might be wondering what the differences are between lake-houses (covered in Chapter 5), warehouses (covered in Chapter 6), and eventhouses and when it would make sense to choose each of these items. Don't worry: we cover the key use cases and implementation scenarios in Chapter 18.

Figure 8-8. System overview page of a Fabric eventhouse

The great thing about the System overview page is that it provides all the key information at a glance. Therefore, you can immediately see the running state of the eventhouse, OneLake storage usage (further broken down per individual KQL database level), compute usage, most-active databases and users, and recent events.

If we switch to the Databases page, we'll be able to see a high-level overview of KQL databases that are part of the current eventhouse, as shown in Figure 8-9.

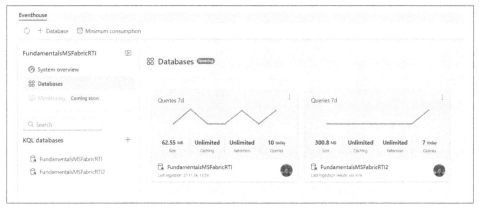

Figure 8-9. Databases page showing all KQL databases in the eventhouse

You can create multiple eventhouses in a single Fabric workspace. Also, a single eventhouse may contain one or more KQL databases (see Figure 8-10).

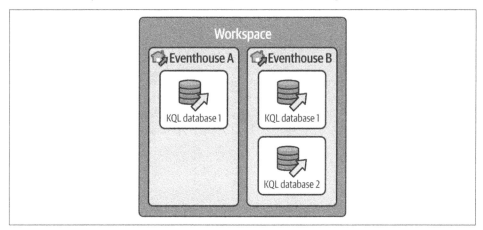

Figure 8-10. Eventhouses containing one and more than one KQL databases

Let's wrap up the story about eventhouse by explaining the concept of *minimum consumption*. By design, eventhouses are optimized to auto-suspend services when not in use. Therefore, when these services are reactivated, it might take some time for the eventhouse to be fully available again. However, there are certain business scenarios in which this latency is not acceptable; think of real-time stock trading or credit card fraud detection, where every second matters. In those scenarios, you should make sure to configure the minimum consumption setting.

By specifying a minimum consumption level, the service is always available, but you are in charge of determining the minimum level, which is then available for

KQL databases inside the eventhouse. Table 8-1 shows the options for configuring minimum consumption (*https://oreil.ly/lfZMg*).

Table 8-1. Minimum consumption options for a Fabric eventhouse

Minimum consumption level	Minimum CUs	SSD capacity of free storage (in GBs)
XXXS (Extra extra extra small)	2.25	25
XXS (Extra extra small)	4.25	50
XS (Extra small)	8.5	200
S (Small)	13	800
M (Medium)	18	3,500–4,000
L (Large)	26	5,250–6,000
XL (Extra large)	34	7,000–8,000
XXL (Extra extra large)	50	10,500–12,000

SSD capacity of free storage is essentially a limited premium storage included in this service.

 If you choose to go this route and configure the minimum consumption on your own, you'll always pay for the selected minimum compute level, unless you go above the specified minimum consumption level. In that case, you'll pay for the actual consumption. This may have an impact on your decision about Fabric capacity size, since the XXS level, for example, won't work below F8 capacity.

KQL Database

Now that you've learned about the eventhouse container, let's focus on examining the core item for storing real-time analytics data—the KQL database.

But first, let's take a step back and explain the origin of the name. While most data professionals have heard of SQL (which stands for Structured Query Language), we are quite confident that KQL is way more cryptic than its "structured" relative.

You might have rightly assumed that *QL* in the abbreviation stands for Query Language. But, what does this letter *K* represent? It's an abbreviation for *Kusto*. We hear you, we hear you: what is Kusto?! Although the urban legend says that the language was named after the famous polymath and oceanographer Jacques Cousteau (his last name is pronounced "Kusto"), we couldn't find any official information from Microsoft to confirm this story. What is definitely known is that it was the internal project name for the Log Analytics Query Language (*https://oreil.ly/__bYI*).

While we're talking about the past, let's share some more history lessons. If you've ever worked with Azure Data Explorer (ADX), you're in luck: KQL database in Microsoft Fabric is the official successor to ADX. Similar to many other Azure data services that were rebuilt and integrated into the SaaS-ified nature of Fabric, ADX provided a platform for storing and querying real-time analytics data for KQL databases. The engine and core capabilities of the KQL database are the same as those in ADX. The key difference is the management behavior: ADX represented a PaaS (platform as a service), whereas KQL database is a SaaS solution.

Although you can store any data in a KQL database (unstructured, semi-structured, and structured), its main purpose is to handle telemetry, logs, events, traces, and time series data. Under the hood, the engine leverages optimized storage formats, automatic indexing and partitioning, and advanced data statistics for efficient query planning.

Let's now examine how to leverage the KQL database in Microsoft Fabric to store and query real-time analytics data. Creating a KQL database in Fabric is as straightforward as it could be. Figure 8-11 illustrates the two-step process.

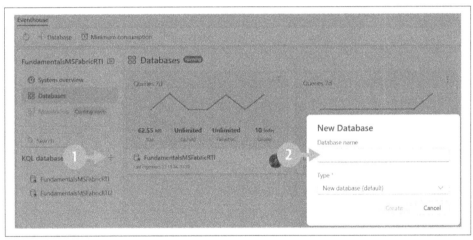

Figure 8-11. Two-step process for creating a KQL database

1. Click on the "+" sign next to "KQL databases."
2. Provide the database name and choose its type. Type can be the default "New database" or a shortcut database. A shortcut database is a reference to a different database that can be either another KQL database in Real-Time Intelligence in Microsoft Fabric or an Azure Data Explorer database.

Don't confuse the OneLake shortcuts we discussed in Chapter 3 with the shortcut database type in Real-Time Intelligence! While the latter simply reference the entire KQL/Azure Data Explorer database, OneLake shortcuts allow the use of the data stored in Delta tables across other OneLake workloads, such as lakehouses and warehouses, or even external data sources (ADLS Gen2, Amazon S3, Dataverse, Google Cloud Storage, to name a few). This data can then be accessed from KQL databases using the `exter nal_table()` function.

Let's now take a quick tour of the key features of the KQL database from the user interface perspective. Figure 8-12 illustrates the main points of interest.

Figure 8-12. Key features of the KQL database

1. Tables displays all the tables in the database.

2. Shortcuts shows tables created as OneLake shortcuts.

3. *Materialized views* represent the aggregation query over a source table or another materialized view. A materialized view consists of a single `summarize` statement.

4. *Functions* are user-defined functions stored and managed on a database level, similar to tables.

5. "Data streams" shows all streams that are relevant for the selected KQL database.

6. Data Activity Tracker shows the activity in the database for the selected time period.

7. "Tables/Data preview" enables switching between two views. Tables displays the high-level overview of the database tables, whereas "Data preview" shows the top 100 records of the selected table.

Query and Visualize Data in Real-Time Intelligence

Now that you've learned how to store real-time analytics data in Microsoft Fabric, it's time to get our hands dirty and provide some business insight out of this data. In this section, we'll focus on explaining various options for extracting useful information from the data stored in the KQL database, introduce common KQL functions for data retrieval, and explore Real-Time dashboards for visualizing the data.

KQL Queryset

The KQL queryset is the Fabric item used to run queries and view and customize results from various data sources. As soon as you create a new KQL database, the KQL queryset item will be provisioned. This is a default KQL queryset that is automatically connected to the KQL database under which it exists. The default KQL queryset doesn't allow multiple connections.

On the flip side, when you create a custom KQL queryset item, you can connect it to multiple data sources, as shown in Figure 8-13.

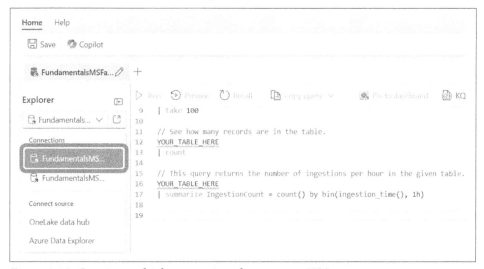

Figure 8-13. Creating multiple connections for a custom KQL queryset

Let's now introduce the building blocks of KQL and examine some of the most commonly used operators and functions. KQL is a fairly simple yet powerful language. To some extent, it's similar to SQL, especially in terms of using schema entities that are organized in hierarchies, such as databases, tables, and columns.

The most common type of KQL query statement is a *tabular expression* statement. This means that both query input and output consist of tables or tabular datasets. Operators in a tabular statement are sequenced by the "|" (pipe) symbol. Data flows (is piped) from one operator to the next, as shown in this code snippet:

```
MyTable
| where StartTime between (datetime(2024-11-01) .. datetime(2024-12-01))
| where State == "Texas"
| count
```

 The piping is sequential, and the data flows from one operator to the next. This means that the query operator order is important, as it may have an impact on both the output results and the performance.

In the previous code example, the data in MyTable is first filtered on the StartTime column and then filtered on the State column, and, finally, the query returns a table containing a single column and single row, displaying the count of the filtered rows.

Do I Need KQL If I Already Know SQL?

A fair question at this point would be, What if I already know SQL? Do I need to learn another language just for the sake of querying real-time analytics data? The answer is, as usual, it depends.

Luckily, we have good and great news to share here!

The good news is: you *can* write SQL statements to query the data stored in a KQL database. But, the fact that you *can* do something doesn't mean you *should*… By using SQL-only queries, you are missing the point and limiting yourself from using many KQL-specific functions that are built to cope with real-time analytics queries in the most efficient way.

The great news is: by leveraging the explain operator, you can "ask" Kusto to translate your SQL statement into an equivalent KQL statement, as shown in Figure 8-14.

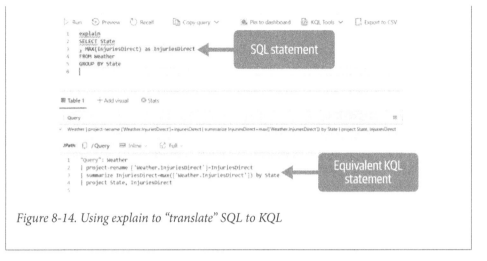

Figure 8-14. Using explain to "translate" SQL to KQL

In the following examples, we query the sample Weather dataset, which contains data about storms and damage in the US. Let's start simple and then introduce some more complex queries. In the first example, we count the number of records in the Weather table:

```
//Count records
Weather
| count
```

Wondering how to retrieve only a subset of records? You can use either the take or limit operator:

```
//Sample data
Weather
| take 10
```

Please keep in mind that the take operator will not return the *top n* records, unless your data is sorted in a specific order. Normally, the take operator returns *any n* records from the table.

In the next step, we want to extend this query and return not only a subset of rows but also a subset of columns:

```
//Sample data from a subset of columns
Weather
| take 10
| project State, EventType, DamageProperty
```

The project operator is the equivalent of the SELECT statement in SQL. It specifies which columns should be included in the result set.

In the following example, we create a calculated column, `Duration`, which represents a duration between `EndTime` and `StartTime` values. In addition, we want to display only the top 10 records sorted by the `DamageProperty` value in descending order:

```
//Create calculated columns
Weather
| where State == 'NEW YORK' and EventType == 'Winter Weather'
| top 10 by DamageProperty desc
| project StartTime, EndTime, Duration = EndTime - StartTime, DamageProperty
```

Now is the right moment to introduce the `summarize` operator. This operator produces a table that aggregates the content of the input table. Therefore, the following statement will display the total number of records per state, including only the top five states:

```
//Use summarize operator
Weather
| summarize TotalRecords = count() by State
| top 5 by TotalRecords
```

Let's expand on the previous code and visualize the data directly in the result set. We'll add another line of KQL code to render results as a bar chart, as shown in Figure 8-15.

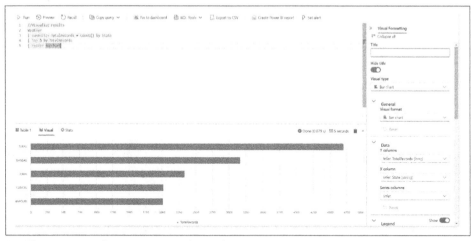

Figure 8-15. Visualizing query results in the query view

As you may notice, the chart can be additionally customized from the Visual Formatting pane on the right-hand side, which provides even more flexibility when visualizing the data stored in a KQL database.

In some scenarios, you may need to perform a conditional count. It's fairly simple to do this in KQL using the `countif` function:

```
//Conditional count
Weather
| summarize StormsWithCropDamage = countif(DamageCrops > 0) by State
| top 10 by StormsWithCropDamage
```

Let's wrap up KQL queryset examples by showing how to calculate the maximum number of injuries per state, renaming the column along the way:

```
//Max injuries per state
Weather
| project-rename ['Weather.InjuriesDirectRenamed']=InjuriesDirect
| summarize InjuriesDirectRenamed=max(['Weather.InjuriesDirectRenamed']) by State
| project State, InjuriesDirectRenamed
```

The first pipe leverages the `project-rename` operator to rename the column in the output result set. Then, we group the data by state and retrieve the maximum value of the renamed column for each state. Finally, the last pipe specifies that only `State` and `InjuriesDirectRenamed` columns should be included in the result set.

These were just basic examples of using KQL language to retrieve data stored in an eventhouse and KQL databases. We can assure you that KQL won't let you down in more advanced use cases when you need to manipulate and retrieve real-time analytics data.

 We understand that SQL is the lingua franca of many data professionals. And although you can write SQL to retrieve the data from the KQL database, we strongly encourage you to refrain from doing this. As a quick reference, we are providing you with a SQL to KQL cheat sheet (*https://oreil.ly/GzMsk*) to give you a head start when transitioning from SQL to KQL.

Real-Time Dashboards

While KQL querysets represent a powerful way to explore and query data stored in eventhouses and KQL databases, their visualization capabilities are pretty limited. Yes, you *can* visualize results in the query view, as you've seen in one of the previous examples, but this is more of a "first aid" visualization that won't make your managers and business decision-makers happy.

Fortunately, there is an out-of-the-box solution in Real-Time Intelligence that supports advanced data visualization concepts and features. Real-Time Dashboard is a Fabric item that enables the creation of interactive and visually appealing business-reporting solutions.

Let's first identify the core elements of the Real-Time Dashboard. A dashboard consists of one or more tiles, optionally structured and organized in pages, where each tile is populated by the underlying KQL query.

As a first step in the process of creating a Real-Time Dashboard, you'll need to enable the feature in the Admin portal of your Fabric tenant, as shown in Figure 8-16.

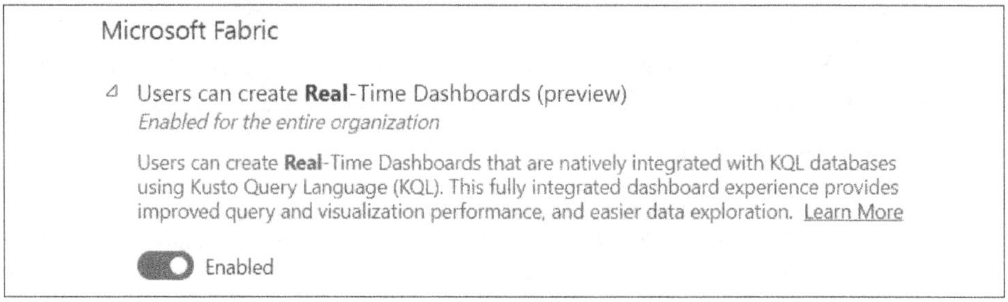

Microsoft Fabric

◿ Users can create **Real**-Time Dashboards (preview)
Enabled for the entire organization

Users can create **Real**-Time Dashboards that are natively integrated with KQL databases using Kusto Query Language (KQL). This fully integrated dashboard experience provides improved query and visualization performance, and easier data exploration. Learn More

Enabled

Figure 8-16. Admin portal: Enable setting for creating Real-Time Dashboards

Next, you should create a new Real-Time Dashboard item in the Fabric workspace. From there, let's connect to our Weather dataset and configure our first dashboard tile. We'll execute one of the queries from the previous section to retrieve the top 10 states with the conditional count function. Figure 8-17 shows the tile settings panel with numerous options to configure.

1. KQL query to populate the tile

2. Visual representation of the data

3. Visual formatting pane with options to set the tile name and description

4. Visual type drop-down menu to select the desired visual type (in our case, it's table visual)

Once you are happy with the tile look and settings, confirm your changes by clicking the "Apply changes" button in the top right corner of the screen. Let's now add two more tiles to our dashboard. We'll copy and paste two queries that we previously used. The first will retrieve the top five states per total number of records, while the second will display the damage property value change over time for the state of New York and for event type, which is winter weather.

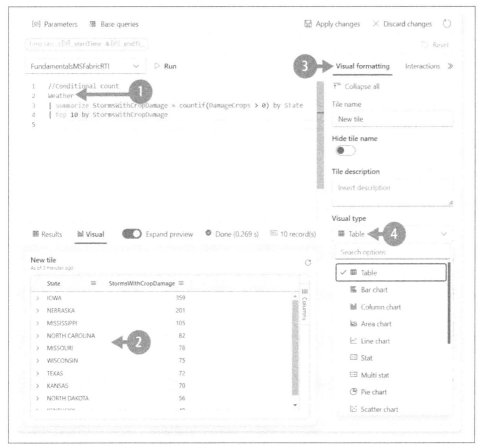

Figure 8-17. Configuration options for a tile in a Real-Time Dashboard

Figure 8-18 displays the Real-Time Dashboard, which consists of three tiles.

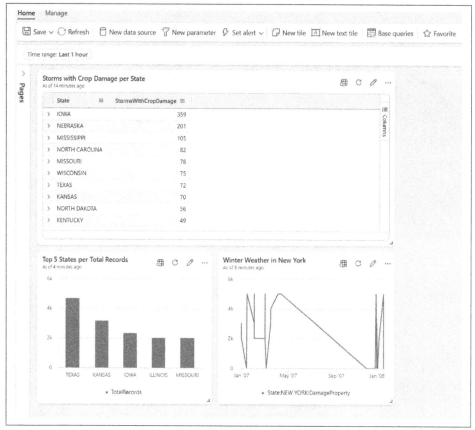

Figure 8-18. Real-Time Dashboard with three tiles

You can also add a tile directly from the KQL queryset to the existing dashboard, as illustrated in Figure 8-19.

Figure 8-19. Pinning the query from the KQL queryset to the existing dashboard

Let's now focus on the various capabilities you have when working with Real-Time Dashboards. In the top ribbon, you'll find options to add a new data source, set a new parameter, and add base queries. However, what really makes Real-Time Dashboards powerful is the ability to set alerts. If the conditions defined in the alert are met, you can trigger a specific action, such as sending an email or a Microsoft Teams message. An alert is created using the Activator item. We'll cover Activator in more detail in the next section.

Figure 8-20 illustrates how to configure the alert on a Real-Time Dashboard tile.

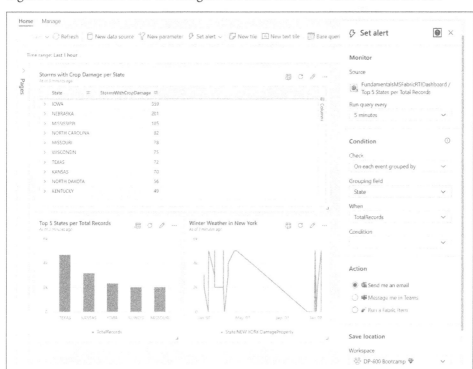

Figure 8-20. Setting the alert on a Real-Time Dashboard tile

You can additionally improve the dashboard performance by leveraging *parameters*. For example, you can parameterize the query and filter the data as early as possible. Hence, the dashboard will render faster. Another handy feature of Real-Time Dashboards is *auto refresh*, which enables you to set an automatic data update so you don't need to refresh the page manually. Auto refresh can be configured from the Manage tab in the top ribbon, as shown in Figure 8-21.

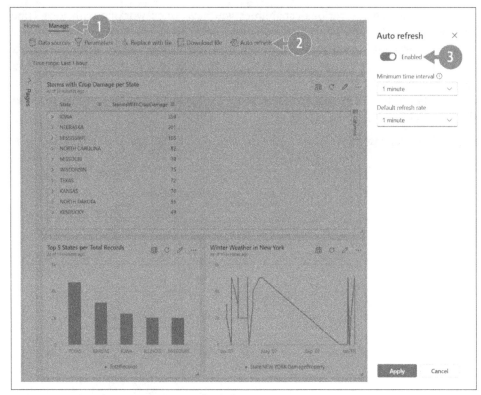

Figure 8-21. Configuring the auto refresh feature

To wrap up the story about Real-Time Dashboards, let's examine the option to export the dashboard. When you export a dashboard, a new JSON file will be created, containing all the details about the dashboard. You may find this feature useful in the following two scenarios:

Dashboard template
> The exported file can be used as a template for creating new dashboards.

Version control
> The exported file can be used to restore the dashboard to a specific version.

Visualize Data with Power BI

Power BI is a mature and widely adopted tool for building robust, scalable, and interactive business reporting solutions. We cover Power BI in more depth in Chapter 9. In this section, we specifically focus on examining how Power BI works in synergy with the Real-Time Intelligence workload in Microsoft Fabric.

Creating a Power BI report based on the data stored in a KQL database couldn't be easier. You can choose to create a Power BI report directly from the KQL queryset, as displayed in Figure 8-22.

Figure 8-22. Creating a Power BI report directly from a KQL queryset

Each query in the KQL queryset represents a single table in the Power BI semantic model. From here, you can build visualizations and leverage all the existing Power BI features to design an effective, visually appealing report.

Obviously, you can still leverage the "regular" Power BI workflow, which assumes you're connecting from the Power BI Desktop to a KQL database as a data source. You'll need to open a OneLake data hub and select KQL Databases as the data source, as illustrated in Figure 8-23.

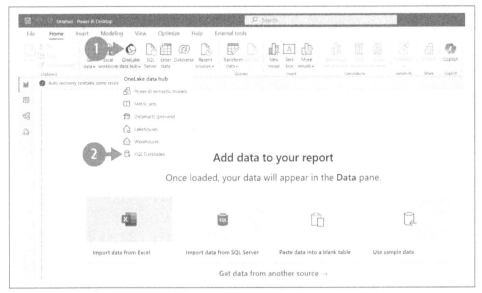

Figure 8-23. Creating a Power BI report by connecting from Power BI Desktop

As with SQL-based data sources, you can choose between the Import and Direct-Query storage modes for your real-time analytics data. Import mode creates a local copy of the data in Power BI's database, while DirectQuery enables querying the KQL database in near real-time.

Activator

How many times have you opened the fridge only to realize there is no milk left? Wouldn't it be great if you could have somehow been warned before you ran out of milk so you could react accordingly and buy more?

This is, in a nutshell, a perfect use case for Activator. Sounds awkward, right? But, we're sure you'll understand it by the end of this chapter, once we explain the core concepts and modus operandi of Fabric Activator.

In plain English, Activator is a no-code solution in Microsoft Fabric that enables not only monitoring the status of your data but also, as its name suggests, *taking actions* based on changes in the status of the data. Activator runs rules against real-time data, and in most cases you won't notice any latency. However, please bear in mind that in some circumstances, latency can be up to 10 minutes. You can learn more about latency in Activator on the Microsoft website (*https://oreil.ly/xQL0z*).

Going back to our milk example, Activator would work similarly to the workflow depicted in Figure 8-24.

Figure 8-24. Simplified overview of the Data Activator workflow

In this chapter, we will discuss how Activator can be leveraged to enrich Microsoft Fabric solutions by incorporating a digital intelligent system for monitoring and acting across all data sources.

Before we proceed, a word of warning when using Activator in Microsoft Fabric. Depending on the configuration settings, it may happen that a high-volume event ingestion causes significant resource consumption. Therefore, always make sure to review the number of events streamed to the Activator items. Sometimes, the events' volume or frequency might be reduced without impacting the business requirements.

Core Activator Concepts

Activator itself is just a service built on top of four core concepts that seamlessly integrate to enable data-driven actions:

Events
> From an Activator perspective, every data source represents a sequence of events, where each event is nothing but the observation of the status of the particular object. In our "fridge and milk" example, an event would be the fridge scanning to determine the status of the milk inside it.

Objects
> The object is the "item of interest" in Activator. This can be a physical object, such as milk in our example, but it can also be an abstract concept like a marketing campaign or user session. If we need to monitor multiple instances of the same object (e.g., if we have more than one fridge to store the milk), each fridge is considered an *object instance*.

Triggers
> Triggers are at the core of Activator. We set triggers to monitor the data and related events, and when the defined threshold is reached, they trigger specified actions.

Properties
> Properties enable reusability of the implemented logic across multiple triggers.

Understanding the Activator Item

As you've already learned in the previous chapters, each Microsoft Fabric experience relies on the concept of items that represent the building blocks of any Fabric solution. Hence, in Data Engineering, you can create items such as lakehouses, notebooks, Spark jobs, and so on. In Power BI, some of the available items are semantic models, reports, and dashboards, and in the Data Warehouse, you can create a warehouse, mirrored databases, and so on.

In Activator, the choice is narrowed down to a single item—Activator. Creating an Activator item requires configuring all the details for connecting to a data source, monitoring conditions, and performing actions. In real life, you would probably want to configure an Activator item for each segment or process you plan to monitor.

Figure 8-25 depicts how triggers, conditions, and actions work in synergy in the Activator to transform your data-driven scenarios from passive to active.

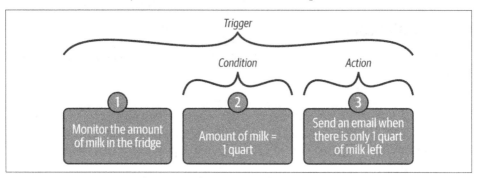

Figure 8-25. Triggers, conditions, and actions working in synergy

Working with Power BI Data

One of the most common scenarios for using Activator is to trigger the action based on data changes in the Power BI report. If you are curious to learn about Power BI in Microsoft Fabric, don't worry, as we cover all the details and provide you with a jump-start in Chapter 9. Here, we'll assume that you are already familiar with basic Power BI concepts and workloads and that your goal is to leverage Activator capabilities on top of the data in a Power BI report.

Let's use our example with milk in the fridge to understand how Activator works with Power BI data. For the sake of simplicity, I'll use an Excel file as a data source for my Power BI report. As shown in Figure 8-26, the Excel file contains the data about the current amount of various beverages in my fridge, such as beer, juice, and milk.

Date	Item	Count
25/09/2024	Beer	6
25/09/2024	Juice	10
25/09/2024	Milk	5
26/09/2024	Beer	5
26/09/2024	Juice	10
26/09/2024	Milk	5
27/09/2024	Beer	3
27/09/2024	Juice	9
27/09/2024	Milk	4
28/09/2024	Beer	2
28/09/2024	Juice	7
28/09/2024	Milk	4
29/09/2024	Beer	2
29/09/2024	Juice	5
29/09/2024	Milk	2
30/09/2024	Beer	2
30/09/2024	Juice	5
30/09/2024	Milk	4
01/10/2024	Milk	1
01/10/2024	Beer	2
01/10/2024	Juice	5

Figure 8-26. Data source for the Power BI report

I'll create a clustered column chart to display the quantity of beverages for each date, as shown in Figure 8-27.

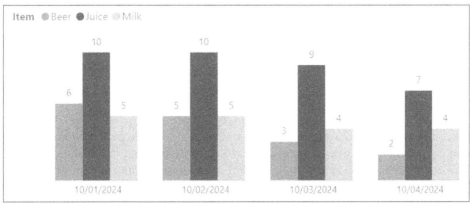

Figure 8-27. Power BI visual displaying the current status of items in the fridge

Once the report is published to Power BI Service, we can configure alerts when the threshold is met. You can see in Figure 8-28 the steps necessary to create an Activator alert.

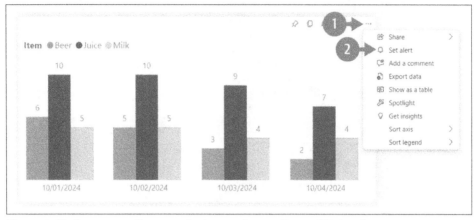

Figure 8-28. Steps to configure an Activator alert on Power BI visual

Let's stop for a moment and examine Figure 8-29, which depicts the various Activator components that we previously examined and the parameters that must be defined when configuring the alert.

1. Specify the visual from the report page that should be monitored. In our case, it's the Total Count per Date clustered column chart.

2. Specifying the condition starts with defining the measure that we want to check. In our case, this is the total quantity.

3. The Operator identifies the logical operator we want to apply. You can choose between multiple options, such as "Becomes greater than," "Becomes less than," "Changes from," "Changes to," and "Changes," to name a few. In our example, we want to be alerted when the quantity is lower or equal to one.

4. In the Value area, enter the threshold value. In our case, that's the number 1.

5. Specify the type of Action you want to take place: send an email or a Microsoft Teams message.

6. Specify the recipients of the alert.

Once the alert has been created, you can open it straight from the Activator item and customize it further. In our example, I want to specify the threshold only on one column from the chart—milk—as I'm currently not interested in monitoring the status of juice or beer. Figure 8-30 shows how the alert can be additionally configured.

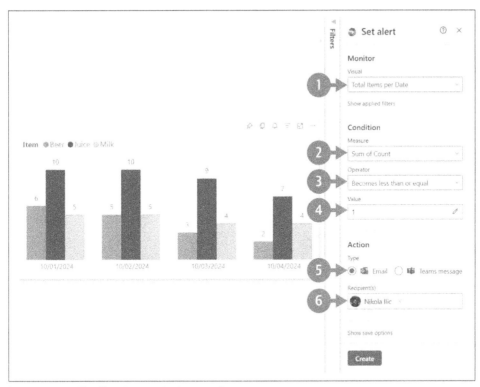

Figure 8-29. *Configuring an Activator alert*

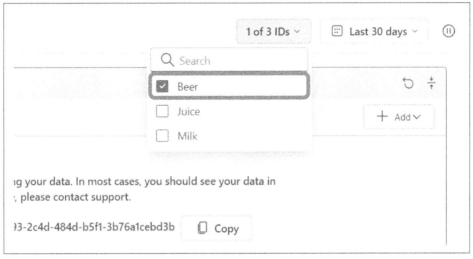

Figure 8-30. *Additional customization of the alert*

I'll now insert new records into my data source, and let's say there is only one quart of milk left in the fridge on September 29. After I refresh my Power BI semantic model, our monitored visual looks as displayed in Figure 8-31.

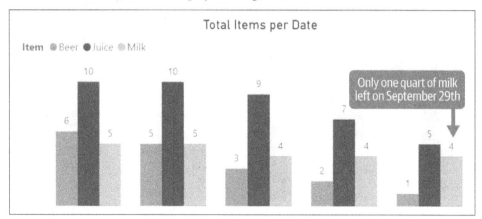

Figure 8-31. The action should be triggered at this point

You can open the Activator item and apply all the necessary configurations directly, or you can simply observe the data as it's being fed from the Power BI report. Figure 8-32 displays the Data view in the Activator item.

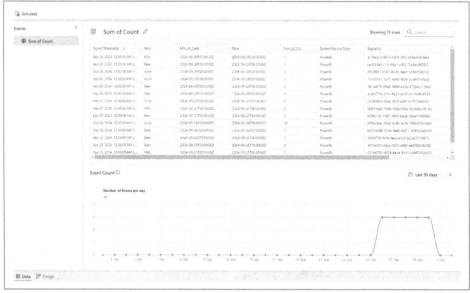

Figure 8-32. Data view of the Activator item

After the trigger condition was met, I received an email message, notifying me that the current count of milk is less than or equal to 1.

You may ask, What happens with the trigger if the milk count doesn't change in the next period? Will the email notification be sent over and over until the milk count increases above 1? The answer is no! The Activator item will check the values in the Power BI visual every 60 minutes, and if the milk value has not changed, it will not trigger the action and won't send another email notification.

Working with Real-Time Hub Data

As you've already learned, Activator was introduced in Microsoft Fabric to address the ever-growing need to act in real time, or as close to real time as possible, based on data changes. It wouldn't be wrong to say that handling real-time data properly has become one of the key requirements for most organizations, regardless of their size.

Hence, though Power BI is a widely adopted business reporting tool, it's commonly used to visualize data with some latency. *Latency* is the time between when the data in the source system changes and the moment that the Power BI semantic model is refreshed and your report shows up-to-date figures.

To return to our milk example, let's say that we are refreshing our Power BI report every 6 hours, starting at 8 A.M. We had 2 quarts of milk in the fridge at 8 A.M., when the Power BI semantic model was refreshed, but then at 9 A.M. there was only 1 quart left. We won't be aware of this change because the action defined in the Activator won't be triggered for another 5 hours—at 2 P.M.—when our next Power BI semantic model refresh operation is scheduled to run.

As we learned earlier in this chapter, Real-Time hub in Microsoft Fabric enables efficient handling of streaming data. Let's take a look at how a Real-Time hub items can be leveraged as a data source for Activator scenarios.

The first thing you may notice is that there are numerous built-in connectors to ingest the data from various sources, both internal to Microsoft Fabric events and external, to bring the streaming data from other cloud vendors or other Microsoft streaming services that are not part of Fabric, such as Azure Event Hubs and IoT hubs.

Figure 8-33 illustrates how the Real-Time hub allows for creating streams for various data sources and how after the stream has been created, you can process, analyze, visualize, and set alerts on these streams.

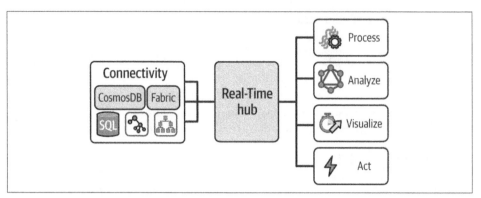

Figure 8-33. A common workflow with Real-Time hub and Activator

Beyond Basic Scenarios

While using Activator in conjunction with Power BI and Real-Time hub will probably be the most frequent scenario you'll encounter, there are many more potential use cases in which you'd want to take a specific action based on the scope of the data change. In this section, we'll examine a few of these ad hoc scenarios.

Trigger Fabric Items

In Chapters 4 and 5, you learned about various data ingestion options in Microsoft Fabric, namely data pipelines and notebooks. We won't get into the scenarios in which to use them (that's in Chapter 18), but we will look at two possible use cases for triggering data pipelines and notebooks with an Activator item:

Trigger the data pipeline when new files arrive at an Azure storage account.
Let's imagine that you want to ingest the data from an Azure storage account into OneLake as soon as the files arrive. You can create an Activator item and then choose a Fabric item as the action type in the rule definition, as shown in Figure 8-34.

Then, you may choose Azure storage events to monitor and, based on the status, trigger the execution of the pipeline that will ingest the data into OneLake.

Trigger the notebook when you identify data quality issues in Power BI reports.
If a certain condition is met in the Power BI report, a notebook can be triggered to clean the data and resolve the issue.

Figure 8-34. Choosing Fabric item as the Action type

Create Custom Actions to Trigger Power Automate Flows

Activator triggers can also be leveraged to initiate specific actions outside of the Microsoft Fabric ecosystem. One of the commonly used solutions for automating processes and operations is Power Automate. Explaining Power Automate is out of the scope of this book, but in a nutshell, it's part of the Power Platform palette of products, and it represents a low-code Microsoft solution for automating and orchestrating business processes. You can find more details about Power Automate on the Microsoft website (*https://oreil.ly/cFT4S*).

What does Power Automate provide that Activator alone can't achieve? In fairness, Power Automate is a more mature and comprehensive solution than Activator. Hence, there are certain areas where Activator simply can't compete with Power Automate.

Two good examples where Power Automate easily beats Activator are:

- Sending notifications using systems other than email and Microsoft Teams
- Calling Power Apps as part of the business process

As a prerequisite for using Activator in a Power Automate flow, you first need to create a custom action in Activator and provide all the necessary information needed for the downstream execution in the Power Automate flow, as depicted in Figure 8-35.

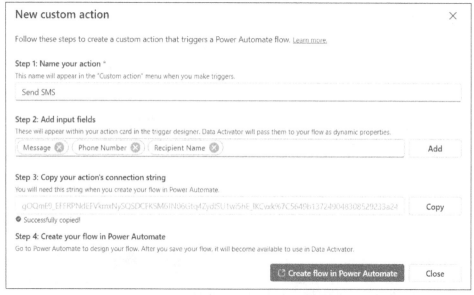

Figure 8-35. Creating a custom action for Power Automate flow

The next step is to use the defined Activator action in the Power Automate flow. As shown in Figure 8-36, once the action triggers, a mobile notification will be sent to the specified user.

Figure 8-36. Using an Activator action in the Power Automate flow

Once created, this custom action can be used as a template across different Activator triggers.

Summary

Real-Time Intelligence—something that at one time was part of the "Synapse experience" in Microsoft Fabric—is now a separate, dedicated workload. That tells us a lot about Microsoft's vision and roadmap for Real-Time Intelligence!

Initially, Real-Time Analytics was included under the Synapse umbrella, together with Data Engineering, Data Warehousing, and Data Science experiences. However, Microsoft thought that handling streaming data deserved a dedicated workload in Microsoft Fabric, which absolutely makes sense considering the growing need to deal with *data in motion* and provide insight from this data as soon as it is captured. In that sense, Microsoft Fabric provides a whole suite of powerful services as the next generation of tools for processing, analyzing, and acting on data as it's generated.

We are quite confident that the Real-Time Intelligence workload will become more and more significant in the future, considering the evolution of data sources and the increasing pace of data generation.

In Chapter 9, we will dive into the wonderful world of visualizing Microsoft Fabric data using Power BI.

Power BI

If you worked with Microsoft Power BI before Microsoft Fabric was announced, you might be (rightly) wondering, What's all the fuss about? Nothing has really changed from the UI perspective, and all of the features and functionalities are still available just as they were in the pre-Fabric era.

And you're absolutely right! The Fabric user interface was built on top of the existing Power BI service UI. To be more precise, all the other experiences and workloads, such as Data Engineering, Data Warehouse, and Real-time Intelligence, which we covered in Chapters 5 to 8, were incorporated into the well-known Power BI experience. Once you navigate to Microsoft Fabric (*https://oreil.ly/YJKnD*) and choose Power BI from the home page, things will look quite familiar to anyone who has ever logged in to the Microsoft Power BI service.

Does this mean that Power BI remained the only unchanged island in the vast sea of innovations that Microsoft Fabric introduced? Absolutely not!

In this chapter, we'll discuss how pre-Fabric Power BI workloads were integrated into the new ecosystem, as well as introduce brand new concepts and features that Microsoft Fabric brought into the Power BI game. We'll also note some points to consider when planning your future analytics solutions and examine various scenarios for leveraging Power BI capabilities in the era of Microsoft Fabric.

Power BI Workloads in the Pre-Fabric Era

Dear reader, if you have never used Microsoft Power BI, we suggest you take a step back and find the Power BI learning resource that best suits your needs—be it a book, an online course, or live training. If you prefer books, we wholeheartedly recommend *Data Modeling with Microsoft Power BI* (*https://oreil.ly/N5T6z*) by Markus Ehrenmueller-Jensen (O'Reilly) or *Learning Microsoft Power BI* (*https://*

oreil.ly/6WuMX) by Jeremey Arnold (O'Reilly). You can also check out other Power BI resources on the O'Reilly learning platform.

In this section, we are giving you the 10,000-foot view of Power BI and its main components so you can continue your Fabric journey feeling well equipped to dive deeper into specific concepts and features of Power BI if necessary. We'll also share some additional resources that we consider useful for learning Power BI.

In a nutshell, Power BI represents a suite of tools and services for business reporting. The main mantra of Power BI is "5 minutes to WOW!" To put it simply, it should take no longer than five minutes from the moment you connect to any of the various disparate data sources until you have nice-looking and visually appealing charts that provide insight from the underlying data. Of course, in reality, it's usually more than five minutes, but the emphasis here is on the ease of use and pace of the development process.

We're not exaggerating when we say that Power BI has managed to live up to its promise. Gartner (*https://oreil.ly/nfwdp*) recognized Microsoft Power BI as an undisputed leader in the analytics and business intelligence platforms "magic quadrant" for multiple years in a row. According to Gartner's definition, a *magic quadrant* is a tool that enables a graphical, competitive positioning of technology providers to help investors make smart investment decisions.

In the context of Fabric, we are talking about Microsoft Power BI as a mature and well-established product that democratizes data analytics workloads. The level of Power BI adoption is already high, and the vibrant community of data professionals using Power BI ensures that the product gets more and more popular over time.

To understand what has changed in Power BI workloads from a Fabric perspective, we first need to examine typical workflows in the pre-Fabric era. Let's kick it off with storage modes. A *storage mode* determines how your data is stored in Power BI semantic models. There are three main options to choose from: Import, DirectQuery, and Dual. We'll first introduce the Import mode, which is the default storage mode in Power BI.

Import Mode for Blazing Fast Performance

When using Import mode, once you connect to a data source, Power BI creates a local copy of the data and stores this local copy in the instance of a tabular Analysis Services model. Analysis Services is an analytical data engine developed by Microsoft and has been used in numerous Microsoft business intelligence solutions since the beginning of this century.

You can apply various transformations, such as replacing values, removing duplicates, and adding new columns, to shape your data and implement additional business logic to enrich the existing data model. The important thing to keep in mind is that, since you are working with a local copy of the data, all the transformations and changes you've applied are relevant *only* to this local copy in the Analysis Services tabular database that Power BI uses for storing the data. Therefore, you don't need to worry that changes made to the Excel file stored in Power BI will be pushed back to the original Excel file stored on your local drive.

Once the data is stored in the Analysis Services tabular database, Power BI keeps it in cache memory, in the columnar, in-memory database called VertiPaq. As you can see in Figure 9-1, all queries generated by the Power BI report will then retrieve the data from this in-memory storage, without even "knowing" about the "real" data source. In this scenario, the only data source is the instance of Analysis Services tabular database, and all the queries will refer to it for data retrieval.

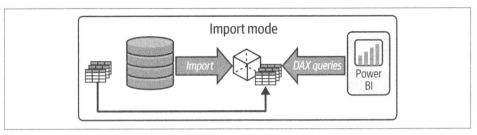

Figure 9-1. Import mode workflow

Since the data is stored in cache memory, the main advantage of using Import mode is that you get the best possible performance of DAX queries. On the flip side, there are certain downsides when going the Import mode route. The most obvious one is *data duplication*, because we are essentially creating a copy of the data from the data source in Power BI's tabular database, as well as *data latency*, because when you import the data from the original data source into Power BI, it is a snapshot *as of that moment*.

Let's illustrate this: imagine that you've imported data from an Excel file stored on your local PC on Monday at 9 A.M. At that time, you had 1,000 records in the Excel file. What happens if you insert another 100 records into the Excel file at 10 A.M.? Well, Power BI doesn't know about those records until you *refresh* the local copy of the data stored in Power BI. This means that between Monday at 9 A.M. and the next data refresh (let's say on Tuesday at 9 A.M.), Power BI will query and display the data as of Monday at 9 A.M.

To wrap up, Import mode provides the best possible experience from the performance point of view, but it also comes with two considerable shortcomings: data duplication and data latency. In addition, depending on the Fabric capacity size, there is a hard limit on the maximum semantic model size. For example, if you're using an F2, F4, or F8 capacity, the maximum model size is 3GB; it's 5GB on F16, 10GB on

F32, 25GB on F64, and so forth. This limit applies to an individual semantic model, not the sum of the memory footprint of all the models in the capacity.

DirectQuery Mode for Real-Time Reporting

DirectQuery mode solves the shortcomings of Import mode.

As you can see in Figure 9-2, there is no duplication, because no data is moved from the original data source into Power BI. Power BI stores metadata only and retrieves the necessary data directly from the source at query time. This means that data resides in its original data source before, during, and after query execution.

There is no latency, either. Since Power BI retrieves the data at query time, whatever data is available from the source at that time will also be available in the Power BI report.

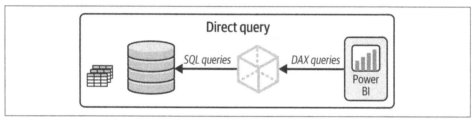

Figure 9-2. DirectQuery workflow

As you can see in Figure 9-2, all DAX queries generated by Power BI are simply translated on the fly into the SQL code and executed directly on the source database.

This is great, isn't it? No data duplication and no data latency, so why don't we simply switch all our semantic models to DirectQuery? The answer is fairly simple: in most cases, the performance of DirectQuery semantic models is *significantly* worse than in Import mode. First of all, it highly depends on the data source's performance capabilities, as well as network bandwidth and latency. Throw in the potential bottleneck of an on-premises data gateway, and we are talking about performance degradation on an order of magnitude; DirectQuery will usually go multiple times slower than Import mode when reporting over the same data.

Therefore, choosing between Import and DirectQuery mode is usually a trade-off between the performance and real-time reporting requirements, as depicted in Table 9-1.

Table 9-1. Import versus DirectQuery mode comparison

Storage mode	Advantages	Disadvantages	Use case
Import	• Best possible performance • All DAX functions supported	• Data latency • Data duplication • Max model size (depends on the capacity size)	• Suitable for most scenarios
DirectQuery	• No data latency • No data duplication	• Significantly worse performance • Not all DAX functions supported • Data modeling limitations	• Real-time reporting requirements • Data size too large for Import mode

Additionally, not all DAX functions are supported in DirectQuery mode because certain DAX functions can't be "translated" into SQL language.

Last but definitely not least, some data sources don't support any querying language. Think of good old Excel; Power BI doesn't provide an interface for querying Excel files. Hence, your DAX queries can't be translated into a language that Excel "understands." As a consequence, you can't use DirectQuery mode if your data source is an Excel file or any similar file type, such as CSV.

Truth be told, the choice might be more nuanced, as Power BI allows you to mix and match Import and DirectQuery modes in the form of the composite model. A *composite model* uses two or more connections to different source groups. As shown in Figure 9-3, a source group is considered any individual DirectQuery source, such as SQL Server or Oracle, whereas all imported data is considered one source group.

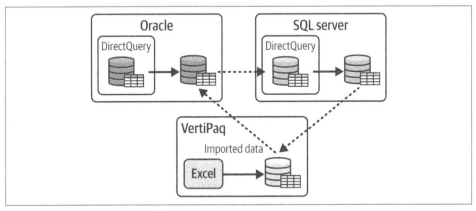

Figure 9-3. A composite model in Power BI

Although this "combo" may come in handy in various semantic model design scenarios, it still doesn't resolve the individual shortcomings of Import and DirectQuery modes. Composite models can also be built on top of Power BI semantic models. In this scenario, you are establishing a DirectQuery connection to published Power BI semantic models in the Power BI service and then combining that data with other DirectQuery and/or imported data. However, this approach comes with many potential caveats due to complex dependencies, so we suggest you implement it with special care.

There is also a third storage mode option, called Dual, that represents a hybrid version of Import and DirectQuery. Dual is widely used in composite models to resolve the constraints of limited relationships between tables in the semantic model. Explaining the shortcomings of limited relationships is outside the scope of this book.

Dual storage mode is commonly used for dimension tables in composite models. In this case, Power BI keeps two copies of the same table—one in Import mode and the other in DirectQuery mode—and, depending on whether a query retrieves data from the Import mode or DirectQuery fact table, the "dual" table "behaves" the same as a fact table, ensuring that queries can take advantage of the regular relationships.

Power BI Workloads in Microsoft Fabric

In Chapter 1, you learned that Microsoft Fabric integrated many of existing data services and solutions and unified them under one umbrella. However, Fabric also introduced many brand-new concepts and features that may be considered a next step in the ever-evolving ecosystem of modern data platforms.

 All the storage modes we examined so far—Import, DirectQuery, and Dual—are here to stay, and they are all still relevant in the era of Microsoft Fabric.

Understanding Direct Lake Mode

Direct Lake undoubtedly represents one of these new features. The aim of Direct Lake is straightforward: to exploit the benefits and overcome the downsides of both Import and DirectQuery modes, which we examined in the previous section. We want the performance of Import mode to match the "no data duplication and no data latency" of DirectQuery mode. Sounds fairly simple, right? However, there is a whole range of resolutions and processes required in the background to enable this magic to happen. Let's start by looking at Figure 9-4.

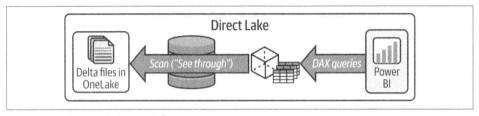

Figure 9-4. Direct Lake workflow

As in the DirectQuery scenario, in Direct Lake mode, Power BI doesn't store a physical copy of the data in the Analysis Services tabular database, and all DAX queries are executed directly against the files stored in OneLake, be it a lakehouse or a warehouse.

However, the way the data is stored in Delta tables (in Parquet files or, as Microsoft prefers to call it, Delta Parquet format) is very similar to the way it's stored in the proprietary format of the Analysis Services tabular database (*.idf* format). Therefore, the engine is capable of transcoding the data from OneLake on the fly with minimal effort and overhead and then storing the data in memory, the same as in Import mode! Hence, we get the performance of Import mode (or very close to Import mode) without creating a copy of the data and without needing to refresh our Power BI semantic model (although we'll soon explain the concept of refresh in Direct Lake mode).

Although you might see in Microsoft presentations that Direct Lake is labeled a "perfect" solution because it takes the best characteristics of both Import and DirectQuery, we consider this too bold of a statement, and we'll stick with an unbiased and less-markety approach in our interpretation of Direct Lake. We'll examine Direct Lake limitations at the end of this chapter.

Prerequisites

Before we dive deep into Direct Lake and examine how it works behind the scenes, let's first understand the prerequisites for using it.

First, and most importantly, you need either a Premium capacity (P SKU) with the "Users can create Fabric items" setting explicitly enabled in the Admin portal or a Fabric capacity (F SKU). (Note that P SKUs were officially retired at the beginning of 2025 and can't be renewed anymore, although there are still a significant number of organizations with active P SKU subscriptions.) Individual licenses, such as Premium-per-user, don't support Direct Lake storage mode.

Then, your data must be stored in OneLake inside a lakehouse and/or a warehouse.

Next, data must be stored in *Delta tables*. If your data is stored in any format other than Delta, such as Parquet, CSV, or JSON, Direct Lake cannot be used.

Finally, Delta tables should be V-Ordered. We are intentionally using the word *should* because V-Order is not a hard requirement for Direct Lake. This means that even if your Delta tables are not V-Ordered, Direct Lake could still work, but you might experience performance degradation. We cover V-Order in detail in Chapter 18.

Two "Flavors" of Direct Lake

Direct Lake in Microsoft Fabric comes in two "flavors":

- Direct Lake on OneLake
- Direct Lake on SQL

Let's examine the key differences between these two implementation options. First and foremost, when using Direct Lake on OneLake, you are connecting *directly* to OneLake Delta tables, whereas if you choose a SQL flavor, the data is accessed *via the SQL analytics endpoint* of the lakehouse or warehouse. This distinction impacts many of the available functionalities of Direct Lake semantic models.

Probably the most significant difference is that with Direct Lake on OneLake, a semantic model may contain tables coming from multiple Fabric items. For example, imagine you have a Customer table stored in lakehouse A, a Product table stored in lakehouse B, and a Sales table stored in warehouse C. All these tables can be part of a single Direct Lake on OneLake semantic model. This is not the case with the Direct Lake on SQL semantic models, which may contain tables only from a single Fabric item. Going back to our previous example, you would have to create a shortcut in lakehouse A that points to the Product table in lakehouse B, and bring Sales table data into lakehouse A as well, if you want to use all of them in the Direct Lake on SQL semantic model.

Next, the Direct Lake behavior, which we're going to examine in more detail later in this chapter, is completely different between these two flavors. In Direct Lake on OneLake models, it's not possible to leverage DirectQuery mode for queries that can't use Direct Lake mode: it's Direct Lake or nothing. Whereas with Direct Lake on SQL, queries can still "talk" with the SQL analytics endpoint; thus, DirectQuery fallback behavior is a viable option.

Last but not least, Direct Lake on OneLake models are authored and managed in the Power BI Desktop. On the flip side, Direct Lake on SQL models can be created from the Fabric web interface exclusively; once created, they can be edited in the Power BI Desktop.

A decision about which Direct Lake flavor to use depends on various criteria. We summarize some of the common considerations in Table 9-2.

Table 9-2. Decision criteria for Direct Lake on OneLake versus Direct Lake on SQL

Criteria	Direct Lake on OneLake	Direct Lake on SQL
Number of data sources to create a semantic model	Multi-source	Single-source
DirectQuery requirements	Not supported	Supported
Use database views as a data source	Not supported	Supported (will fall back to DirectQuery)
Permission model	Depends on the data source	Depends on the SQL analytics endpoint of the data source
Model authoring	Power BI Desktop	Fabric Web UI

Creating a Direct Lake on OneLake semantic model starts by opening the OneLake catalog from Power BI Desktop and choosing the Fabric item you want to use from the drop-down menu, as shown in Figure 9-5.

Figure 9-5. Choosing the Fabric item from OneLake catalog

The next step is crucial because it determines whether you are going the OneLake or SQL route. Figure 9-6 illustrates the two options available when connecting to the Fabric lakehouse.

Let's say we've decided to create a Direct Lake on OneLake semantic model. Once we pick the tables from the selected lakehouse, the entire process of creating and managing a semantic model doesn't vary much from the process of creating any other semantic model type, such as Import or DirectQuery. The only difference is that, once it's created, you don't need to publish the model to the Fabric workspace—it will be automatically saved in the workspace you specified during model creation.

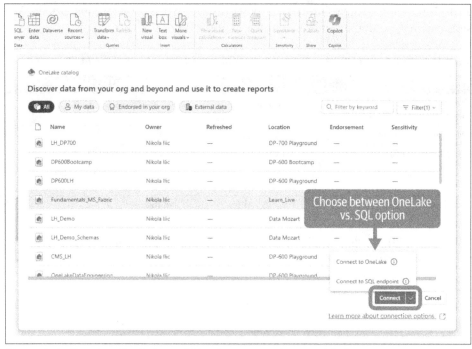

Figure 9-6. Choosing OneLake or SQL when connecting to a lakehouse

You can also enhance the semantic model by creating typical model objects, such as relationships, measures, or calculation groups, to name a few. However, bear in mind that any changes you apply to the model in Power BI Desktop are immediately saved back to the model in the service, so all Power BI reports that are live-connecting to that model will instantly include all the updates—for better or for worse.

On the other hand, if you try to create a brand-new Direct Lake on SQL semantic model from Power BI Desktop by selecting the same lakehouse item, you won't be allowed to do that, since Power BI will prompt you to choose between the Import and DirectQuery modes in that case. However, you *can* connect and edit the existing Direct Lake on SQL semantic model, which was previously created and saved in the Fabric workspace.

Default Versus Custom Semantic Model

Once you create a new lakehouse or warehouse item in the Fabric workspace, don't be surprised when you see unexpected neighbors in the workspace. Each lakehouse comes with two additional companions, a SQL analytics endpoint and a default semantic model; creating a warehouse results in only once additional companion, a default semantic model.

This behavior might be quite baffling for someone who worked with Power BI before Microsoft Fabric and who has just embarked on their Fabric journey.

Let's illustrate this with an example: you are a Power BI developer in a retail company, and you've just created your nice-looking report in Power BI Desktop using the Import mode. You named your report "Sales Overview." You hit the Publish button in Power BI Desktop and choose the workspace where you want your report to be published. If you navigate to the selected workspace, you should see two items with the same name: the report itself and a semantic model. The semantic model item contains the *real* data and other model definitions, including, but not limited to, relationships, hierarchies, and calculated columns and measures. The report item contains the report definitions, such as visuals, filters, and report themes. Behind the scenes, these two items, the report and the semantic model, are tightly coupled and bound.

An important thing to keep in mind is that *the report can't exist without a semantic model*, while the opposite is not true. You *can* use the "Sales Overview" semantic model as a blueprint for multiple unrelated reports by leveraging the *live connection* feature. This enables you to connect to already published Power BI semantic models (and other instances of Azure Analysis Services or SQL Server Analysis Services databases) and build a report on top of an existing semantic model. This report is called a *thin report*.

 You can try it yourself! Delete the report from the workspace, and you'll see that the semantic model is still there. Inversely, if you delete a semantic model from the workspace, you'll notice that the report was also automatically removed. Beware: if you're trying this with real items, make sure to back up your semantic model before you delete it from the workspace.

There are no default versus custom semantic models in the pre-Fabric world. However, for the sake of clarity, we'd like to explain that there is no item named *custom* semantic model. We are simply using this label to draw a distinction between a default semantic model and semantic models that are not created automatically when provisioning a new lakehouse or warehouse. Therefore, whenever you see the word *custom* next to the semantic model, be aware that we are referring to any semantic model that is not a default semantic model.

While the default semantic model may be useful for some basic data exploration and ad hoc requests, we strongly encourage creating custom semantic models for enterprise-grade reporting and regular business use cases.

A custom semantic model should be your go-to choice since it provides a full set of functionalities and can be managed more flexibly than the default semantic model.

This includes, but is not limited to, leveraging popular external tools, such as Tabular Editor, for managing and maintaining Direct Lake semantic models.

The fastest way to create a custom Direct Lake on SQL semantic model is to use the web UI in the Power BI service, although be aware that not all modeling features are available in the web UI compared to Power BI Desktop. As shown in Figure 9-9, you may simply choose the option "New semantic model," which will initiate a similar workflow to the one shown in Figure 9-7. However, this time, you must specify a name for your semantic model. In addition, you may choose to store the semantic model in a workspace other than the one where your lakehouse or warehouse resides. This is important in scenarios where access to workspace items is defined through workspace roles, and you should differentiate between users who should have access to the lakehouse and SQL analytics endpoint objects versus access to the semantic model only.

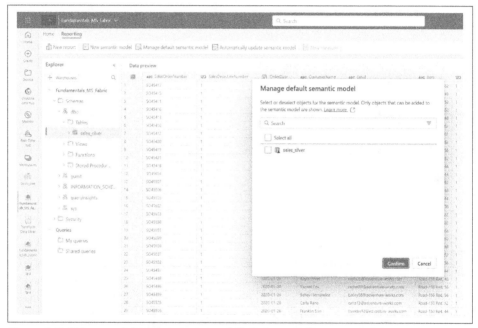

Figure 9-7. "Manage default semantic model" dialog window

Once you add objects to the semantic model, you can proceed with managing the model and enhancing it with relationships, DAX measures, Calculation groups, etc.

To conclude this topic, we summarize the key differences between default and custom semantic models in Table 9-3.

Table 9-3. Key differences between default and custom semantic models

Feature	Default semantic model	Custom semantic model
Automatically created	Yes	No
Can be managed with external tools	No	Yes
Can be stored in a different workspace than the lakehouse	No	Yes
Uses Direct Lake as a default storage mode	Yes	Yes

Syncing the Semantic Model with OneLake

When you create a lakehouse or warehouse, if you stick with the default configuration settings, a default semantic model is just a shell; it doesn't contain any objects. You can add objects to the default semantic model in two ways, as shown in Figures 9-8 and 9-9.

Figure 9-7 showed how to manually add objects using the "Manage default semantic model" feature in the SQL analytics endpoint of the lakehouse. Figure 9-8 uses the property "Sync the default Power BI semantic model" as an option to automatically add new lakehouse objects to a default semantic model.

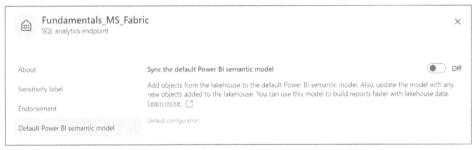

Figure 9-8. Syncing the default Power BI semantic model

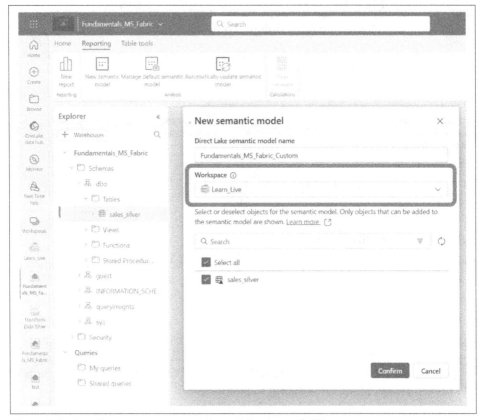

Figure 9-9. Creating a custom semantic model using web UI

Bear in mind that this property is disabled by default, which means any new tables you create in the lakehouse will *not* be automatically included in the default semantic model. To include newly created objects in a default semantic model, you should either enable this property or manually add tables, as shown in Figure 9-8.

Enabling the "Sync the default Power BI semantic model" property will cause permanent background traffic between the default semantic model and OneLake, which might incur additional One-Lake consumption costs.

Direct Lake Key Concepts

Now that we've introduced Direct Lake mode from a high-level perspective, it's time to dig deeper and explain the various concepts behind this feature. Understanding these concepts will not only help you build scalable and efficient semantic models in Fabric but also enable you to implement techniques to build more robust and performant analytics solutions.

How Does Direct Lake Work?

"Performance of the Import mode!" This is how Microsoft will *sell* you the Direct Lake feature. Hence, wondering how that could be possible would be a natural reaction. The answer is fairly simple, although the technical implementation is definitely not.

The key ingredient is the Delta Parquet format. Simply said, data is stored within Delta Parquet files in a way very similar to that in the proprietary format of Power BI's VertiPaq database.

In Figure 9-10, we break down the entire workflow relevant to query processing. Please keep in mind that this workflow doesn't apply exclusively to Power BI but also applies to other Microsoft Fabric workloads.

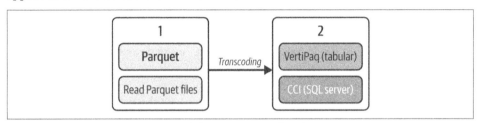

Figure 9-10. Query-processing workflow in Microsoft Fabric

From a Direct Lake perspective, we are interested in both steps of the workflow.

Let's explain this by using an example. Say we have a Power BI report named "Sales Overview." The report is created on top of a Direct Lake semantic model of the same name. Your manager opens the report and starts interacting with visuals. Initially, there is no data in the semantic model. Remember, the physical data is stored in One-Lake, which is based on the "one copy" approach, which we introduced in Chapter 3. Let's assume that the report page contains a table with four columns: Calendar Year, Product Name, Total Revenue, and Total Sales Quantity. Once the report page opens, Power BI will load the data from OneLake *on demand*, meaning Power BI will load only the columns needed by the report. During data loading, the underlying data structures will be transcoded.

Transcoding is the process of translating data stored in Delta Parquet files into the VertiPaq native format. This process is not expensive in terms of time and resources. As we already learned, the way the data is stored in Delta Parquet files is quite similar to VertiPaq's native format. Once the data is transcoded and loaded into VertiPaq, every subsequent report query that targets the same columns will be served from VertiPaq. This is of paramount importance because this is exactly the same modus operandi as in Import mode! Hence, "the performance of Import mode" proclaimed by Microsoft starts to make sense.

 When using Direct Lake, the first queries will take longer to execute because of the time needed for transcoding. Once the data is paged into memory (VertiPaq), from a technical point of view, there is no difference between the Direct Lake and Import storage modes.

Direct Lake Semantic Model Refresh (aka Framing)

One of the biggest points of confusion when discussing Direct Lake use cases is, How do we *refresh* a Direct Lake semantic model? This is a fair question, especially coming from Power BI professionals from the pre-Fabric era, who used to deal with regular and ad hoc refreshes of their Import mode semantic models.

As a quick reminder, when you publish an Import mode semantic model to a workspace, you are just publishing a snapshot of the data at a certain point in time. Then, you need to ensure that the data is up-to-date with the data source, either by refreshing the semantic model on a schedule (e.g., every four hours, every day) or by manually triggering the refresh process. Assuming that you didn't implement an incremental refresh or apply custom partitioning of the tables in the semantic model, each table consists of a single partition that contains all the data. Hence, when you are refreshing a semantic model, all the rows and columns from each table will be reloaded from the data source.

To illustrate, let's imagine that you have a semantic model called Sales Overview in Import mode, which consists of the tables specified in Table 9-4.

Table 9-4. Example tables of the Sales Overview Import semantic model

Table name	Number of rows	Number of columns	Size in MB
DimCustomer	50,000	20	3
DimProduct	3,000	25	1
DimDate	7,000	20	2
FactSales	100,000,000	10	2,000

The following things happen when you initiate a refresh of the Sales Overview semantic model, which is approximately 2 GB in size:

- Power BI will keep a read-only replica of the model during the refresh process so that users can continue using their reports during the refresh window. This implies that you need approximately 4 GB of memory available during the refresh window: 2 GB for the semantic model you are currently refreshing and 2 GB for the read-only replica.

- The entire table will be refreshed if you haven't configured an incremental refresh or applied custom partitioning of the tables. In our case, this means that we need to load 100 million rows in our FactSales table each time we refresh the semantic model.

- Those 100 million data records will be *physically* stored in the FactSales table in the Power BI semantic model.

Therefore, depending on data volumes and some other semantic model design decisions, refreshing Import mode semantic models may be an extremely costly operation, both in terms of time and resources.

The data refresh concept is totally different for Direct Lake semantic models. Since this is not a *real* data refresh, but only a metadata refresh, we will refer to the process of bringing the latest data into Direct Lake semantic models as *framing*.

 Don't confuse framing with syncing! As we've already explained in this chapter, *syncing* enables you to add new tables to your semantic model, while *framing* enables you to have the latest version of the data in a particular table.

However, to understand how framing works in reality, we first need to explain some of the intricacies of data storage in Delta Parquet files. We'll again use our Sales Overview model as an example. This time, we'll focus on the table DimCustomer, which stores data about customers, including attributes such as first name, last name, email address, phone number, ZIP code, and so on. Table 9-5 displays the data for customer Aaron Adams.

Table 9-5. Abbreviated view of the DimCustomer table

Customer key	First name	Last name	Email address	Phone	ZIP code
1	Aaron	Adams	aaron48@adventure-works.com	1-123-4567	12345

If you take a look at Figure 9-11, you may notice that it consists of two Parquet files. Additionally, you'll spot an item called *_delta_log*, which enables tracking of all the changes that happened to the DimCustomer table.

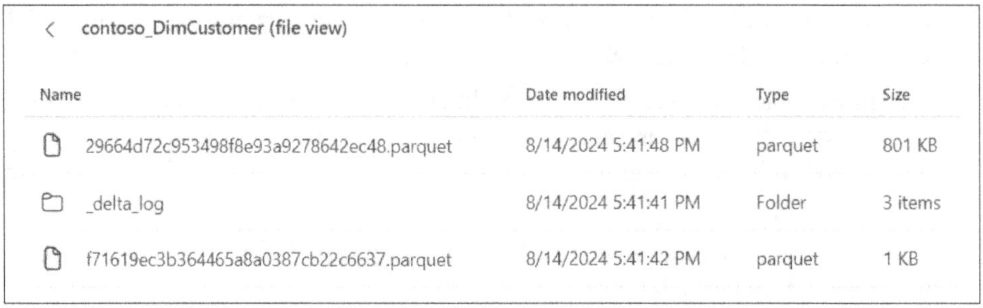

Figure 9-11. DimCustomer table (file view) in OneLake

If we open a *_delta_log* folder, we can spot a number of *.json* files inside. The number of files depends on how frequently the data changes in the specific table. This might sound weird at first glance, but let's not forget that a table in OneLake is nothing but a Parquet file or collection of Parquet files. Parquet files are immutable; when we update a record in the file, the actual file doesn't change to reflect the update. What happens is that a *new version* of the file is created, and that new version contains the updated record.

In Figure 9-12, you can see that the *_delta_log* for the DimCustomer table contains two versions of the file.

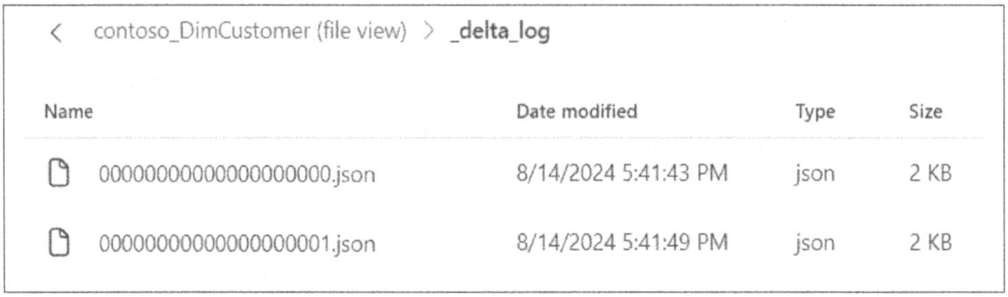

Figure 9-12. Multiple versions of the DimCustomer table stored in the _delta_log folder

Finally, we created a custom semantic model with tables from the lakehouse and a very basic report that shows the information about the customer Aaron Adams, as shown in Figure 9-13.

Figure 9-13. Information about the customer displayed in a Power BI report

Let's say that our customer Aaron Adams changed his email address from *aaron48@adventure-works.com* to *aaron49@adventure-works.com*. In Figure 9-14, you can see that a new file version ending with 002 has been added to the *_delta_log*.

Name	Date modified	Type	Size
00000000000000000000.json	8/14/2024, 5:41:43 PM	json	2 KB
00000000000000000001.json	8/14/2024, 5:41:49 PM	json	2 KB
00000000000000000002.json	8/14/2024, 7:52:39 PM	json	3 KB

Figure 9-14. New file version added to a _delta_log

What happens now with the Power BI semantic model? Will this email address update be automatically reflected in our Sales Overview report? It depends!

If we stick with the default semantic model configuration settings, the answer is yes. In Figure 9-15, you can see that the default behavior of the Refresh setting is to enable Power BI to detect changes to the underlying Delta table and automatically update the Direct Lake semantic model.

> ◢ Refresh
>
> **Keep your Direct Lake data up to date**
>
> Configure Power BI to detect changes to the data in OneLake and automatically update the Direct Lake tables that are included in this semantic model. Learn more
>
> ⬤ On
>
> **Configure a refresh schedule**
>
> Define a data refresh schedule to import data from the data source into the semantic model. Learn more
>
> ◉ Off

Figure 9-15. Power BI's default setting to update the semantic model to incorporate the latest data

However, this might not be something that you want. Let's say that you need to ensure that the Power BI semantic model is updated only *after all the underlying Delta tables are processed*. Think of a scenario where you first process the FactSales table and then the DimCustomer table. With this setting enabled, as soon as you process a fact table, all changes will be reflected in the Power BI semantic model, whereas the DimCustomer table will still contain the previous version of the data. Hence, you might want to disable this option and implement a semantic model refresh as a standalone processing step once all data preparation tasks are completed.

Nevertheless, regardless of which option you choose, the refresh process itself is entirely different from that in Import mode semantic models. In Import mode models, the physical data is stored in the model, while in Direct Lake mode, only metadata is stored and refreshed.

Figure 9-16 illustrates what is considered part of the Direct Lake semantic model.

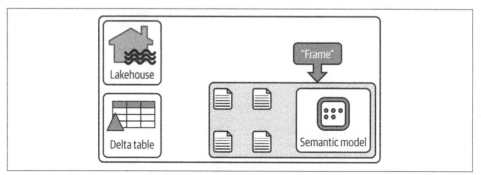

Figure 9-16. Direct Lake model including four existing files

As you can see, there are four files currently *framed* in the context of the Direct Lake semantic model. Once a new file enters OneLake, like in our case when we updated a record in the DimCustomer table, this *frame* will have to be extended to incorporate the latest file version. Figure 9-17 shows the extended frame version, which includes the newly added file.

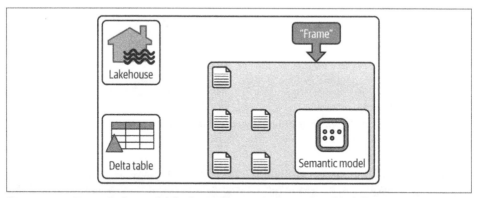

Figure 9-17. Direct Lake model "reframed" to include newly added files

The *reframing* process has multiple implications for the semantic model. First and foremost, whenever framing occurs, all the data currently stored in memory (we are referring to a cache memory) is dumped from the cache. This is of paramount importance for the transcoding concept, which we are going to discuss next.

Since the Direct Lake "refresh" is a metadata-only refresh, it's usually a low-intensity operation and shouldn't consume too much time and resources. Even if you deal with a billion-row table, you aren't refreshing billions of rows of data in the semantic model; you are refreshing only *the information* about that gigantic table.

Transcoding (Loading Columns into Memory)

Now that we know how to synchronize the data from a lakehouse with the semantic model (syncing) and how to include the latest metadata in the semantic model (framing), it's time to understand what really happens behind the scenes once you put your Direct Lake semantic models to action.

This is the selling point of the Direct Lake feature, right? Performance of the Import mode, but without copying the data.

In plain English, *transcoding* represents the process of loading parts of the Delta table or the entire Delta table into cache memory.

When we say "parts of the Delta table," we are referring to particular columns of the table. Let us briefly absorb this fact and put it in the context of Import mode workloads:

- Loading data into cache memory is the ingredient that ensures the best possible performance provided by the Import mode.
- In Import mode, if you haven't enabled "Large" for the "Semantic model storage format" option, the entire semantic model is stored in cache memory, and it must fit memory limits. In Direct Lake mode, only columns needed by the queries are stored in cache memory, the same as for Import mode models with "Semantic model storage format" set to "Large."

Let's break down these two bullet points further. The first bullet point means that once columns from the Direct Lake semantic model are loaded into cache memory, from a technical perspective, this is absolutely the same as Import mode. The second bullet point means that the cache memory footprint of the Direct Lake semantic model could be significantly lower than, or, in the worst case, the same as that of the Import mode equivalent. However, this lower memory footprint comes with a price—increased waiting time for the initial data loading because of the transcoding operation.

To demonstrate the difference between the memory footprint of the Import and Direct Lake semantic models, I've prepared two identical semantic models based on a Medicare Part D dataset available from *Data.CMS.gov* (*https://oreil.ly/AwQTS*).

Both semantic models consist of exactly the same set of tables, columns, relationships, and DAX measures. The only difference is the storage mode.

To analyze the semantic model size, I'll be using a free external tool, DAX Studio, which you can downloaded from the DAX Studio website (*https://oreil.ly/ETKOA*). One of the built-in features of DAX Studio is VertiPaq Analyzer, an open source tool for capturing information about a semantic model. Explaining DAX Studio and VertiPaq Analyzer is outside of the scope of this book, so we'll focus solely on functionalities relevant to understanding the differences between the Import and Direct Lake storage modes.

Figure 9-18 shows the total size in memory of the Import mode model.

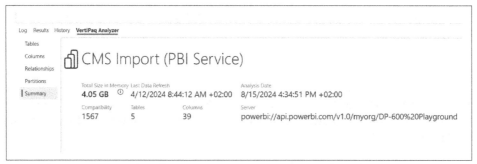

Figure 9-18. The size of the Import mode semantic model, captured by VertiPaq Analyzer

As you can see, the size of the model is 4.05 GB. Once I perform the same check on the Direct Lake semantic model, in Figure 9-19, you will notice that the difference in total size in memory is enormous.

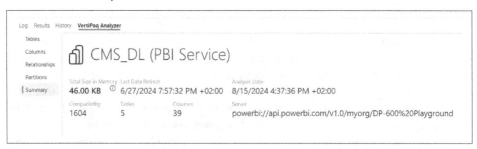

Figure 9-19. The size of the Direct Lake semantic model, captured by VertiPaq Analyzer

Instead of 4.05 GB, the size is now 46 KB! That's because the Direct Lake semantic model includes metadata only.

However, before you jump to quick conclusions based on these two figures, let me introduce you to another major concept in Direct Lake, called temperature, that may have an impact on the memory footprint of semantic models.

Temperature

The concept of *temperature* assumes that each column in the semantic model has a temperature. The more the column is queried, the higher its temperature is. This property enables the Power BI engine to decide which columns stay in cache memory and which are kicked out back to OneLake. The higher the temperature of the column, the greater the chances are that it stays in cache memory.

You can identify columns with the highest temperature by querying dynamic management views (DMVs) in the Power BI tabular model. You can use the aforementioned DAX Studio or SQL Server Management Studio to obtain the data about the semantic model. Figure 9-20 shows the initial results, before any query against my Direct Lake semantic model was executed.

Log **Results** History VertiPaq Analyzer

TABLE_NAME	COLUMN_NAME	DICTIONARY_TEMPERATURE	DICTIONARY_LAST_ACCESSED
cms_provider_drug_costs_star	provider key (153)	11.776046449508	8/15/2024 2:37:36 PM
cms_provider_drug_costs_star	geo key (152)	11.7634536217433	8/15/2024 2:37:36 PM
cms_provider_drug_costs_star	drug key (151)	11.7601463096407	8/15/2024 2:37:35 PM
cms_provider_dim_provider	provider key (132)	9.84744116984676	8/15/2024 2:37:37 PM
cms_provider_dim_geography	geo key (123)	9.84047983617322	8/15/2024 2:37:37 PM
cms_provider_dim_drug	drug key (137)	9.83911142265133	8/15/2024 2:37:37 PM
cms_provider_dim_year	Year (115)	9.83834816630207	8/15/2024 2:37:37 PM
cms_provider_drug_costs_star	Tot Drug Cst (149)	8.80125628501773	8/15/2024 2:37:32 PM
cms_provider_drug_costs_star	Tot Day Suply (148)	8.76096680819967	8/15/2024 2:37:28 PM
cms_provider_drug_costs_star	Tot Clms (147)	8.7561848028686	8/15/2024 2:37:27 PM
cms_provider_drug_costs_star	Tot Benes (146)	8.75414224101502	8/15/2024 2:37:27 PM
cms_provider_drug_costs_star	Tot 30day Fills (145)	8.7528266975918	8/15/2024 2:37:27 PM
cms_provider_drug_costs_star	GE65 Tot Drug Cst (144)	8.74853615486052	8/15/2024 2:37:26 PM
cms_provider_drug_costs_star	GE65 Tot Day Suply (143)	8.72076704059215	8/15/2024 2:37:23 PM
cms_provider_drug_costs_star	GE65 Tot Clms (142)	8.71742501873666	8/15/2024 2:37:23 PM
cms_provider_drug_costs_star	GE65 Tot Benes (141)	8.71584843310062	8/15/2024 2:37:23 PM
cms_provider_drug_costs_star	GE65 Tot 30day Fills (140)	8.71425714622247	8/15/2024 2:37:23 PM
cms_provider_drug_costs_star	GE65 Sprsn Flag (139)	8.71161217152472	8/15/2024 2:37:22 PM

Figure 9-20. Analyzing column temperature values

To obtain the results in Figure 9-20, we used the following query:

```
SELECT DIMENSION_NAME AS [TABLE_NAME]
, COLUMN_ID AS [COLUMN_NAME]
, DICTIONARY_SIZE
, DICTIONARY_TEMPERATURE
, DICTIONARY_LAST_ACCESSED
FROM $SYSTEM.DISCOVER_STORAGE_TABLE_COLUMNS
ORDER BY DICTIONARY_TEMPERATURE DESC
```

Let's quickly decipher the results in Figure 9-20. We focus on the column DICTIO-NARY_TEMPERATURE, which shows how "hot" a specific column is. Without going any further, you may notice that the "key" columns (provider key, drug key, etc.) dominate the top of the result set. The reason is simple: these columns are used to establish relationships between the tables in the semantic model. Hence, Power BI keeps them "warm" to enable quick filter propagation between the tables.

If no queries against the Direct Lake semantic model are executed, the temperature value will decrease over time. If I query the same dynamic management view after an hour of model inactivity, the temperature value may drop to nearly zero.

But what happens if we activate the model and start interacting with the report built on top of it? Figure 9-21 shows the result of querying the same dynamic management view once we have created a plain table visual to show the total number of records per year.

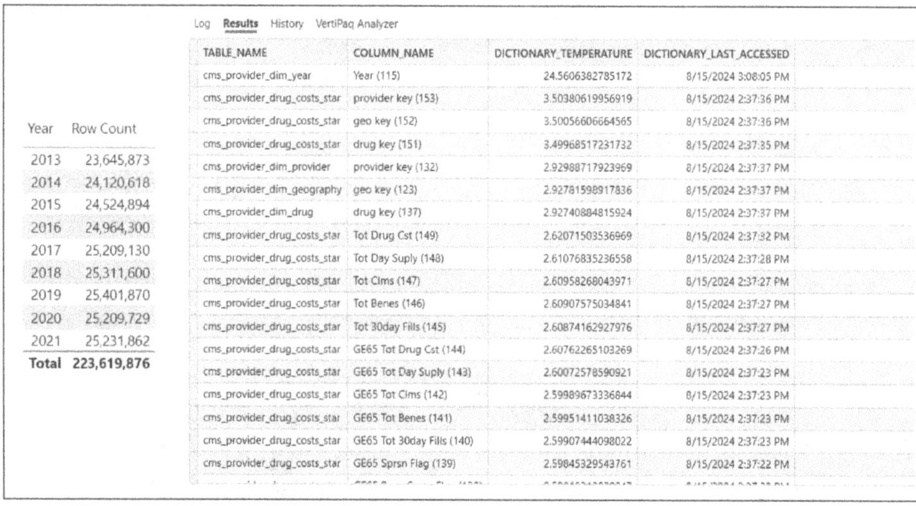

Figure 9-21. Analyzing column temperature values after interacting with the model

By adding a Year column to the report, we caused its temperature to skyrocket; it is now approximately eight times higher than the next column from the model. This way, the engine ensures that the most frequently used columns will stay in cache memory and be served from there so that report performance will be the best possible for the end user.

A fair question at this point would be, What happens when all our users go home at 5 P.M. and no one interacts with Direct Lake semantic models until the next morning? The answer is simple: the first semantic model user will have to sacrifice for all the others and wait a little bit longer for the initial run. Then, everyone could potentially benefit from having warm columns ready in the cache. But what if the first user in the morning is your manager or a company CEO? We definitely don't want to make this type of user wait for long to see their KPIs and figures!

The good news is that there is a fairly straightforward solution to this problem. By *pre-warming* our model early in the morning, before any of the users open their reports, we can load the most frequently queried columns into cache memory and have them ready in advance. This can be done in multiple ways, but probably the most convenient one is to leverage a semantic link feature, which we examined in Chapter 7, and execute DAX code from the Fabric notebook. It doesn't have to be any fancy DAX. A plain COUNTROWS of the table, or COUNT over a specific column or set of columns, will serve the purpose and enforce the data to be loaded into the cache. Then, you can schedule this notebook to run every morning at 8 A.M. before any users start interacting with the Direct Lake model.

Since we covered a couple of very important concepts relevant to Direct Lake workloads in Power BI, let's wrap up this section by compiling a high-level overview of all the key concepts. Figure 9-22 illustrates each concept you need to know when working with Direct Lake semantic models in Microsoft Fabric.

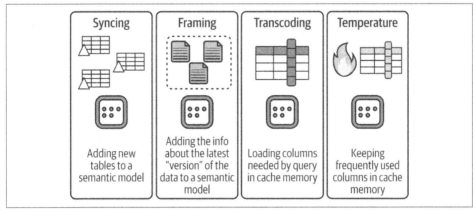

Figure 9-22. Key Direct Lake concepts at a glance

Direct Lake Guardrails

A complex query over huge amounts of data may wreak havoc on your workload. We should not forget that Power BI is just one piece of the Microsoft Fabric puzzle and there might be dozens of other operations and tasks running in parallel, each consuming its fair share of capacity units. However, Microsoft imposes resource and memory guardrails that should enable the smooth running of your Fabric capacity workloads and ensure that no one gets throttled in the process. Table 9-6 lists all the guardrails that might prevent your semantic models from using Direct Lake.

Table 9-6. Direct Lake guardrails

Fabric SKU	Parquet files per table	Rows per table (millions)	Max model size in OneLake (GB)	Max memory (GB)	Max memory per query (GB)
F2	1,000	300	10	3	1
F4	1,000	300	10	3	1
F8	1,000	300	10	3	1
F16	1,000	300	20	5	2
F32	1,000	300	40	10	5
F64	5,000	1,500	Unlimited	25	10
F128	5,000	3,000	Unlimited	50	10
F256	5,000	6,000	Unlimited	100	10
F512	10,000	12,000	Unlimited	200	20
F1024	10,000	24,000	Unlimited	400	40
F2048	10,000	24,000	Unlimited	400	40

Whenever your semantic model or query hits any of the limits specified in Table 9-6, Direct Lake mode will not be used. What happens with our queries if Direct Lake is not in place? It depends. We'll examine available options in the next section, but here's a quick hint. If your semantic models are using Direct Lake on SQL flavor and you don't change the default configuration, whenever Direct Lake mode cannot be used, queries will fall back to DirectQuery storage mode. If your models are using Direct Lake on OneLake option, then no fallback to DirectQuery is possible.

It's not only about hitting resource and memory limits. Certain features and use cases are not yet supported for Direct Lake scenarios. The best example is T-SQL views, a commonly used database object for encapsulating complex query logic. While Power BI will not prevent you from using T-SQL views in Direct Lake on SQL semantic models, you should be aware that any query that retrieves the data from a T-SQL view will not be able to use Direct Lake mode. As a reminder, views are not even available as a data source for Direct Lake on OneLake semantic models.

We'll examine other limitations in the closing part of this chapter.

Control DirectLakeBehavior for Direct Lake on SQL Semantic Models

As we've already explained, if we stick with the default settings for our Direct Lake on SQL semantic models, whenever Direct Lake can't be used, whether because of resource or memory limit violation or using unsupported features, queries will fall back to DirectQuery storage mode.

However, we can modify this behavior by configuring the DirectLakeBehavior property of the semantic model. This property can be configured in three ways:

Automatic
> This is a default value. If Direct Lake can't be used, all queries will use a DirectQuery mode.

DirectLakeOnly
> All queries must use Direct Lake mode. If Direct Lake mode is not available, queries won't run, an error will be thrown, and the report won't render. This behavior may come in handy when you need to identify resource-exhaustive queries before exposing them to the end user.

DirectQueryOnly
> This is the opposite of *DirectLakeOnly*. All queries must use DirectQuery mode. The typical use case for this option is testing the performance of those queries that will exceed Direct Lake limits and will be served by DirectQuery mode.

Figure 9-23 shows what happens with queries against the Direct Lake semantic model once Direct Lake mode can't be used.

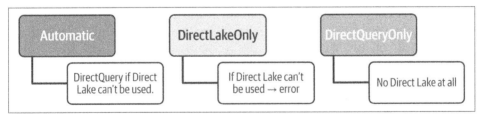

Figure 9-23. Controlling Direct Lake model behavior

The DirectLakeBehavior property can be configured from the web UI in Power BI Service, from the Power BI Desktop, or by using an external tool such as Tabular Editor.

Direct Lake Limitations

Direct Lake is one of those features that you might think of when you wonder, Where have you been all my life? We believe that you already understand how powerful the concept of Direct Lake mode is. However, before you jump all-in to Direct Lake, let's examine the list of current limitations that might make you think twice before you hop on this train.

 This section covers technical limitations only. For architectural considerations and decision guidance for using Direct Lake over Import mode and vice versa, please refer to Chapter 18.

The key thing to keep in mind is that Microsoft Fabric is still an immature product that is rapidly evolving. The same applies to the Direct Lake feature. Therefore, we would like to emphasize that some of the currently listed limitations may be lifted in the future. Hence, always make sure to check the list of current limitations on the official Microsoft Learn site (*https://oreil.ly/G6ed4*):

Only Delta tables from the Fabric lakehouse or warehouse are supported.
> The emphasis is on both Delta *and* tables. Simply put, no Delta format, no Direct Lake. Similarly, T-SQL views, as already explained in the previous section, will also prevent Direct Lake queries (for Direct Lake on SQL models) or will not be available at all (for Direct Lake on OneLake models).

No DAX calculated columns and DAX calculated tables.
> Since these two data structures are calculated and persisted during the semantic model refresh process, and we've already learned that there is no data refresh process in Direct Lake semantic models, you need to implement the logic of calculated columns and/or tables further upstream, in the Delta table stored in the Fabric lakehouse or warehouse. This doesn't apply to special types of DAX calculated tables, such as calculation groups, what-if parameters, and field parameters, which are all supported in Direct Lake.

Primary key columns must contain unique values.
> Regardless of how awkward this sounds, constraints in Microsoft Fabric are not enforced. Hence, it might happen that your primary key columns contain duplicate values. In these circumstances, DAX queries will fail.

Summary

We covered a lot in this chapter. This is not a coincidence, as the majority of Fabric users will be Power BI professionals.

If you are one of them, the good news is that your transition to Power BI workloads in Microsoft Fabric should be smooth sailing. If nothing else, the user interface and most of the functionalities remained the same as in the pre-Fabric era. Import and DirectQuery storage modes are here to stay, and from that perspective, nothing has changed in the way we design and build our Power BI items.

Yet, one of the most significant enhancements that Microsoft Fabric introduced to the data analytics world is specifically relevant to Power BI. If you've read this entire chapter, you know that we are referring to the Direct Lake mode—a revolutionary feature that aims to supplement Import and DirectQuery scenarios by exploiting and combining their strengths and overcoming their weaknesses.

At this point, we would like to emphasize two points:

- Direct Lake is *not* a replacement for Import and DirectQuery storage modes. It's just another option for implementing Power BI solutions.
- We strongly encourage you to broaden your existing Power BI knowledge and learn *when* and *how* to use Direct Lake mode, since this will become a necessary skill for every successful Power BI professional.

From a future-proof point of view, we are quite confident that Power BI will continue to dominate the BI reporting tools market. Tight integration with other Microsoft Fabric components and the introduction of new, groundbreaking features, such as Direct Lake, will ensure increased adoption of Power BI and expand the number of use cases.

In Chapter 10, we'll take another turn with the more conventional data workloads, as we examine databases in Microsoft Fabric.

SQL Databases

In Chapter 9, we talked about Power BI, which is the most well-known feature in the Fabric landscape since it has been around for more than 10 years. In this chapter, we'll introduce one of Fabric's newest features: SQL databases.

SQL databases in Fabric bring together the trusted power of SQL Server and Azure SQL Database engines and integrate them into the Fabric ecosystem. This integration offers the familiarity and strength of SQL within a robust, scalable platform, unlocking advanced analytics and smooth data integration opportunities. They therefore bridge the gap between the analytical world, which we've mostly focused on in this book, and the operational data world, allowing you to bring them to the same place.

In a nutshell, SQL databases give us the capabilities of SQL Server and Azure SQL, but with fewer knobs and handles. As a result, we profit from more simplicity, but in exchange we have less control. Their combination of automation, AI integration, governance, and seamless data operations makes these databases a suitable solution for enterprise-scale applications while maintaining efficiency and reliability.

In application development scenarios, developers can leverage SQL databases in Fabric to modernize and improve their operations. With the introduction of built-in vector data types, teams can store and query product and customer information to enable advanced semantic search, enhancing AI-driven functionalities.

A *vector data type* stores multiple numerical values in a specific order, making it useful for mathematical operations, AI, and spatial data. Unlike single-value scalars, vectors enable efficient computations including similarity search, transformations, and indexing. This is useful for tasks such as recommendation systems, anomaly detection, natural language processing, and image recognition, where fast comparisons of complex data are needed. For example, in a music streaming app, vector data helps recommend songs by comparing user listening patterns with similar users.

For organizations modernizing their analytics workflows, SQL databases in Fabric streamline processes by integrating directly with OneLake. When building a new app that uses SQL databases in Fabric as its datastore, for example, that data will automatically be mirrored to OneLake, so you can use the data through analytical experiences like data engineering. This can eliminate the need for traditional ETL pipelines (however, it only eliminates the need to copy data; it doesn't alleviate the need to transform or load data into another platform like a data lake), reducing complexity and improving efficiency. Operational data stored in SQL databases can feed directly into Power BI for real-time reporting, enabling businesses to respond quickly to dynamic situations. Additionally, governance tools like Microsoft Purview ensure data management practices remain compliant and secure, empowering organizations to scale confidently.

 As with most sources, there are limitations to the mirroring of a SQL database in Fabric. At the time of writing for example, the maximum number of tables that can be mirrored from a database was one thousand. You can find the most current list of limitations in the Microsoft documentation (*https://oreil.ly/8S0Lo*).

Over the course of this chapter, we'll first discuss the reasoning behind SQL databases in Fabric, followed by a look at their key features and how to work with data in them. We'll round this out by walking you through all the steps required to get started with your first SQL database in Fabric.

Why SQL Databases in Fabric?

The introduction of SQL databases in Fabric was a response to evolving business needs and the need for operational efficiency. With predictions of one billion new applications (*https://oreil.ly/QWB93*) being developed in the next five years, 87% of organizational leaders believe AI will play a critical role (*https://oreil.ly/pLCgU*) for maintaining competitive edges.

The Role of AI

Fabric's SQL databases empower developers to focus on building applications rather than managing complex infrastructure. By leveraging familiar T-SQL syntax and widely used tools like SSMS, developers can streamline their workflows and reduce the learning curve. To further simplify this development process, features like Copilot accelerate development by simplifying database and application design processes, while the inclusion of graph capabilities expands the potential for advanced relational modeling. Artificial intelligence supports developers along the entire lifecycle of developing solutions using SQL databases in Fabric, opening this world to developers without a strong SQL background.

Operational Efficiency

Operational efficiency is another cornerstone of SQL in Fabric. Autonomous operations—including automatic indexing, backups, and patching—minimize manual intervention, allowing teams to focus on innovation rather than maintenance. This combination of streamlined development, AI integration, and operational efficiency positions SQL databases in Fabric as a game-changing solution for modern application development.

As you can see in Figure 10-1, SQL databases in Fabric deliver a fully grown Azure SQL database that natively integrates with your Fabric workspace and capacity.

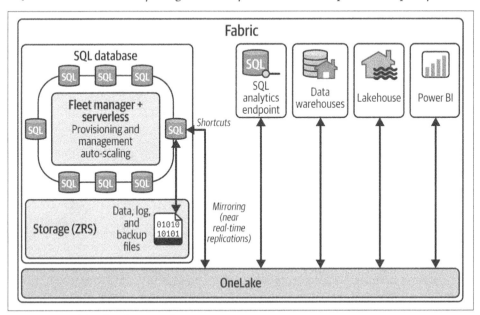

Figure 10-1. SQL databases architecture

As you can also see in Figure 10-1, SQL databases currently use a serverless deployment with *zone-redundant storage* (ZRS).

 In Microsoft Azure, ZRS is a redundancy option for storing data that replicates it synchronously across multiple availability zones within a region. This ensures higher availability and resiliency against failures in a single data center.

This seamless integration also includes the pricing component. Your SQL database will consume its capacity units (2.61 CUs per vCore) and be billed as part of your Fabric capacity. We will explain the concepts of billing and capacity units in more depth in Chapter 14.

Key Features of SQL Databases

SQL databases in Microsoft Fabric integrate advanced database management features with modern automation and intelligence, addressing the technical demands of enterprise-scale data operations. This section outlines the primary technical capabilities of SQL databases in Fabric.

Simplicity and Autonomous Operation

Database creation and management in Fabric are designed to be efficient and user-friendly. With minimal input, a database can be provisioned in seconds. The platform incorporates advanced automation to optimize performance and reduce the need for manual intervention, streamlining database administration for developers.

Integrated Copilot assists with tasks such as query generation, database design, and optimization, enabling developers to perform these operations more efficiently. The system supports autoscaling, which dynamically adjusts compute and storage resources based on workload demands, ensuring consistent performance.

Fabric's auto-provisioning establishes robust, fault-tolerant databases that remain operational during server failures and allow for rolling updates with no disruption to applications. Auto-configuration further refines database performance by tailoring memory usage, data formats, and access structures to specific workloads, enabling users to load data and begin operations immediately.

Auto-indexing, powered by machine learning, identifies and implements missing indexes that can improve query performance. It validates each index before applying changes, continuously learning to refine its recommendations. These features collectively optimize database operations without requiring manual oversight.

Automation extends to critical aspects such as the following:

Data protection

Continuous monitoring of sensitive and regulated data through a unified management interface

Security

Built-in encryption for databases, backups, and connections, safeguarding data against external threats and unauthorized access

Backups and recovery

Automatic daily backups with on-demand options, supporting point-in-time recovery within a seven-day window

Patching and failover

Updates applied without downtime, while failover mechanisms ensure seamless transition during server disruptions, meeting a 99.995% SLA (service level agreement)

These automation capabilities enhance database reliability, performance, and security while minimizing administrative overhead.

AI Integration and Optimization

SQL databases in Fabric are designed to facilitate the development of AI-enhanced applications. Support for vector data types allows developers to store embeddings from AI models and implement features like semantic search and recommendation systems. These capabilities enable the creation of applications with advanced AI-driven functionality.

Integration with Azure AI and OpenAI allows databases to incorporate external AI models. This enables the combination of relational data with AI-generated insights, enriching the scope of applications built on the platform. Developers can utilize Copilot assistance to interact with data using natural language queries, generate scripts, and receive design recommendations, reducing the complexity of implementing AI in applications.

Additionally, SQL in Fabric supports the creation of AI-powered applications with built-in features for integrating AI models and vector data. Coupled with tools like LangChain, these capabilities allow developers to embed artificial intelligence into their applications, enabling functionality such as semantic search, recommendation engines, and other AI-driven experiences.

Integrated Governance and Security

Fabric provides centralized security and compliance controls through its Microsoft Purview governance layer. Databases are encrypted by default, both in storage and transit, with support for TLS 1.2 ensuring secure data communication. TLS 1.2

(Transport Layer Security version 1.2) is a protocol designed to secure network communications by encrypting data exchanged between systems. Its significance lies in safeguarding sensitive information, like passwords and financial details, from unauthorized access or tampering.

Zone-redundant setups provide high availability and disaster recovery, ensuring uninterrupted operations and robust data protection. While there is no equivalent to firewall rules, databases in Fabric use Entra authentication only, so you can use conditional access rules to limit database access.

We will also talk about governance and security in more depth in Chapters 15 and 16.

DevOps Integration

SQL databases in Fabric are built to align with modern DevOps practices, enabling streamlined database management and agile workflows. Every database is fully integrated with source control, allowing teams to version databases, track changes, and collaborate efficiently. This integration ensures that database schema and configurations are part of the broader development lifecycle, enabling consistent deployments and reducing errors across environments.

By integrating with CI/CD pipelines, SQL databases in Fabric support automated testing, deployment, and monitoring. This compatibility enables organizations to implement robust DevOps strategies, ensuring rapid iteration and reliable database operations.

Unified Data Storage with OneLake

All SQL databases in Fabric are tightly integrated with OneLake. This setup ensures real-time data replication across workloads, eliminating the need for traditional ETL processes. As a result, databases can directly support analytics in Power BI and other Fabric tools, simplifying data access and improving overall efficiency.

GraphQL Interface

SQL databases in Fabric also include a built-in GraphQL interface, offering a flexible and efficient way to query and interact with data. (For more information on GraphQL in Fabric, refer to Chapter 12.) This interface enables developers to fetch precisely the data they need with a single query, minimizing the over-fetching and under-fetching issues often encountered with traditional REST APIs.

The GraphQL interface simplifies data integration for modern applications, especially those with complex frontend requirements or microservice architectures. By combining the relational power of SQL with the flexibility of GraphQL, developers can seamlessly build data-driven applications, enabling rapid iteration and streamlined communication between database and application layers.

This especially opens up a lot of capabilities for developers who are not as familiar with SQL; we'll expand on these later in this chapter.

Ingesting and Querying Data

Data can be inserted into SQL databases in Fabric using a variety of methods. Since the engine provides a regular SQL endpoint, developers and analysts can use any SQL-compatible tool to interact with the database. This includes traditional tools like SSMS and sqlcmd, as well as modern data pipeline solutions such as Azure Data Factory pipelines and pipelines in Microsoft Fabric. Even legacy tools like SSIS remain fully compatible, allowing organizations with existing ETL processes to seamlessly integrate with Fabric's SQL databases.

On the consumption side, data stored in SQL databases is mirrored in OneLake, Fabric's unified data storage layer. This mirroring, which we'll explain in more depth in Chapter 11, enables real-time availability of data for analytics and other workloads without requiring traditional ETL processes to copy the data.

 Keep in mind that mirrored data will retain the same structure as its source, so you may still need to run some additional transformations to fulfill your analytical requirements.

Users can query the database directly using SQL tools or leverage OneLake to feed data into visualization tools like Power BI or other Fabric services. The seamless integration with OneLake ensures that data is always accessible for analytics, reporting, or machine learning applications, making it easier for organizations to implement modern data workflows without disrupting established practices.

A Step-by-Step Guide to Building and Managing SQL Databases

As in previous chapters, let us do a step-by-step walkthrough on how to get started.

When you select "Create" and scroll down or search for "database," you'll find the SQL database artifact (see Figure 10-2).

Figure 10-2. Create new SQL database

After selecting "SQL database" on that page, all you need to provide is a name for the new SQL database (Figure 10-3).

Figure 10-3. Creating a new SQL database and giving it a name

We'll call our database BookSQL and select Create on that screen. The system creates everything for us, and after a few seconds, the provisioning is complete. The provisioning automatically creates a semantic model and a SQL analytics endpoint for us (see Figure 10-4).

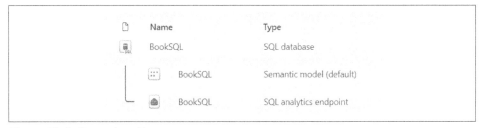

Figure 10-4. Created artifacts

Our SQL database effectively has two different SQL endpoints: the SQL analytics endpoint, which you're already familiar with from lakehouses, as well as the SQL endpoint of the SQL database itself. Just as in other experiences we discussed earlier, the analytics endpoint is read-only, while the endpoint of the SQL database does not allow cross-querying over the SQL database and, for example, another lakehouse. This means the "correct" endpoint will depend on your use case.

While this may be different in edge cases, it's probably simplest to use the SQL database for OLTP-like workloads and the analytics endpoint for all analytical workloads. Of course, there are also situations, like iterating over a metadata table, where both endpoints will get you the same result. While we have seen slightly better performance on the SQL database over the SQL analytics endpoint in such cases, it won't make a huge difference due to the usually very small amount of data involved in such scenarios. We'll talk more about the decision-making process behind this in Chapter 18.

Once you create the SQL database, it takes you to a welcome screen with multiple options, similar to previous experiences.

For users with a strong background in SQL, the connection strings are usually the first stop to connect to the new database using the tools we are comfortable with.

For this instance, we'll add some sample data by clicking "Sample data" on the welcome screen, as shown in Figure 10-5.

Figure 10-5. SQL database welcome screen

This will automatically trigger the AdventureWorksLT database to be populated to your database. You can also see this when expanding your database in the explorer view on the left (see Figure 10-6).

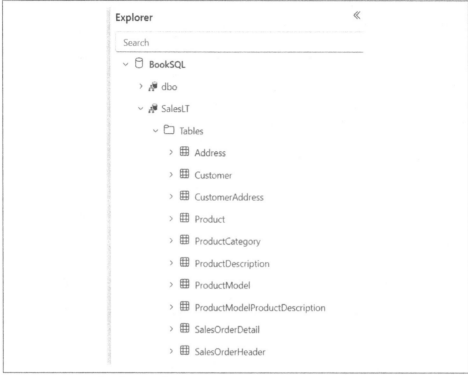

Figure 10-6. SQL database explorer

The main menu (see Figure 10-7) also provides shortcuts to open the database, or rather connect to it, using VS Code or SSMS, as well as starting a new SQL editor in the browser (using "New Query").

Figure 10-7. SQL database main menu

The SQL editor (shown in Figure 10-8) comes with Copilot support as well as regular IntelliSense.

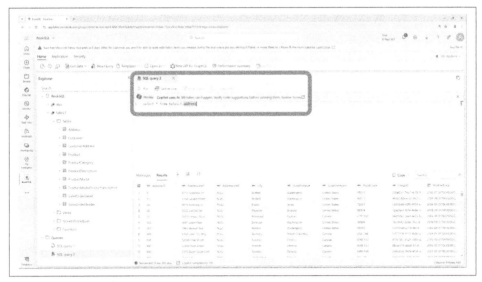

Figure 10-8. SQL editor

It can be used for any T-SQL operation like querying and manipulating data as well as to create or modify tables and other objects.

The main menu also has a link to the performance summary (shown in Figure 10-9) which gives you a first impression of your database's state with regard to performance and consumption. At the very bottom of that summary, you will find a link to the Performance Dashboard.

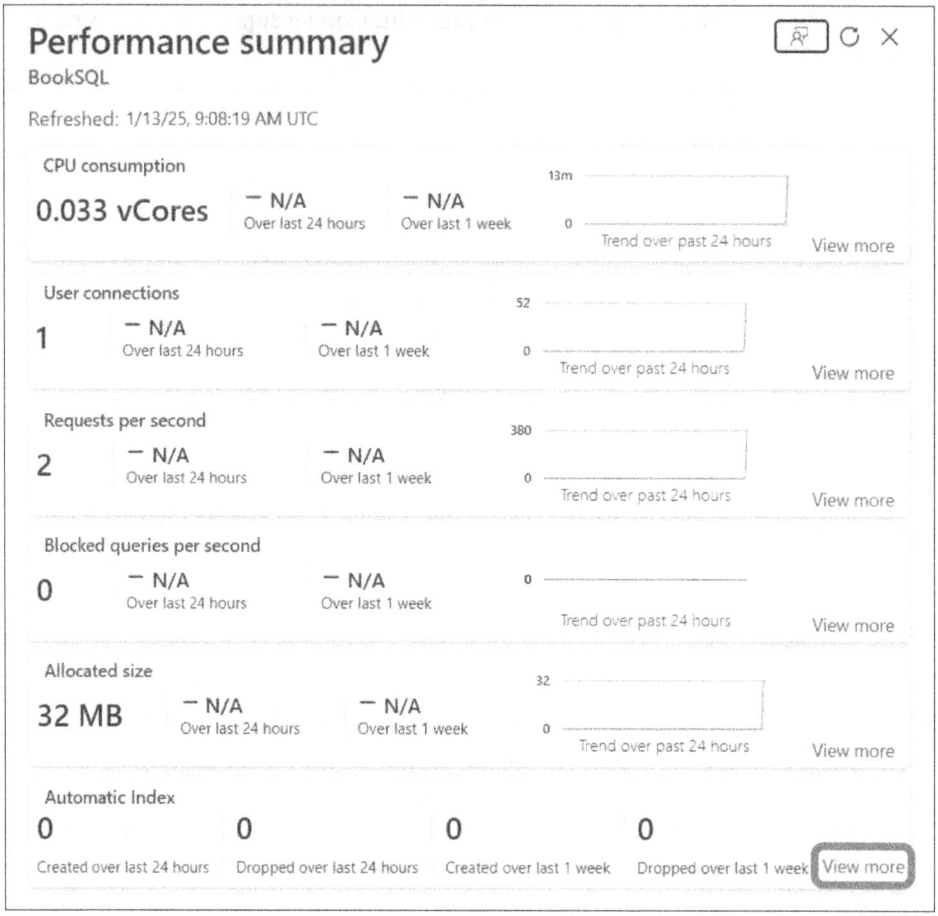

Performance summary
BookSQL

Refreshed: 1/13/25, 9:08:19 AM UTC

CPU consumption

0.033 vCores   — N/A   — N/A
                      Over last 24 hours   Over last 1 week

13m

0   Trend over past 24 hours   View more

User connections

1   — N/A   — N/A
     Over last 24 hours   Over last 1 week

52

0   Trend over past 24 hours   View more

Requests per second

2   — N/A   — N/A
     Over last 24 hours   Over last 1 week

380

0   Trend over past 24 hours   View more

Blocked queries per second

0   — N/A   — N/A
     Over last 24 hours   Over last 1 week

0   Trend over past 24 hours   View more

Allocated size

32 MB   — N/A   — N/A
           Over last 24 hours   Over last 1 week

32

0   Trend over past 24 hours   View more

Automatic Index

0   0   0   0

Created over last 24 hours   Dropped over last 24 hours   Created over last 1 week   Dropped over last 1 week   View more

Figure 10-9. Performance summary

The Performance dashboard provides a more detailed view of the state of your database, as illustrated in Figure 10-10.

The main menu also has an option for Replication, from which you can reach the replication monitor. This will show you the current status of database mirroring (more on that in Chapter 11), which is enabled by default (see Figure 10-11). The replicated data is available directly in OneLake as well as through the SQL analytics endpoint that got created for us.

Figure 10-10. Performance dashboard

Figure 10-11. Replication monitor

We can immediately see data show up in our OneLake explorer (see Chapter 3) as it is being replicated there (Figure 10-12).

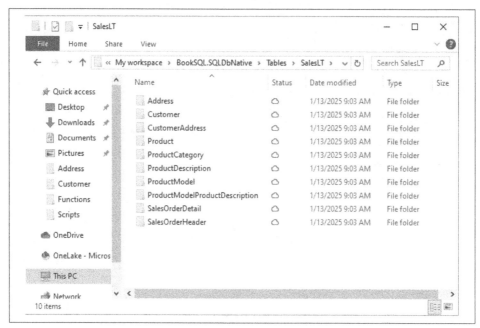

Figure 10-12. Mirrored data in OneLake explorer

We will not go into the details of AI capabilities on SQL databases and vectors—that would warrant a book by itself. However, we do want to point out the simplicity of the GraphQL integration. To create a new GraphQL API, you can either right-click any table or the "New API for GraphQL" button in the main menu (see Figure 10-13).

Figure 10-13. Initiating the GraphQL API wizard

We'll use an Address table, which prompts for a name to call the new API (Figure 10-14), and we'll choose BookAPI.

New API for GraphQL

Name *

Create   Cancel

Figure 10-14. The new API wizard

Then we need to select the data that should be available through that API. In our case, the Address table is preselected because it is where we started the wizard from (Figure 10-15). This selection can be modified later.

To use the selected table, we click Load on that same screen.

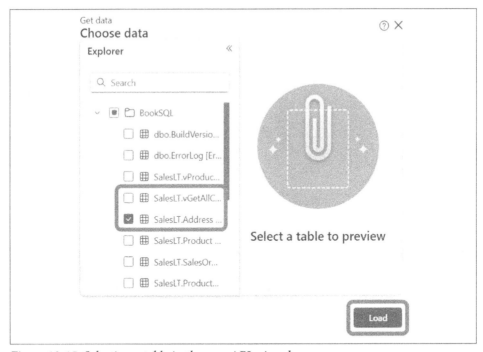

Figure 10-15. Selecting a table in the new API wizard

This has created an endpoint that we can query from a multitude of languages and platforms. The main menu of this screen has a "Generate code" button (Figure 10-16).

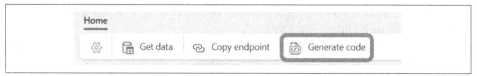

Figure 10-16. The GraphQL API main menu

This will autogenerate ready-to-use code using Python or Node.js to query this exact endpoint (Figure 10-17).

Generate code ✕

Python ⌄

```python
from azure.identity import InteractiveBrowserCredential
import requests
import json

# Acquire a token
# DO NOT USE IN PRODUCTION.
# Below code to acquire token is for development purpose only to test the GraphQL endpoin
# For production, always register an application in a Microsoft Entra ID tenant and use t
# https://learn.microsoft.com/en-us/fabric/data-engineering/connect-apps-api-graphql#crea

app = InteractiveBrowserCredential()
scp = 'https://analysis.windows.net/powerbi/api/user_impersonation'
result = app.get_token(scp)

if not result.token:
    print('Error:', "Could not get access token")

# Prepare headers
headers = {
    'Authorization': f'Bearer {result.token}',
    'Content-Type': 'application/json'
}
```

🗋 Copy

Figure 10-17. The GraphQL API code generator

Similar to the SQL editor, the graph editor comes with IntelliSense (see Figure 10-18).

Figure 10-18. Graph editor

The following code, for example, would query the AddressID, AddressLine1, and City properties from the Address table:

```
query {
  addresses {
    items {
      AddressID
      AddressLine1
      City
    }
  }
}
```

The result when running this query would be a JSON document (see Figure 10-19).

```
Results
1    {
2      "data": {
3        "addresses": {
4          "items": [
5            {
6              "AddressID": 9,
7              "AddressLine1": "8713 Yosemite Ct.",
8              "AddressLine2": null
9            },
10           {
11             "AddressID": 11,
12             "AddressLine1": "1318 Lasalle Street",
13             "AddressLine2": null
14           },
```

Figure 10-19. Result from GraphQL query

For more details on GraphQL, take a look at Chapter 12.

Summary

SQL databases in Microsoft Fabric integrate SQL Server and Azure SQL Database engines into a scalable, modern platform for advanced analytics and AI-driven applications. Developers can use familiar SQL tools alongside features like vector data types for semantic search and machine learning integration for personalized recommendations. With native OneLake integration, SQL databases can help to eliminate some traditional ETL workflows, enabling real-time analytics and efficient data sharing across Fabric components, including Power BI.

Designed for enterprise-scale applications, Fabric's SQL databases simplify management with tools like Copilot and autonomous features such as auto-indexing and autoscaling. Security and governance are built in, with encryption, automated backups, and compliance tools like Microsoft Purview. The platform aligns with modern DevOps practices, offering CI/CD pipeline integration and source control for streamlined workflows.

With support for AI model integration, a GraphQL interface for flexible querying, and real-time data replication via OneLake, SQL databases in Fabric empower organizations to build intelligent, efficient, and secure applications while modernizing their data strategies.

In the next chapter, we'll look into a feature called mirroring, which allows you to replicate data into OneLake without using traditional ETL tasks.

## CHAPTER 11

Mirroring

We looked into SQL databases in Chapter 10, and this chapter will focus on a feature that allows you to seamlessly integrate operational data from other sources with Fabric through a smart mechanism called mirroring.

Imagine a global retail company with operations spanning multiple regions, each store with its own dedicated OLTP database, running in that store's closest Azure region on Azure SQL database. The company headquarters, located in the United States, frequently runs complex analytical queries to assess worldwide sales trends and inventory status. Instead of creating manual ETL tasks for each of the stores or relying on slow cross-region queries, the company leverages mirroring in Microsoft Fabric. By mirroring the key datasets from the organization's globally distributed operational databases to the US-based data warehouse in Fabric, analysts can access fresh data from all regions seamlessly without using any ETL.

This approach eliminates the latency and complexity of querying remote datasets or manually moving data in real time, providing a centralized view of global operations while ensuring the data remains localized for regional workloads. The simplicity and efficiency of mirroring transform the company's global analytics strategy, making it faster and more scalable without extensive data movement or complex integration.

What Is Mirroring?

Mirroring creates a near real-time, read-only copy of a dataset from an external source within a Fabric workspace, allowing users to access and analyze live data without impacting the source system. While there is a small impact on the operation systems caused by the replication of the source data, all analytical queries are made against Fabric and therefore have no impact on the source. The source dataset can consist of an entire source database or only specific tables, as illustrated in Figure 11-1.

 Mirroring in Fabric is not the same technology that you may be using in SQL Server (SQL Server database mirroring).

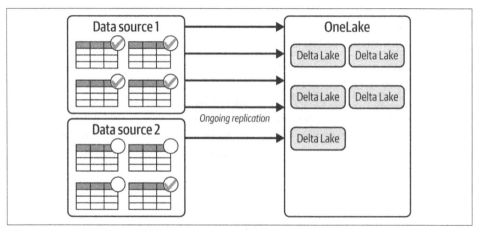

Figure 11-1. Mirroring in Fabric

Ok, that sounds great. But what does that mean, exactly?

Mirroring allows you to replicate your data from supported sources directly into Parquet files in OneLake without writing any ETL or copy tasks or pipelines. At the time of writing, the supported sources are Azure SQL Database, Azure SQL Managed Instance, SQL databases in Fabric (which we discussed in Chapter 10), Azure Cosmos DB, Azure Databricks, and Snowflake.

Besides those sources that are supported out of the box, there is also a concept called *open mirroring* that enables you to write your own applications to mirror data from other sources. This extensible and customizable capability leverages the open Delta Lake table format to integrate existing data into OneLake, facilitating continuous replication and synchronization. You can learn more about open mirroring and its capabilities in the official Microsoft documentation (*https://oreil.ly/PXSXJ*).

Since the supported sources are being expanded constantly, make sure to check the Microsoft documentation for the latest types of mirroring (*https://oreil.ly/k3l02*).

Unlike a shortcut that exclusively keeps the data at its source, mirrored data does get replicated to OneLake. Therefore, you have an actual copy of your data, which requires additional storage. To offset the additional cost assigned to mirrored data, Microsoft provides you with 1 TB of free storage for mirrored data per capacity unit purchased. This means you get 2 TB of free mirror storage with an F2 and 64 TB with an F64.

The amount of free mirror storage is accurate at the time of writing, but like all licensing and cost information, it's subject to change!

Mirroring is a continuous process, so any changes to your source data will be reflected in almost real time (depending on the number and complexity of changes, latency, etc.). The fact that data is being replicated rather than linked to through a shortcut does imply that in some cases your data may be more accurate and up-to-date at the source than it is in Fabric. If no updates occur in the source tables, the replicator engine will gradually reduce its polling frequency, extending up to an hour. It will automatically return to regular polling frequency as soon as it detects new data updates.

The outlier with regard to mirroring is Azure Databricks. Unlike the other sources, Databricks only mirrors the metadata (called Unity Catalog). So despite the (slightly misleading) name *mirroring*, it works more like a value-added shortcut.

Mirroring Requirements

While the entire process of mirroring is fairly straightforward, there are some prerequisites in addition to having a Fabric warehouse and a compatible source system.

Enabling Mirroring in Your Tenant

To make sure you can use mirroring, go to your Admin portal as highlighted in Figure 11-2.

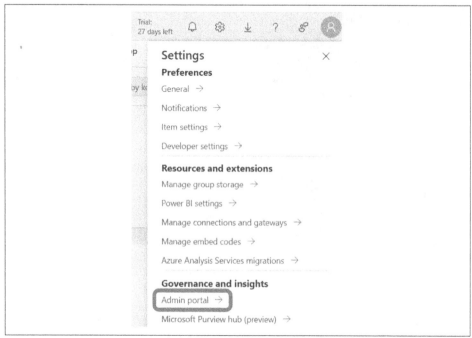

Figure 11-2. Admin portal

The Admin portal is searchable, so you can search for just "API" to find the setting "Service principals can use Fabric APIs" (among others; see Figure 11-3). Make sure this setting is enabled.

Figure 11-3. Search results for "API" in the Admin portal

Networking

Although the networking requirements are fairly basic, your source system must be reachable from your Fabric capacity, so set your firewall rules accordingly.

The networking side can also add to the cost of mirroring. While, at the time of writing, there are no ingress charges in Fabric, there can be egress charges on the source (e.g., for an Azure SQL Database that is not in the same region as the Fabric capacity).

At the time of writing, mirroring doesn't support source systems behind an Azure Virtual Network or private networking.

Source Data Limitations

Mirroring supports only tables. No other objects, such as views, functions, or procedures, can be replicated into Fabric through mirroring, and security settings won't be replicated in Fabric either.

In addition, there are limitations and restrictions that depend on the source system being used. For example, when using Azure SQL Database as your source, all tables used with mirroring must have a primary key. While this sounds fairly minor, it could be a huge issue because many source systems simply don't use primary keys or handle them differently, and you may not be able to simply add them. Some data types are currently unsupported to be either a primary key or for the entire replication process.

As the limitations per system change rather frequently, please refer to the official documentation with regard to the latest restrictions for Azure SQL DB (*https://oreil.ly/lSbNq*), Azure SQL Managed Instance (*https://oreil.ly/V3bB9*), Cosmos DB (*https://oreil.ly/biKTu*), Databricks (*https://oreil.ly/OYo0w*), and Snowflake (*https://oreil.ly/P7h3x*) in the context of mirroring.

A Step-by-Step Guide to Mirroring from Azure SQL DB

Given that it's probably the most widely used offering among the supported source systems, and the easiest to deploy, we've decided to use Azure SQL Database in our step-by-step instructions on how to enable mirroring.

If you don't have an Azure SQL Database, you can create a new single database (*https://oreil.ly/zwJQH*). There is a free tier available, so this won't incur any additional charges.

System Assigned Managed Identity (SAMI)

To publish data to Fabric OneLake, the System Assigned Managed Identity (SAMI) of your Azure SQL logical server must be enabled and designated as the primary identity.

In the Azure portal, go to your logical SQL Server, select Security in the resource menu, then choose Identity and switch Status to "on" under "System assigned managed identity" (shown in Figure 11-4).

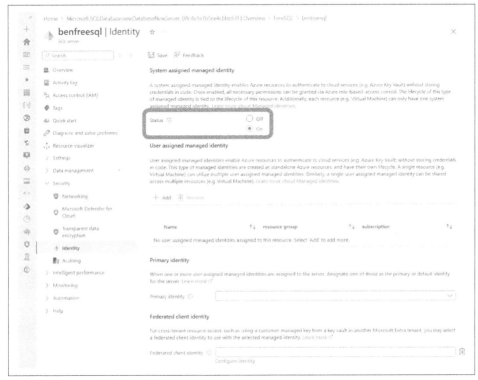

Figure 11-4. Enabling SAMI on your Azure SQL Server

You can confirm that SAMI is set as the primary identity by executing this T-SQL query:

```
SELECT * FROM sys.dm_server_managed_identities
```

Grant Access for Fabric Through a Database Principal

You can either use a SQL authenticated user or an Entra account to authenticate against your Azure SQL DB. We will use a SQL account here for simplicity (you can create SQL accounts yourself, but Entra authentication may require support from your admin team).

In a production environment, we highly recommend using Entra authentication due to the added security features and benefits.

Connect to the master database of your Azure SQL Server using your tool of choice, like SSMS (*https://oreil.ly/Zy6Vk*).

Run the commands in Example 11-1 to create a login and assign the required role to it.

Example 11-1. Create a login and the corresponding role

```
CREATE LOGIN fabric_mirror WITH PASSWORD = 'VerySecretPassword'
ALTER SERVER ROLE [##MS_ServerStateReader##] ADD MEMBER fabric_mirror
```

Then, using the code in Example 11-2, switch your context to the user database you want to mirror and create a user and the corresponding permissions based on the newly created login.

Example 11-2. Create a user and the corresponding permissions

```
CREATE USER fabric_mirror FOR LOGIN fabric_mirror
GRANT CONTROL TO fabric_mirror
```

In SQL Server, the GRANT CONTROL TO statement gives a principal full control over an object, including all permissions such as SELECT, INSERT, UPDATE, DELETE, EXECUTE, and ALTER, as well as the ability to grant or revoke permissions for others. It also allows modifying or dropping the object and accessing child objects within a schema. However, CONTROL does not permit transferring ownership, which remains exclusive to the object's owner.

Create a Mirrored Azure SQL Database

In Fabric, select the Create icon, scroll to the "Data Warehouse" section, and then select "Mirrored Azure SQL Database" (see Figure 11-5).

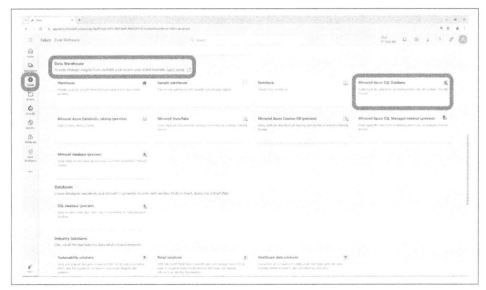

Figure 11-5. Creating a mirrored Azure SQL Database in Fabric

To enable mirroring, select "Azure SQL database" as your new source in the first step of the wizard, shown in Figure 11-6.

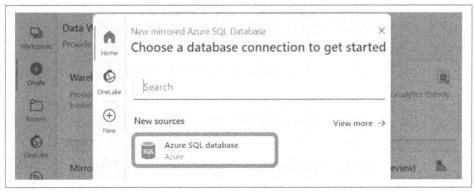

Figure 11-6. Selecting a new source for mirroring

In the next step, connect to the Azure SQL logical server from Fabric to establish a link between the Azure SQL Database and Fabric (see Figure 11-7).

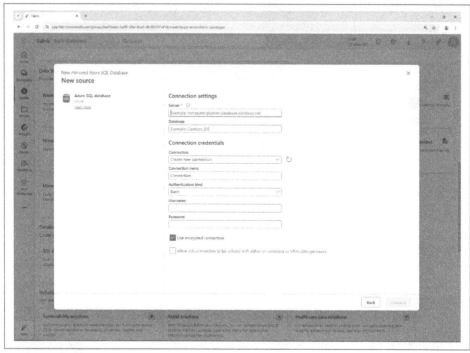

Figure 11-7. Specifying connection settings

Fill in your connection details and click Connect.

In the next step of the wizard (Figure 11-8), configure which tables you want to have mirrored into Fabric. By default, all tables are selected. Optionally, you can choose to automatically mirror all future tables. Note that some tables, which are (partially) unsupported due to unmet requirements, are marked with an exclamation mark or a red X icon.

Figure 11-8. Configuring mirroring

In our case, we'll go ahead and select all tables and confirm with Connect.

There is a limit to the number of tables that can be mirrored. At the time of writing, for Azure SQL Database, this limit is 500 tables. If you select all tables and there are more than 500, only the first 500 in alphabetical order will be mirrored. Make sure to check the most current limitations (*https://oreil.ly/q7fOc*) in the documentation.

On the next screen (see Figure 11-9), we can define a name for our mirrored database and confirm by clicking "Create mirrored database."

As everywhere in Fabric, make sure to establish a proper naming convention for your mirrored items.

Figure 11-9. Naming the mirrored database

This will initialize the mirror, which will take a few minutes to run. The screen will inform you of the progress, as shown in Figure 11-10.

Figure 11-10. Mirrored database is starting

Once the initialization is completed, click Refresh to display the replication status. It should look similar to what you see in Figure 11-11.

Figure 11-11. Monitor replication

Once the initial replication is completed, you should see the number of rows as well as the last replication timestamp when refreshing the view.

Your mirrored database is an artifact by itself that you can find in your workspace along with a default semantic model and a SQL analytics endpoint, both of which get automatically created for every mirrored database (see Figure 11-12).

Figure 11-12. Mirrored database in workspace

If you select it, you will go to the screen that enables you to stop, configure, or monitor your replication (see Figure 11-13).

Figure 11-13. Existing mirror settings

If you select the SQL analytics endpoint that was created for this mirrored database, you can browse and query your tables like any other warehouse in Fabric (see Figure 11-14). Of course, you can also directly access those files like any other file in OneLake through OneLake explorer (as we explained in Chapter 3).

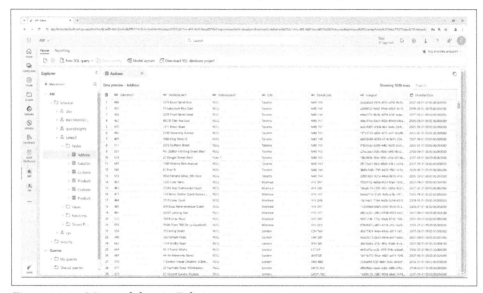

Figure 11-14. Mirrored data in Fabric

Fabric Link Is Not the Same Thing

A similar concept that often gets confused with mirroring is Fabric Link. Fabric Link is a solution specifically for Microsoft Dynamics, an ERP solution, when run as a SaaS solution. Fabric Link also replicates operational data, which gets replicated to another storage level called Dataverse, which is then be accessed through shortcuts. While those shortcuts get automatically created for you, the major difference is that with mirroring, the data gets replicated into Fabric, whereas with Fabric Link, it ends up in Dataverse (see Figure 11-15).

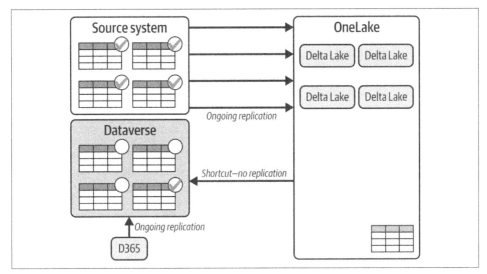

Figure 11-15. Mirroring versus Fabric Link

Summary

In Microsoft Fabric, mirroring is a powerful feature that enables users to replicate near real-time, read-only copies of data from sources like Azure SQL DB, Azure Cosmos DB, Azure Databricks, and Snowflake into a Fabric warehouse without the need for ETL pipelines or manual copying. By storing these replicas in OneLake, Fabric ensures that the data can be analyzed within the platform without impacting the source system, although this requires additional storage, for which Microsoft provides 1 TB of free mirroring storage per capacity unit purchased.

Mirroring differs from shortcuts, as it fully replicates (except when Azure Databricks is the source) the data into Fabric, offering an actual copy rather than a link to the original source. Replication happens continuously, so updates from the source are reflected in Fabric with minimal latency. To enable mirroring, certain prerequisites must be met, including admin settings adjustments and network configurations, and it currently supports only tables from source databases, excluding views and functions. The process also requires specific security settings and connection configurations, but once set up, it enables a variety of analytics capabilities on live data within Fabric. While it does take away the analytical workloads from your source system, the replication process itself does use and require additional resources on your source system.

In our next chapter, Chapter 12, we will take a look at how you can use GraphQL in the context of Fabric.

Microsoft Fabric API for GraphQL

If you have a developer background or role, you may be wondering, We are creating a custom dashboard using code, and we need the data stored inside Microsoft Fabric—can we access it in some way other than via a SQL analytics endpoint?

This is a real-life requirement we've encountered multiple times. And the short answer is, yes, you can! For the longer answer, we encourage you to read this chapter and understand how to leverage the Fabric API for GraphQL feature for an enhanced data retrieval experience compared to the traditional REST API approach.

Honestly, the official name, Fabric API for GraphQL, sounds too scary even for experienced data professionals, let alone someone who just started their Fabric learning journey, unless you are a seasoned application developer. Hence, let's first try to demystify the core concepts of this feature.

First and foremost, GraphQL is a query language. You might have already assumed that from its name (*QL* stands for query language). To take this one step further: it's not any query language—it's a query language for the API. It's an open source protocol and has been successfully implemented in numerous programming languages. Since GraphQL is an API query language, it isn't bound to any particular database engine or vendor.

From a high-level perspective, the main advantages of GraphQL compared to REST APIs are:

Flexibility
    GraphQL allows you to define individual columns that you need to extract, whereas most REST APIs provide a standard response only.

Efficiency

GraphQL enables combining multiple queries in a single call. A simple example is the possibility of joining tables in the GraphQL query. In GraphQL, this will result in a single call, while in the REST API, it would produce multiple calls.

Core GraphQL Operations

GraphQL supports three operation types:

Query

Query is the essential operation type of GraphQL. To some extent, GraphQL queries may remind you of SQL queries, at least from a logical point of view: you can select specific fields from the table, join multiple tables, filter and sort the data, and so on.

Mutation

Mutation corresponds to commands that enable data modification on the server side. Think of this operation as an equivalent to CREATE, UPDATE, and DELETE statements in SQL.

Subscription

Subscription allows subscribing to real-time data. You can subscribe to a particular event, such as data deletion or user creation, and whenever the event occurs, the server will send the data to a GraphQL query.

 At the time of writing, Microsoft Fabric supports only Query and Mutation operation types for GraphQL, although it's very likely that the Subscription operation will be supported in the future for Real-Time Intelligence workloads.

Working with GraphQL in Fabric

Before we explain how to create and execute GraphQL queries in Microsoft Fabric, let's first take a brief overview of the currently supported operations based on the Fabric item type. Table 12-1 shows which GraphQL operations can be performed in Fabric items.

Table 12-1. Supported GraphQL operations for various Fabric items

Fabric item type	GraphQL operation type
Warehouse	Query/Mutation
Lakehouse	Query
Mirrored database	Query

Fabric item type	GraphQL operation type
SQL database in Fabric	Query/Mutation
Azure SQL DB	Query/Mutation

Notice that only Fabric warehouse, Azure SQL Database, and SQL database in Fabric currently allow for modifying the data.

A single GraphQL item can be leveraged to query multiple warehouse, lakehouse, mirrored database, and SQL database items simultaneously, although it is not possible to create relationships between these items. Relationships are currently supported only in the scope of a single item.

Let's now put the GraphQL feature into action. As you can see in Figure 12-1, as a prerequisite, the feature has to be enabled in the Admin portal of your Fabric tenant.

Figure 12-1. Enabling API for GraphQL in the Admin portal

Once enabled, API for GraphQL is available for *all* Fabric item types that support this feature as specified in Table 12-1. That is, it's not possible to implement a more granular control and enable GraphQL only for, say, lakehouses or warehouses.

Query Data with API for GraphQL

Let's first retrieve the data from individual Fabric warehouse tables. As a starting point, we first need to create the API for GraphQL item in Microsoft Fabric. Once we provide the item name, choose the data source (e.g., lakehouse or warehouse), and pick particular tables from the source, we are ready to query the data.

The following code snippet, executed directly inside the API for GraphQL item's development environment, will retrieve the data from specific columns of the dim Products and dimCustomers tables:

```
query {
    dimProducts {  #Table 1 name
     items {        #Columns to be included in the query
      ProductKey,
      EnglishProductName,
      Color,
      Class
        }
     }
     ,
    dimCustomers { #Table 2 name
       items {      #Columns to be included in the query
        CustomerKey,
        FirstName,
        LastName,
        Gender
        }
     }
  }
```

This basic query will retrieve all the records from the columns defined in the query. However, what if we are interested in only a subset of records or, potentially, in a single record from the table? We have good and bad news here: the bad news is that you can't rely on *traditional* operators, such as >, >=, <, or <=. However, the good news is that we can still filter the data by substituting these operators with their verbose relatives. Hence, = becomes eq, > becomes gt (greater than), < becomes lt (less than), and so on, as shown in Table 12-2.

Table 12-2. API for GraphQL logical operators

GraphQL operator	Operation
eq	Equal to
neq	Not equal to

GraphQL operator	Operation
gt	Greater than
lt	Less than
gte	Greater than or equal to
lte	Less than or equal to
isNull	Check if the value is null

Imagine that you need to retrieve the data for customers whose first name equals Adam. Here is the code snippet that will meet this requirement:

```
query {
    dimCustomers
    (filter: {FirstName:  {
        eq:"Adam"
    }}) {
    items {
     CustomerKey,
     FirstName,
     LastName,
     Gender
        }
    }
}
```

Figure 12-2 displays the results retrieved by the query.

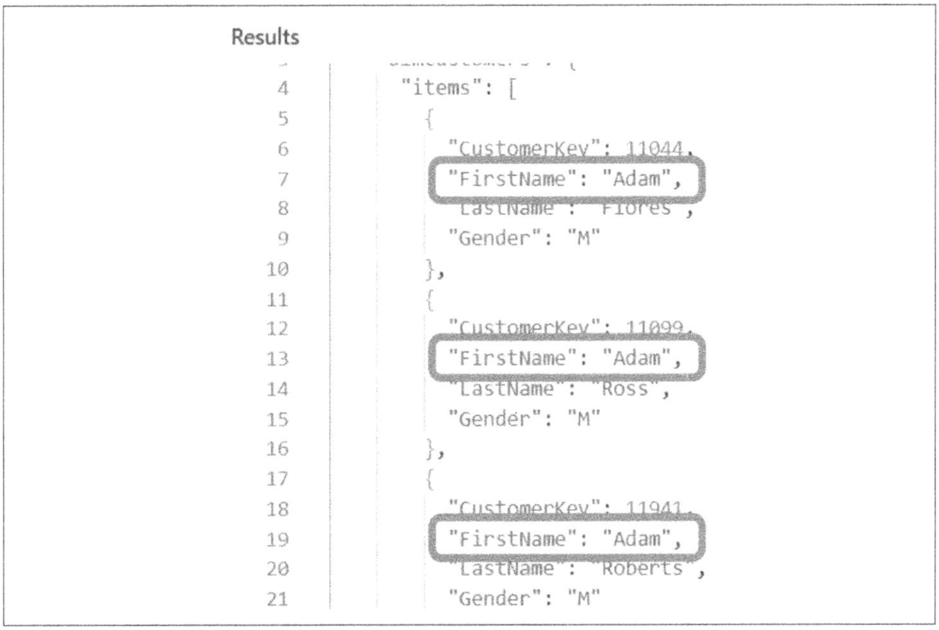

Figure 12-2. Results giving only those customers whose first name is Adam

Creating Relationships

Relationships in API for GraphQL, like those in traditional RDBMSs, allow combining data from multiple tables in the same query. When you open the API for GraphQL item, the relationship properties are configured from the "New relationship" dialog, as displayed in Figure 12-3. First click on the three dots next to the schema name and then select the "Manage relationships" option.

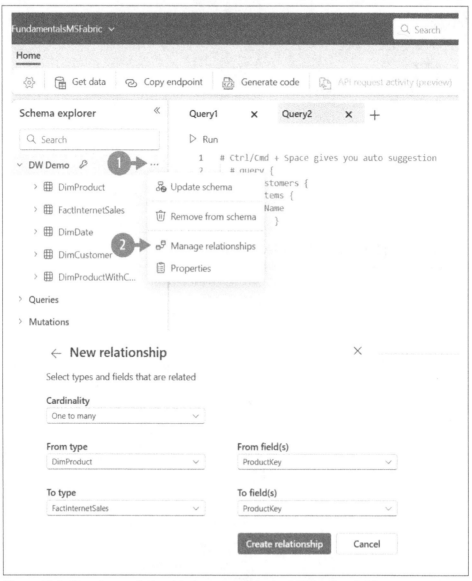

Figure 12-3. Creating a relationship between tables in API for GraphQL

Here, we are establishing a relationship with one-to-many cardinality between the DimProduct and FactInternetSales tables on the common column ProductKey.

Let's now generate a query that will retrieve combined data from both DimProduct and FactInternetSales. The following code snippet represents the query that retrieves all blue products and relevant sales order numbers from the FactInternet Sales table, including the SalesAmount value. Additionally, we are sorting the data on the SalesAmount column in descending order:

```
query {
    dimProducts
        (filter: {Color:{eq:"Blue"}}) {
    items {
    Color,
    EnglishProductName
    factInternetSales
        (orderBy: {SalesAmount: DESC}){
        items{
            SalesOrderNumber,
            SalesAmount
        }
    }
        }
    }
}
```

Making Changes Using Mutations

Mutations are a very powerful feature of API for GraphQL, as they enable data manipulation in the Fabric warehouse. As shown in Figure 12-4, mutations for executing the CREATE statement are automatically included in the Schema explorer of the GraphQL item.

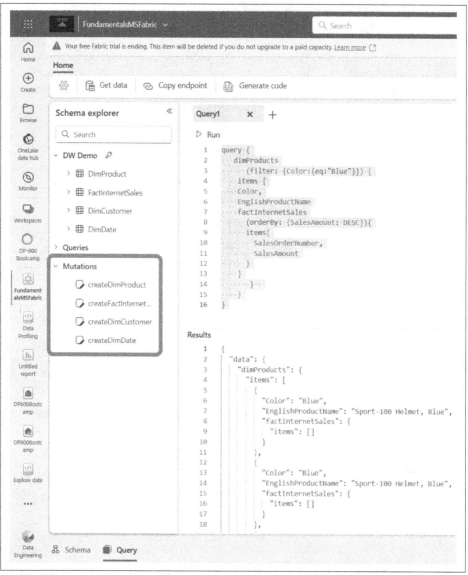

Figure 12-4. Default inclusion of CREATE mutations in the Schema explorer

Hence, if we want to create a new record in the DimProduct table, we can leverage the existing mutation createDimProduct, as shown in the following code snippet:

```
mutation {
    createDimProduct(
      item: { ProductKey: 99999
              , EnglishProductName: "Fundamentals of Microsoft Fabric" })
  {
        result # Required to return the result of the mutation execution
  }
}
```

Figure 12-5 confirms that our record was successfully created in the DimProduct table.

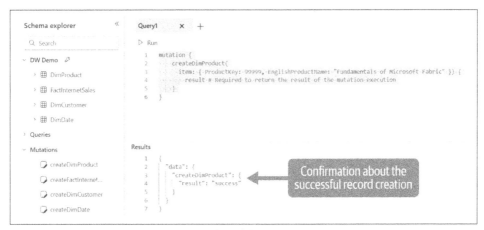

Figure 12-5. Creating a new record in the table

Let's look at deleting records from a specific table. Depending on how your table in the Fabric warehouse was created, this may be performed in two ways:

- If the table was created without a PRIMARY KEY constraint, UPDATE and DELETE operations are *not* available out of the box.

- If the table was created with a PRIMARY KEY constraint, even though this con-straint must be specified as *not enforced* in the Fabric warehouse, UPDATE and DELETE operations are available out of the box.

Let's examine how to apply the mutation operation for both scenarios.

Since DELETE mutations are not available out of the box in the Schema explorer for tables without a primary key, we need to extend our toolbox and leverage stored procedures from the warehouse. (Explaining the concept of stored procedures and the benefits of using stored procedures is outside of the scope of this book.)

To apply DELETE and UPDATE operations with API for GraphQL for tables with no primary key constraint, as a prerequisite, you must encapsulate transaction logic inside regular stored procedures in the Fabric warehouse and then execute these procedures inside the GraphQL item.

We've already created a basic stored procedure called spDeleteProduct. This procedure takes the ProductKey input parameter and deletes the record from the DimProduct table where the ProductKey value is equal to the value defined in the parameter. The following T-SQL code snippet was used in the SQL query editor to create the stored procedure:

```
CREATE PROC [dbo].[spDeleteProduct]
@ProductKey int
AS
BEGIN
DELETE FROM DimProduct
WHERE ProductKey = @ProductKey
END
```

We can now execute this procedure from API for GraphQL and pass the parameter value we want to use. In Figure 12-6, you may notice that I'm deleting the product with the ProductKey 99999 that we previously created.

```
Query1        ✕    +

▷ Run
    1    mutation {
    2        executespDeleteProduct(ProductKey: 99999) {
    3            result
    4        }
    5    }

Results
    1    {
    2      "data": {
    3        "executespDeleteProduct": []
    4      }
    5    }
```

Figure 12-6. Deleting a record from the table by executing the stored procedure

Using similar logic, we can also update the existing records in the table. Again, to achieve this with the API for GraphQL, we need to create a stored procedure in Fabric warehouse as the first step. For the GraphQL item, the execution logic and the code syntax are the same as in the previous example with the DELETE statement—it's only the stored procedure's inner logic that differs from the previous scenario, as you might want to execute the UPDATE statement instead of DELETE.

Let's examine how to perform DELETE and/or UPDATE operations for tables with a primary key constraint. As you'll notice, it's a more straightforward process than in the previous scenario.

Using the following T-SQL code snippet in the SQL query editor, we'll create a new warehouse table, DimProductWithConstraint, and define a primary key constraint on the ProductKey column:

```
CREATE TABLE DimProductWithConstraint
(ProductKey INT NOT NULL
,ProductAlternateKey VARCHAR(100) NOT NULL
,EnglishProductName VARCHAR(100) NOT NULL
)

ALTER TABLE DimProductWithConstraint
ADD CONSTRAINT PK_Product PRIMARY KEY NONCLUSTERED (ProductKey) NOT ENFORCED;

INSERT INTO DimProductWithConstraint
SELECT ProductKey
    ,ProductAlternateKey
    ,EnglishProductName
FROM DimProduct
```

Please be aware that the primary key column can't be nullable, or your query won't work. Additionally, keep in mind that all constraints in Fabric warehouse *must* be wrapped with the NOT ENFORCED clause. If you are coming from a traditional SQL Server world, this may come as a huge shock. However, all key constraints in Fabric warehouse are supported only when NOT ENFORCED is used. You can read more about these requirements in the official Microsoft documentation (*https://oreil.ly/-5xIl*).

Going back to our GraphQL item, when we define a table with a primary key constraint, *all* mutation operations are automatically available in the Schema explorer. Once we updated the schema, as you can see in Figure 12-7, all three mutation operations—CREATE, UPDATE, and DELETE—are available for the DimProduct WithConstraint table.

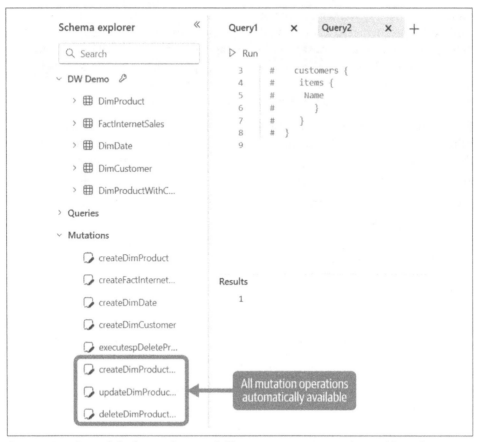

Figure 12-7. Out-of-the-box inclusion of all mutation operations for a table with a primary key constraint

To wrap up this section, if tables in the warehouse were created with primary key constraints, all mutation operations (CREATE, UPDATE, and DELETE) in the GraphQL item will be created automatically. On the flip side, when tables don't have a primary key explicitly defined, only the CREATE operation is available out of the box; for the UPDATE and DELETE operations, you need to use stored procedures.

Going Above and Beyond with Variables

As in other programming languages, you may find the concept of variables helpful in scenarios where you need to filter the data based on user input or when you want to reuse the same query with different parameter values.

Figure 12-8 depicts how you can define variables within the Query variables window of the GraphQL item and pass this value to the mutation operation.

Figure 12-8. Passing the value dynamically to the mutation operation

Variables can also be leveraged in query operations. In the following example, displayed in Figure 12-9, we are dynamically setting multiple filters for the query.

Figure 12-9. Passing multiple values dynamically to the query operation

Let's wrap up this chapter by pointing out a few of the key characteristics of the API for GraphQL item in Microsoft Fabric:

- The API for GraphQL item requires applications to use Microsoft Entra for authentication. Your client application must be registered and configured properly to execute API calls against Microsoft Fabric.

- Once you have tested and prototyped the desired GraphQL operation, the API editor can generate boilerplate Python or Node.js code based on the query or mutation executed in the GraphQL editor.

- The enable/disable feature for queries and mutations provides administrators and developers with granular control over API access and usage. It allows you to selectively activate or deactivate specific queries and mutations within the GraphQL schema.

Summary

Although API for GraphQL might not look like a groundbreaking feature at first glance, and probably won't be frequently used by data engineers and Fabric admins, we still consider it a huge leap forward compared to the traditional way of dealing with API-related scenarios. Therefore, we are convinced that application developers, as the primary target group for this feature, will appreciate the possibility of leveraging GraphQL items in Microsoft Fabric.

Due to its portability and programming-language independence, GraphQL opens a whole new world of options for querying and manipulating the data stored in Microsoft Fabric. Finally, because it provides a rich set of features, such as querying data from multiple tables by sending a single query, creating relationships between tables, applying modifications to the data, and executing stored procedures, we are sure that GraphQL's popularity will increase over time and that it will soon become a de facto standard when working with APIs.

Fasten your seatbelts—in the next chapter, get ready to meet Microsoft Fabric Copilots and other AI-powered features.

## CHAPTER 13

AI and Copilots

"Hey, Copilot, can you summarize this book for me?"

We sincerely hope you won't write a prompt like this, since we firmly believe you should read our book in full. However, we won't blame you much (just kidding, of course we will) if you leverage the latest technology to save yourself some time and effort. As you well know, we can't deny the omnipresence of artificial intelligence (AI) and large language models (LLMs) in every segment of our lives.

In this chapter, we will examine how AI and LLMs can be leveraged in various Microsoft Fabric components, as well as in which scenarios you might consider asking Copilot for assistance. We have to be honest at the very beginning and warn you that this is going to be quite a long chapter—but this is not to scare you off from reading it! On the contrary, we want to assure you that you should expect a thorough overview of the AI features and Copilots in Microsoft Fabric.

Before we dive into exploring various implementations of AI in Microsoft Fabric, let's first take a step back and examine LLMs, as they represent the backbone of Copilot, which we cover in depth in the next section. If we had written this book just two years ago, this chapter almost surely wouldn't have existed. But as of today, it's unthinkable to write practically any tech book without mentioning LLMs. That is how rapidly this new technology has risen to prominence.

In plain English, an LLM is the software that can "talk" to you using natural language. When we say talk, we mean that an LLM is capable of both understanding and responding using human language. LLMs are based on machine learning models trained on large amounts of data—hence, the name "large." Chatting with software is nice, but this is just a minor aspect of LLM use cases. LLMs can be leveraged to generate essays, poems, and programming code, all the way to creating podcasts, videos, or images out of natural language prompts. Whenever we talk about LLMs in the context of creating something based on a natural language prompt, we are essentially talking about *generative AI*, a special type of deep learning model capable of producing text, images, programming code, and audio-visual content in response to a prompt.

 Before we proceed, an important word of warning: generative AI models are usually good at identifying patterns, but sometimes they identify patterns that don't actually exist, or misapply a pattern that is present to an inappropriate use case. This can result in the models providing false information, a phenomenon known as hallucination.

Additionally, generative AI models are only as accurate as the data they are fed, and it is always recommended that you check the output validity, instead of blindly trusting results.

What Is Copilot?

Now that you understand how AI and LLMs can potentially make your life easier, let's examine the way Copilot in Microsoft Fabric can enhance your productivity and make your usual workloads more straightforward. Before we dive deeper into exploring Copilots, we want to answer the question from the section title: what is Copilot?

It's a generative AI chatbot based on LLMs. We want to emphasize that AI and Copilots are infused into every single Fabric experience, so you'll find us examining numerous Copilots throughout this chapter: Copilot for Data Science and Data Engineering, Copilot for Data Factory, Copilot for Data Warehouse, Copilot for Power BI, Copilot for Real-Time Intelligence, and Copilot for SQL database.

Enable Copilot in Microsoft Fabric

Let's first explain how to start using Copilot. Tenant or capacity geolocation plays a crucial role in the default settings for Copilot in Microsoft Fabric. If your tenant is outside the US or France, Copilot is disabled by default. To enable Copilot, you (or your Fabric administrator) need to navigate to the Tenant settings of the Admin portal, as displayed in Figure 13-1.

In addition, there is a setting called "Data sent to Azure OpenAI can be processed outside your capacity's geographic region, compliance boundary, or national cloud instance." Quite a long name for the setting that is applicable only to organizations that want to use Copilot and AI features powered by Azure OpenAI and whose capacity's georegion is outside the European Union (EU) data boundary and the US.

The Microsoft documentation (*https://oreil.ly/XDEAX*) provides additional information about data processing across geographic areas.

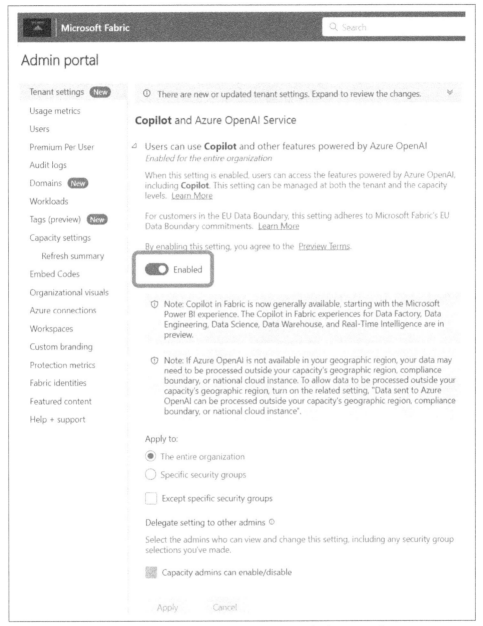

Figure 13-1. Enabling Copilot in the tenant settings outside the US and France

When you enable the "Capacities can be designated as Fabric Copilot capacities" setting, a regular Fabric capacity becomes a special "Copilot capacity" type to enable more streamlined Copilot use and billing.

Geolocation is not the only consideration. At the time of writing, Copilot is supported only for F64 capacities or higher. If you are wondering whether a trial license can be used to try out Copilot, we have to disappoint you: a trial SKU is not eligible for Copilot.

In the remaining sections of this chapter, we'll focus on exploring individual Copilots in Microsoft Fabric.

Copilot for Data Factory

As you learned in Chapter 4, Data Factory allows for seamless data integration and data orchestration processes in Microsoft Fabric. As you may recall, two main Fabric items in the Data Factory experience are Dataflow Gen2 and data pipelines. Copilot in Data Factory is supported for both items. Here are a couple of examples of how Copilot can be used in Data Factory:

Dataflow Gen2
- To create new transformation steps for an existing query
- To create a new query that can reference an existing query
- To provide a summary of a query and its applied transformation steps

Data pipelines
- To create a new pipeline from scratch
- To summarize an existing pipeline by explaining the content and relations between different pipeline activities
- To provide error assistance by troubleshooting data pipeline issues and providing actionable guidance on how to resolve them

Let's first see Copilot in action in the Dataflow Gen2. We'll create a Dataflow called Orders Transform. As you see in Figure 13-2, we're connecting to the Delta table "orders," which is stored in a lakehouse, and we'll immediately open the Copilot pane from the top ribbon.

Let's now put Copilot to the test. In accordance with the recommended practices, I'll first apply data filtering. Currently, the table contains data for three years: 2019, 2020, and 2021. Let's imagine that we want to keep only the records from the year 2021. Therefore, I'll write the following prompt in the Copilot chat window: "Keep only records for the year 2021."

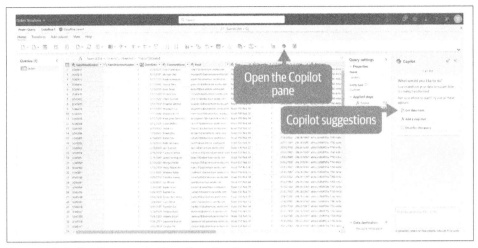

Figure 13-2. Copilot pane in Dataflow Gen2

As you can see in Figure 13-3, it worked! Two things happened behind the scenes based on our conversation with Copilot:

- There is now a transformation step called Filter rows in the Applied steps pane.
- The M code was automatically generated based on the conversation.

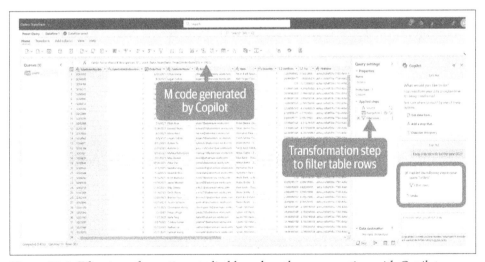

Figure 13-3. Filter transformation applied based on the conversation with Copilot

That's nice, but let's see if Copilot can support us with more sophisticated requirements. Currently, the customer name is stored as a full name, including both the first name and last name of the customer. Let's imagine that we need these two stored separately. In the Copilot chat window, I'll enter the following prompt: "Split the CustomerName column into FirstName and LastName."

Figure 13-4 confirms that Copilot did the job properly again—we have the FirstName and LastName stored as separate columns in the dataset.

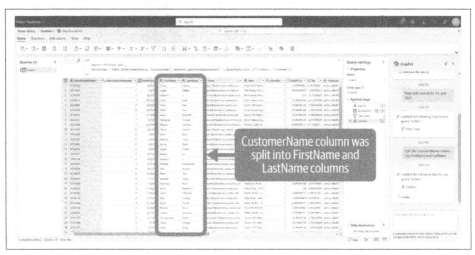

Figure 13-4. Splitting the customer's name into first name and last name

One last thing we want to try is to create a duplicate query named orders_agg based on the orders query, then aggregate the data inside the orders_agg query, so that the total number of orders is displayed per item. We'll enter the following prompt in the Copilot chat window: "Create a duplicate of the orders query and name it orders_agg." This time, Copilot completed the task with some caveats. A new query was created, not as a duplicate of the base query but as a reference. Explaining the difference between the duplicate and reference transformations in Power Query and Dataflows is outside the scope of this book. However, keep in mind that there are subtle differences between these two, especially from the perspective of what happens to the derived query (whether duplicated or referenced) in the case of changes applied to the base query (in our case, the orders query).

Let's wrap it up by aggregating the data. We'll enter the following prompt in the Copilot chat window: "Count the number of orders per item." After Copilot successfully applied the "Group by" transformation to calculate the total number of records per item, we asked it to sort the data per OrderCount in descending order. Figure 13-5 displays the final outcome.

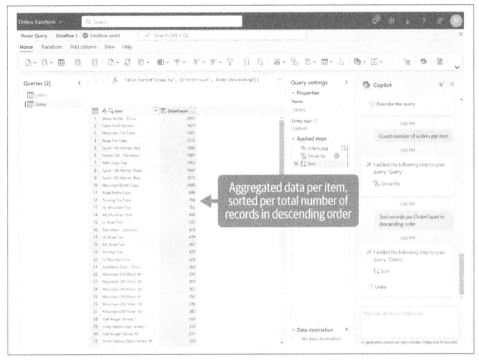

Figure 13-5. Copilot successfully applying the "Group by" and Sort transformations

Code Efficiency with Copilot

Please bear in mind that Copilot might not always generate the most efficient code for the entire transformation pipeline. In some circumstances, the order of transformation steps might determine whether query folding occurs. *Query folding* is the capability of Power Query's engine to generate a single SQL statement that's going to be executed on the data source side. The main benefit of query folding is that it pushes heavy data transformation operations to a data source, thus reducing the amount of work necessary to apply transformations in the Dataflow afterward. Additionally, there might be a more efficient way to perform a particular transformation step than the one implemented by Copilot. Therefore, it's always the responsibility of the developer to check both accuracy and efficiency in order to optimize the query.

Once you're happy with the Copilot-made transformations, you can configure the data destination, such as a lakehouse or warehouse, and publish the Dataflow.

It's now time to learn how to leverage Copilot when working with data pipelines. Figure 13-6 shows how to launch the Copilot pane from the blank pipeline canvas.

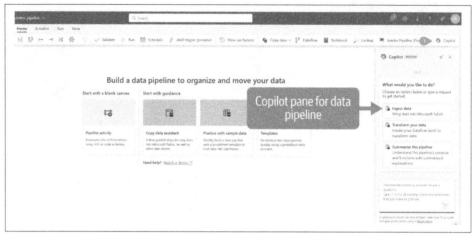

Figure 13-6. Copilot pane for data pipeline

Each of the available options generates a predefined prompt that might be used to instruct Copilot:

- "Ingest data" generates the prompt "Get data using copy data activity."
- "Transform your data" generates the prompt "Transform data with Dataflow Gen2."
- "Summarize this pipeline" generates the prompt "Summarize this pipeline."

Let's start with the "Ingest data" option. As soon as we confirm the predefined prompt, Copilot will insert a "Copy data" activity task on the pipeline canvas, as shown in Figure 13-7.

The "Transform your data" option will add the Dataflow Gen2 task to the pipeline canvas. As you learned in Chapter 4, Dataflow Gen2 is commonly used for implementing data transformations.

The "Summarize this pipeline" option may come in very handy with complex pipelines, where the summarized overview might be helpful to better understand various pipeline tasks and how they correlate with each other.

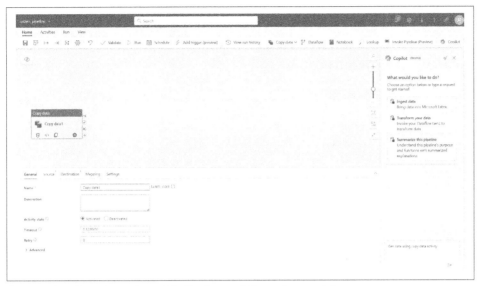

Figure 13-7. Data ingestion with Copilot and Copy data activity

Copilot for Data Engineering and Data Science

We sincerely hope that you already have a good grasp of skills and knowledge about the Data Engineering and Data Science workloads in Microsoft Fabric, which we covered in depth in Chapter 5 and Chapter 7, respectively.

Copilot for Data Engineering and Data Science may assist in providing the answers to the questions you ask about lakehouse tables and Power BI semantic models, as well as generate code snippets for data analysis and data visualization.

The process of interacting with Copilot starts by selecting a Copilot icon in a Fabric notebook and then asking questions in the chat panel. Copilot understands not only the metadata but also the data that you load into the DataFrame. A *DataFrame* is a special temporary data structure in the Python programming language, stored in memory, that consists of rows and columns, similar to a database table or Excel spreadsheet.

Let's see Copilot for Data Engineering and Data Science in action. We'll open the notebook named Star Schema LH and initialize the Copilot chat window. As you can see in Figure 13-8, Copilot provides a list of predefined prompts that you can use to quickly get up and running.

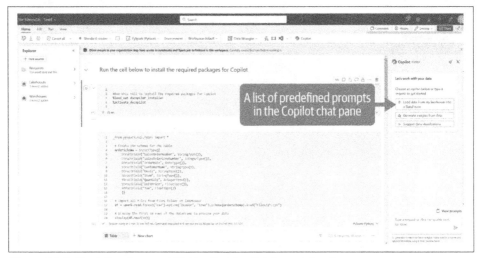

Figure 13-8. Predefined prompt list in the Copilot for notebook

Let's follow the Copilot suggestions and first load the data into a DataFrame. We'll now stop for a moment to examine Figure 13-9.

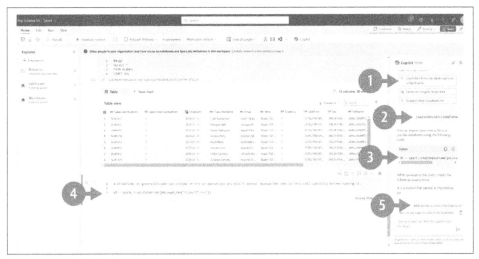

Figure 13-9. Loading data into DataFrame with Copilot

1. We've selected the predefined prompt: "Load data from my lakehouse into a DataFrame."

2. In the prompt window, we've replaced the generic name with the name of our data source (orders).

3. Copilot generated a PySpark code snippet to load the data into a DataFrame.

4. Once we selected "Code insert" in the top left corner of the generated code, a new cell was created in the notebook to include the generated code.

5. Additional prompt suggestions popped up in the Copilot chat pane.

We can perform a quick data profiling with Copilot's assistance, as shown in Figure 13-10, where we check if there are any missing or duplicate values in the DataFrame.

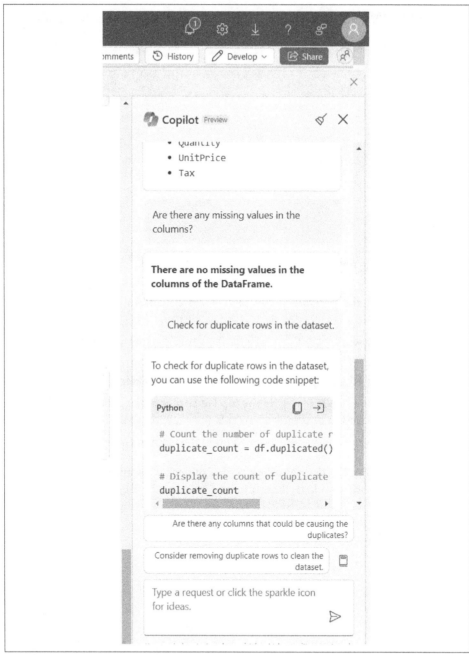

Figure 13-10. Basic data profiling with Copilot

Let's now use Copilot to get some insights from the data. We'll type the following prompt into the Copilot chat pane: "What is the average Unit Price?" Figure 13-11 shows that Copilot first generates the PySpark code that we insert with a single click into the notebook cell and then calculates and displays the average Unit Price value.

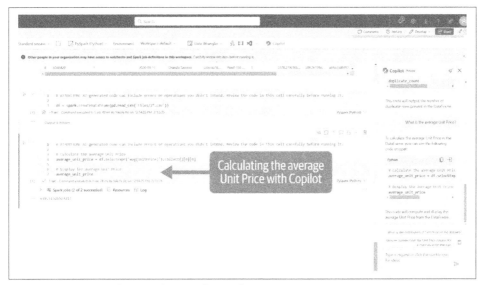

Figure 13-11. Basic data analysis with Copilot

Let's wrap it up by asking Copilot to assist in data visualization tasks. We first used the predefined prompt "Suggest data visualizations." In the chat window, we replaced the generic name with our orders dataset, to get the following prompt: "Analyze orders and suggest ways to visualize the data." Copilot generated eight different suggestions, starting with the sales trends over time all the way to geospatial analysis. Based on Copilot's suggestions, we've entered the following prompt as shown in Figure 13-12: "Plot a line chart showing total sales amount over different time periods (e.g., daily, monthly, yearly) to identify trends and seasonality."

The generated PySpark code snippet looked promising, so we inserted it directly into the notebook cell. However, poor Copilot incorrectly assumed that there is a TotalSalesAmount column in our DataFrame, and this caused the query to throw an error (see Figure 13-12).

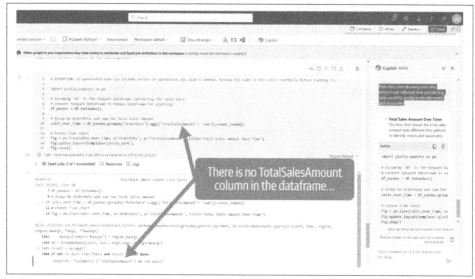

Figure 13-12. An incorrect code snippet generated by Copilot

And, this is why we are constantly repeating: don't blindly trust Copilot! Let's imagine that we're the analyst who's currently working on this notebook. Apparently, we know our dataset well, and we can now use *our own knowledge* to fine-tune Copilot's suggestion and fix this code. We'll swap the nonexistent TotalSalesAmount column with the existing Quantity column, and now the code works like a charm, as you can confirm in Figure 13-13.

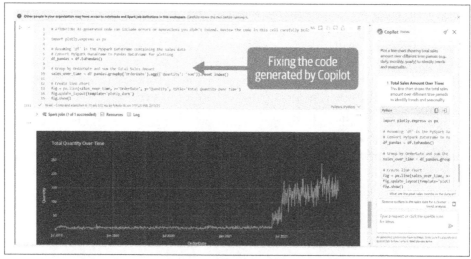

Figure 13-13. Fixing the Copilot generated code to produce the desired results

The moral of this story is: take the warning from line 1 of the generated code snippet seriously!

 AI-generated code can include errors or operations you didn't intend. Review the code in this cell carefully before running it.

Another possibility when using Copilot in a notebook is to write prompts directly in a cell, instead of using the Copilot chat pane. In Figure 13-14, you can see how we're leveraging a magic command within the cell to ask the natural language question directly: "What is the maximum Tax?" The output represents the Copilot-generated response.

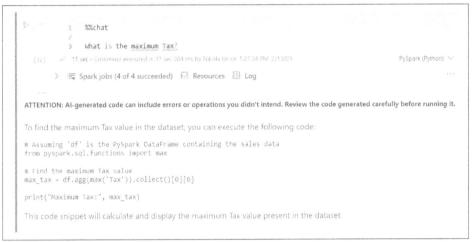

Figure 13-14. Interacting with Copilot directly from the notebook cell

As we saw in Chapter 5, magic commands are special instructions that expand upon the default Python capabilities. The command %%chat is just one of the numerous magic commands available when interacting with Copilot in Microsoft Fabric. You can also generate code by using the %%code magic command, or you can use %%describe to summarize and describe a dataframe. You can find the full list of supported magic commands (*https://oreil.ly/o7pJp*) in the Microsoft documentation.

Copilot for Data Warehouse

If you implemented a warehouse as part of your Fabric architecture, you can use Copilot to assist in numerous use cases.

 Before we examine these cases, please bear in mind that Copilot doesn't use data stored in warehouse tables to generate T-SQL statement suggestions. It relies only on table and column names, along with primary and foreign key metadata, to come up with a T-SQL code suggestion.

Copilot for Data Warehouse can be accessed in three ways:

Chat pane
> Use the chat pane if you want to ask questions using natural language. The generated response is either a T-SQL query or a natural language answer.

Code completion
> Once you start writing T-SQL in the SQL query editor window, Copilot will automatically generate a code suggestion, which you can accept by pressing the Tab key.

Quick actions
> Within the SQL query editor, you will find Fix and Explain options as quick actions. Simply highlight the piece of T-SQL code and choose one of the quick action buttons:
>
> - Explain, to get the natural language explanation of the selected query statement.
> - Fix, to fix errors in the query statement. In addition, Copilot will generate comments to explain fixes and suggest best practices for writing T-SQL code.

Let's warm up Copilot in warehouse with a simple prompt: "How can I ingest data into Fabric Warehouse?" As you see in Figure 13-15, Copilot provides a comprehensive list of all the available ingestion options.

Figure 13-15. The list of data ingestion options, generated by Copilot

Now, we'll move on to some more advanced scenarios. We'll type the following prompt into the Copilot chat window: "How many customers made orders on January 1st 2021?" Figure 13-16 shows how powerful Copilot can be for SQL-based scenarios.

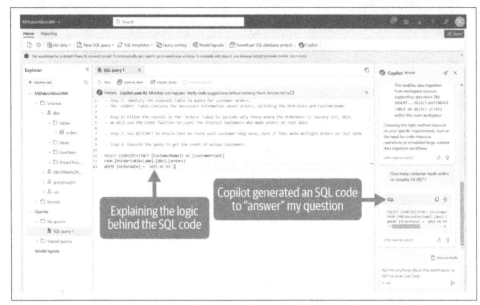

Figure 13-16. Copilot-generated SQL code with an explanation of the code logic

As you can see, Copilot first generated a SQL code snippet as the answer to our natural language question. We can then insert the code in the query window directly from the Copilot chat window. And, as you see, Copilot generated not only the code but also comments explaining the logic behind the generated query.

We'll now expand on the previous query and ask Copilot the following: "How many customers made more than 2 orders on January 1st 2021?" Looking at Figure 13-17, we consider this a wonderful way to not only retrieve the desired results but also to learn and better understand T-SQL code.

Figure 13-17. Very helpful code explanation provided by Copilot

This is nice, but let's now really go wild with Copilot in Warehouse. In Figure 13-18, we're looking into an existing query that could have been written by us or someone else. Let's say that we're not sure what this query is supposed to do. We can simply type /explain in the Copilot chat window, and Copilot will explain the query.

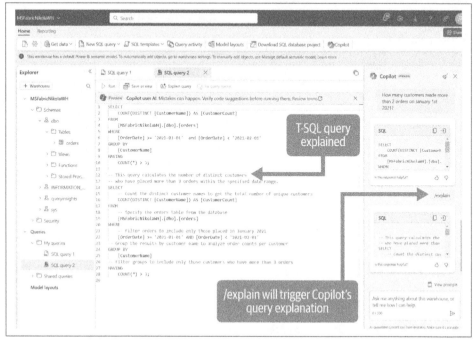

Figure 13-18. Producing a query explanation by Copilot with the /explain prompt

Generally speaking, the "/" commands may be used for numerous advanced use cases. Table 13-1 shows some common examples. Please keep in mind that, when using these commands, they must be at the start of your prompt.

Table 13-1. Commands to generate actions

Command	Generated action
/generate-sql	T-SQL query from the prompt
/explain	Explanation of the active query
/fix	A fix for the active query
/question	Natural language response from the prompt
/help	Links to Copilot documentation

Another use case for Copilot in Warehouse is for code completion. You need to enable "Show Copilot completions" (*https://oreil.ly/K85j-*) in the Warehouse settings. After that, you can check the status at the bottom of the query editor, as displayed in Figure 13-19.

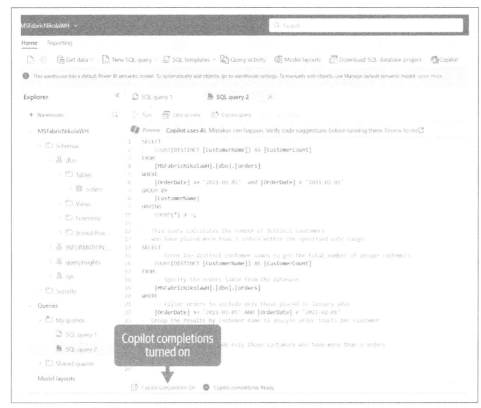

Figure 13-19. Checking whether the Copilot completion setting is turned on

Finally, Copilot quick actions is just a dressed-up implementation of the /explain and /fix commands that we mentioned in Table 13-1. Figure 13-20 shows how to access these actions in the query editor.

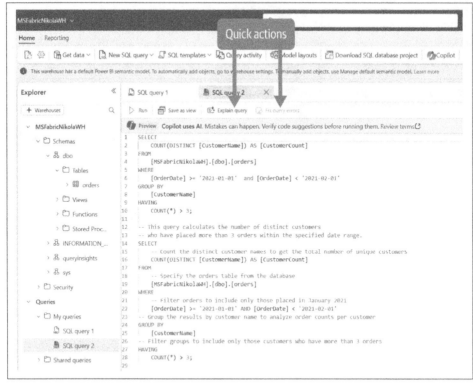

Figure 13-20. Quick actions to explain and/or fix a query

The "Fix query errors" option is disabled by default and becomes enabled only after a query run fails with errors.

Copilot for Power BI

We wouldn't be wrong if we said that Copilot for Power BI is the longest-standing of all Fabric Copilots. And, it's not a coincidence, taking into consideration the solid history of various built-in AI features in Power BI, such as the Q&A feature, Smart Narratives, Analyze feature, Key influencers visual, and many more.

Copilot for Power BI can be leveraged for multiple tasks, both in the Power BI service and Power BI Desktop. In the following sections, we'll examine some of the common scenarios for using Copilot for Power BI.

Prepare Semantic Model for Copilot

The universal truth when working with data is "garbage in, garbage out!" This means that if your data is of poor quality when you start building your analysis, you shouldn't expect that it will somehow be magically fixed and that your end users will get clean, high-quality output. Therefore, it is of paramount importance to invest time and effort in shaping the data before you start performing any analysis on it.

This is absolutely true in every scenario—including scenarios involving Copilot. You should be aware that Copilot is not a magician that can transform your "ugly duck" into "white swan" data.

Table 13-2 provides the list of considerations for various model objects that might have an impact on the results generated by Copilot.

Table 13-2. Semantic model considerations for Copilot

Object	Recommendation	Consideration	Example
Table	Define clear relationships	Ensure proper relationships are established, including relationship cardinality (1:1, 1:M, M:M)	The Sales table is connected to the Customer table on the CustomerKey column
Measure	Standardized calculation logic	Ensure standardized and clear calculation logic	The Total Sales measure is calculated as the sum of the SalesAmount column from the Sales table
Measure	Naming conventions	Ensure the measure name clearly reflects the calculation	Use "Average_Tax_Amount" instead of "AvgTaxAmt"
Fact table	Create a fact table in accordance with the Star schema design	Fact tables should contain measurable data in addition to dimension keys	Orders, Sales, Purchases
Dimension table	Create a dimension table in accordance with the star schema design	Dimension tables should contain descriptive attributes relevant to the object of interest	Customer, Product, Date
Hierarchy	Logical grouping of attributes used for drilling down into data	Ensure the hierarchy has a logical sequence	Calendar hierarchy that consists of Year, Quarter, Month, and Day
Column	Use clear names	Ensure column names are unambiguous and self-explanatory	Use Customer_Name instead of CustomerKey
Column	Use proper and consistent data types	Ensure correct and consistent data types across all tables in the model	Set numeric type for columns used in calculations

In addition, when using Copilot for writing DAX, you should provide clear descriptions of model objects (measures, tables, and columns) so that Copilot "knows" how do you want to handle a particular calculation.

Create Reports in the Power BI Service or Power BI Desktop

Let's create our first Power BI report with Copilot. As a prerequisite, we need a semantic model that will be used as a blueprint for the report. We've created a fairly simple semantic model in Direct Lake storage mode, which consists of four tables:

- FactSales
- DimCustomer
- DimProduct
- DimDate

If you're not sure what Direct Lake storage mode is and how it works behind the scenes, we encourage you to revisit Chapter 9, where we covered Direct Lake storage mode in detail. As you see in Figure 13-21, tables are connected with regular 1:M relationships.

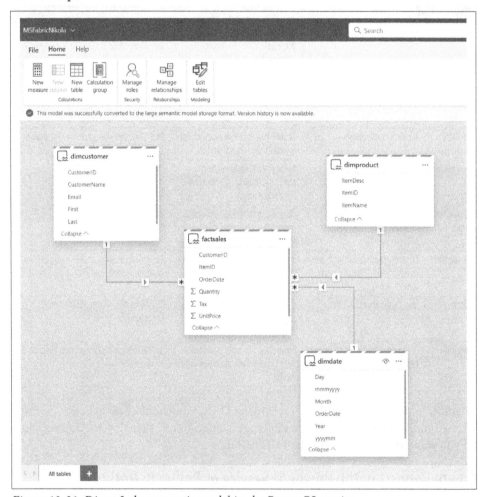

Figure 13-21. Direct Lake semantic model in the Power BI service

We've also created two DAX measures:

- `Total Quantity = SUM(FactSales[Quantity])`
- `Sales Amount = SUMX(FactSales,`
  `FactSales[Quantity] * FactSales[UnitPrice]`
  `)`

We will use this model for all our demos in this chapter. Once we choose the "Create report" option from the semantic model settings, our old buddy Copilot is ready to assist us. Similar to the experience you've seen in the previous sections with other Fabric Copilots, there is a list of predefined prompts in the Copilot chat window, as displayed in Figure 13-22.

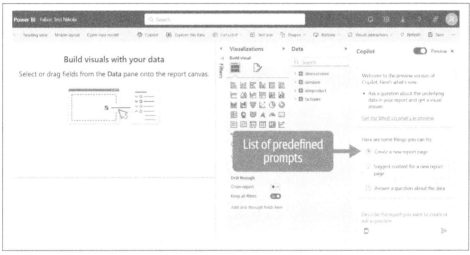

Figure 13-22. Copilot predefined prompts in the Power BI service

Let's give it a try and start with the top suggestion, "Create a new report page." After Copilot performs the model schema scanning, it provides a brief description of the suggested report pages, as you can see in Figure 13-23.

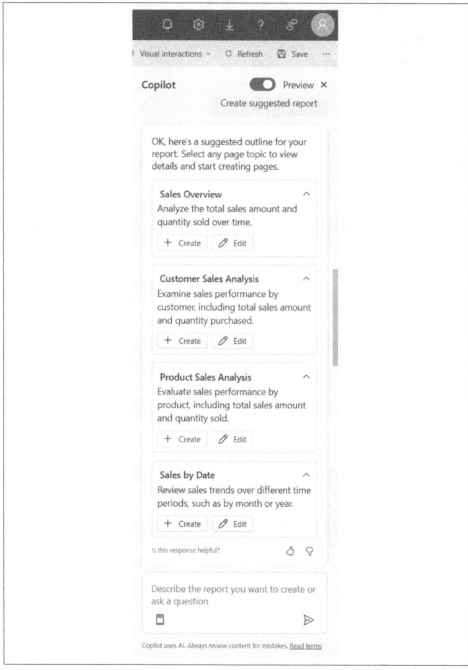

Figure 13-23. Copilot suggesting a report with four pages

We've then asked Copilot to create the suggested report. As you might have noticed in the previous figure, you can choose between the Create and Edit options. Choosing Create will trigger the report page creation, whereas Edit enables you to fine-tune the generated suggestion and customize it according to your needs. In this case, let's keep it simple and see what Copilot comes up with. Figure 13-24 shows the Copilot-generated report.

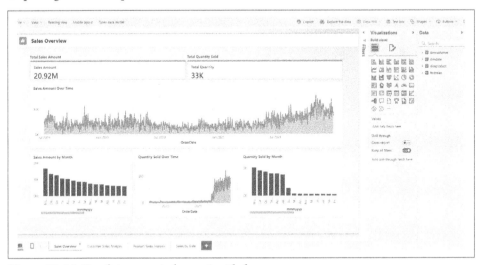

Figure 13-24. Copilot-generated report with four pages

Let's be honest—this looks promising! You can obviously complain about using color X instead of color Y, or choosing visual type A instead of visual type B. But we consider this an excellent starting point, one that you could build upon to make your report look even better.

The next thing we want from Copilot is to suggest the content for the new report page. If you recall, this is one of the predefined prompts. Once we trigger this prompt, Copilot provides four suggestions for additional report pages:

- Customer Demographics
- Sales Tax Analysis
- Product Description Insights
- Order Quantity Trends

We can proceed to create or edit any or all of these pages.

The process of creating a Copilot-generated report in Power BI Desktop is very similar. The key thing to keep in mind when designing reports in Power BI Desktop is that you need to provide a Copilot-compatible workspace, as shown in Figure 13-25.

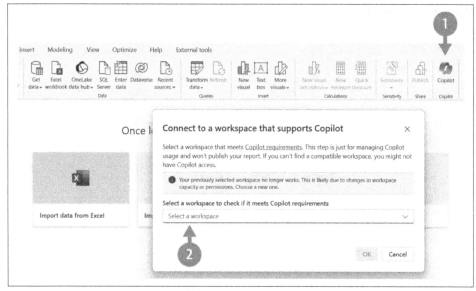

Figure 13-25. Creating a Copilot-generated report from Power BI Desktop

Please be aware that the workspace you select here doesn't necessarily need to be the workspace where the report will be published. It just needs to be a workspace with Copilot enabled.

Summarize Report Content in the Copilot Pane

Sometimes, users don't have permission to edit a Power BI report. However, even in these scenarios, Copilot can be of help by providing a summary of the report in the Copilot chat pane. Figure 13-26 displays Copilot's response to the prompt "Summarize visuals on this page."

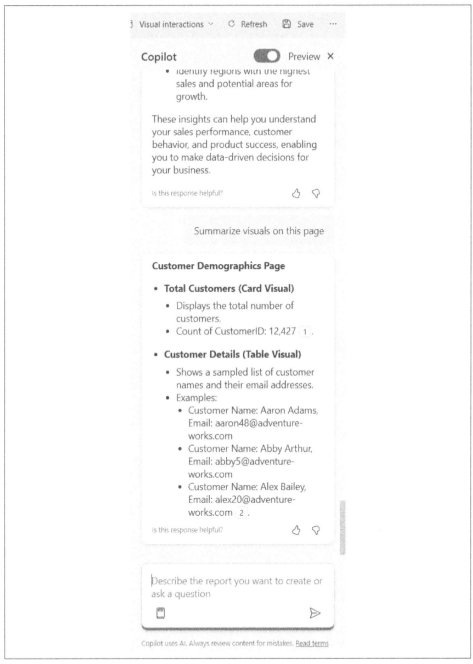

Figure 13-26. Copilot summarizing the report page content

Write DAX with Copilot

"DAX is simple, but not easy!" This sentence, shared by Alberto Ferrari (*https://oreil.ly/95dBe*) and coined by one of his learners, best describes the feelings of the majority of Power BI practitioners. While DAX is definitely not a primary topic of this book, it is without a doubt an integral part of Power BI and probably the most intimidating skill to acquire for many Power BI data analysts. Having a dedicated Copilot for DAX is like a dream come true to ease the burden of writing DAX code and flatten the DAX learning curve.

DAX Copilot is available within the dedicated DAX query view in Power BI Desktop, as shown in Figure 13-27.

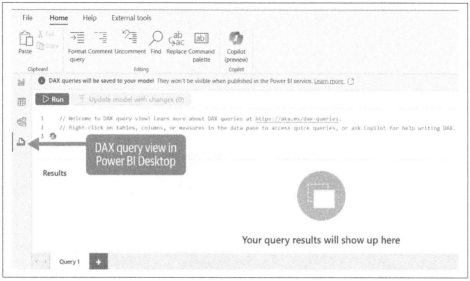

Figure 13-27. DAX query view in Power BI Desktop

We've connected to the semantic model we previously created and used in the previous sections. Once in a DAX query view, we've entered the following prompt in the dialog window: "Total Sales for each product." And, if you take a look at Figure 13-28, you'll notice that Copilot did a wonderful job, as the generated DAX query produced the expected results.

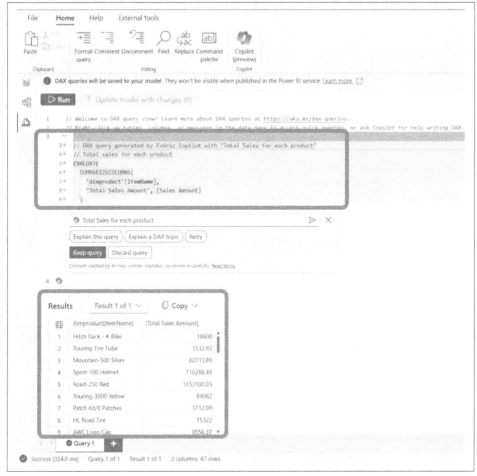

Figure 13-28. DAX query generated by Copilot and its results

Furthermore, we can ask Copilot to suggest measures for our report. Copilot rightly assumed that calculating the average value of the sales amount may be helpful for our end users, but it generated an invalid DAX statement. Since we don't have a sales amount column in the model, Copilot tried to apply the AVERAGE function to the Sales Amount measure, which is not allowed. The query returned the error shown in Figure 13-29.

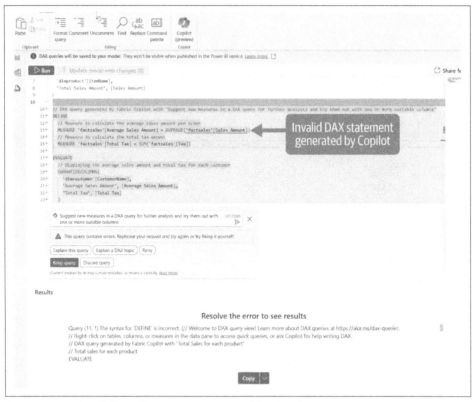

Figure 13-29. Invalid DAX statement generated by Copilot

Again, you shouldn't be too surprised with this behavior. We will emphasize that you should always take Copilot-generated results with a grain of salt, as these results might be incorrect or unexpected.

In addition to assisting with writing DAX code, Copilot may be used as a learning tool. Choosing the "Explain a DAX topic" button will trigger Copilot to provide a narrative summary of the functions used in the previously generated query, as shown in Figure 13-30.

Let's try to summarize our experience of using Copilot in Power BI so far. It's extremely powerful and versatile, covering a wide range of use cases and scenarios. As you saw, we've been able to quickly get up and running with creating multipage reports out of the blue, as well as level up our DAX coding skills. However, we want you to remember two key things about Copilot for Power BI:

- Just as with other Copilot- and AI-generated results, be careful to evaluate and double-check the outcome.

- Building and maintaining a proper semantic model is more relevant than ever in Copilot-based scenarios.

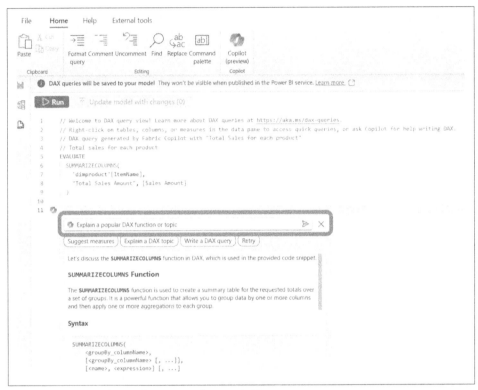

Figure 13-30. Copilot explaining a relevant DAX topic

Copilot for Real-Time Intelligence

With Copilot in the Real-Time Intelligence workload, your natural language queries can be easily translated into KQL language. If you are not sure what KQL is, we suggest you start by reading Chapter 8, where we examine numerous KQL examples.

Like its other Fabric "relatives," Copilot for Real-Time Intelligence enables you to transform conversational interactions into actionable outcomes. In real life, this means you can dynamically refine Copilot-generated queries by adjusting the prompt to provide additional context if needed. Not only that: let's say that the generated KQL query is correct, but you need to explore data in more detail. You can achieve that by asking follow-up questions, either by extending the scope of the original prompt or by adding filters. All of that on top of the previous conversation with Copilot.

Copilot for Real-Time Intelligence can be accessed from the KQL queryset item. If you are not sure what the KQL queryset is, we recommend you first navigate to Chapter 8, which covers all Real-Time Intelligence items, including the KQL queryset, in more depth.

Once we open the KQL queryset, the Copilot chat window can be expanded, as displayed in Figure 13-31.

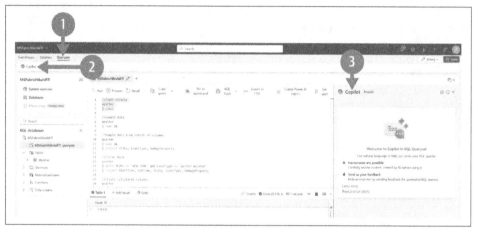

Figure 13-31. Copilot chat window in KQL queryset

1. Open the KQL queryset.

2. Launch Copilot.

3. Expand the Copilot window.

We'll be using the sample Weather dataset provided by Microsoft. Let's start simply by entering the following prompt: "How many storm events happened in 2007?" The generated output is a KQL code snippet, which we may directly insert into the query editor, as shown in Figure 13-32.

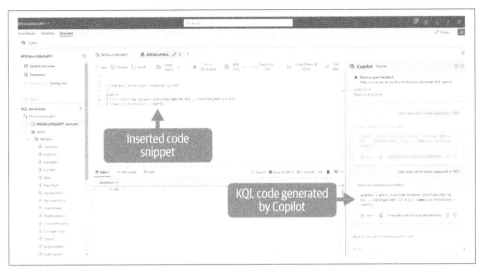

Figure 13-32. KQL code snippet as a response to a natural language question

As previously mentioned, we can ask follow-up questions. For example, let's say that we are interested only in storm events that happened in New York. We've asked Copilot: "How many of those were in New York?" where "those" refers to the result generated based on the previous question. Copilot didn't disappoint and provided the following KQL code snippet to include the additional filter on the State column:

```
// How many of those were in New York?
//
Weather
| where StartTime between (datetime(2007-01-01) .. datetime(2007-12-31))
| where State == "New York"
| summarize EventCount = count()
```

This can be further customized. Let's say that we want to see not only the summarized data but also a detailed overview that includes every single storm event in New York in 2007. We asked Copilot: "Can you list all of them?" Again, pay attention to how the question is phrased: we're not explicitly asking for "New York" and "2007" as filter criteria, but Copilot builds upon the previous conversation:

```
// Can you list all of them?
//
Weather
| where StartTime between (datetime(2007-01-01) .. datetime(2007-12-31))
| where State == "NEW YORK"
| project StartTime, EndTime, EpisodeId, EventId, State,
EventType, InjuriesDirect, InjuriesIndirect, DeathsDirect,
DeathsIndirect, DamageProperty, DamageCrops, Source,
BeginLocation, EndLocation, EventNarrative, StormSummary,
EpisodeNarrative, BeginLon, EndLon, BeginLat,
```

Copilot for SQL Database

Copilot for SQL database works the same way as Copilot for Data Warehouse. Therefore, all the features and use cases that we examined in the Copilot for Data Warehouse section are absolutely relevant in SQL database scenarios as well.

You can learn more about the SQL database in Fabric in Chapter 10.

AI Services in Microsoft Fabric

Azure AI services is the official successor to Azure Cognitive Services. The main goal of AI services is to enable developers and organizations to quickly build intelligent applications using customizable APIs and models.

Microsoft Fabric provides two options for using AI services:

Prebuilt AI models in Fabric
You can leverage numerous prebuilt AI models in Fabric to enrich the existing data. The following prebuilt AI models are currently available:

- Azure OpenAI Service includes widely adopted and used *GPT-35-turbo* and *GPT-4* family of models.

- Text Analytics includes language detection, sentiment analysis, key phrase extraction, personally identifiable information (PII) recognition, named entity recognition, and entity linking.

- Azure AI Translator enables text and document translation across more than 100 languages using a REST API.

Bring your own key (BYOK)
This option allows for provisioning AI services and bringing your own key to use them from Microsoft Fabric.

One of the key considerations when using AI services in Fabric is the consumption rate, which may vary significantly depending on the model you use. We suggest you first check the consumption rate (*https://oreil.ly/MaGGF*) to ease the potential burden on the Fabric capacity.

Data Agent in Microsoft Fabric

The Fabric data agent feature was introduced with the aim of providing even more power and flexibility in implementing generative AI workloads. In a nutshell, Fabric data agent enables creating your own conversational Q&A systems based on the structured data stored in OneLake.

The core idea behind the Fabric data agent item is to provide instructions and examples in advance, thus guiding AI to ensure that the correct answer will be provided to the end user. As with Copilots, Fabric data agent relies on LLMs. We'll explore key differences between Copilot and Fabric data agent in this section.

Figure 13-33 displays a typical workflow in Fabric data agent.

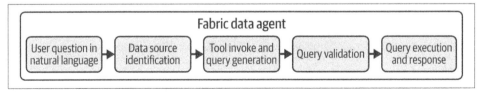

Figure 13-33. A common workflow for Fabric data agent

The process starts with the user asking a question in the Fabric data agent interface using natural language. The system takes this query and leverages the user's credentials to access the data source. It then evaluates the user's question against various data sources, such as lakehouses, warehouses, semantic models, and KQL databases. Then, the Fabric data agent invokes the appropriate tool and generates the query using the proper language: T-SQL for retrieving the data from the lakehouse or warehouse, DAX for querying Power BI semantic models, and KQL for getting the data from KQL databases. The generated query is validated, and finally, after the query is executed, results are displayed in a human-readable way, such as tables, summaries, or key insights.

Here are some examples of the common, real-life questions that you may ask Fabric data agent:

- How many active customers did we have on January 1, 2025?
- Which marketing campaign had the biggest impact?
- What product sells the most units?

From a conceptual point of view, you can think of a Fabric data agent as similar to a Power BI report. When working with Power BI, you first create a report, and then you can share the report with other colleagues in the organization who can generate their own insights based on the original report. It is similar to the Fabric data agent item, which first needs to be created and configured, and then can be shared with others.

Please bear in mind that the Fabric data agent requires some fine-tuning to be able to provide meaningful answers to specific questions. While you may expect the Fabric data agent to provide out-of-the-box responses to reasonable questions, in some specific use cases, it may come up with incorrect answers. This is due to its lack of context about your organization and key data definitions. To overcome this issue and guide the Fabric data agent in the right direction, you should provide the Fabric data agent with specific instructions and examples.

Fabric Data Agent Versus Copilot

With Fabric data agent and Copilot providing a very similar set of functionalities, and both being based on the same technology (generative AI and LLMs), a fair question would be, Which generative AI feature should I use in Microsoft Fabric?

There are two main considerations that might affect your decision:

Flexibility
> Fabric data agent provides much more flexibility with configuration. You can provide it with instructions and examples, so it is fine-tuned to handle your specific use case. On the flip side, Copilot can't be configured to handle particular, organization-specific scenarios.

Scope
> Copilot is bound to Fabric workloads. It can assist you in generating the code for notebooks, writing DAX queries, or analyzing the content of a pipeline. On the other hand, a Fabric data agent works independently; for example, you can connect it to Microsoft Teams and other non-Fabric workloads.

Working with the Fabric Data Agent

Let's see the Fabric data agent item in action. Once we create a new Fabric data agent item, the first step is to ensure that the data source is defined, as shown in Figure 13-34.

The data source can be defined on the individual table level. In this example, we've added four tables from the lakehouse. We're now ready to start asking our questions. Let's start with a simple one: "What is the most expensive product we are selling?" Let us briefly stop here and explain the result you may observe in Figure 13-35:

1. The natural language response generated by the Fabric data agent
2. Explanation of all the steps taken to obtain the result
3. The tabular response generated by the Fabric data agent
4. SQL query generated to obtain the result

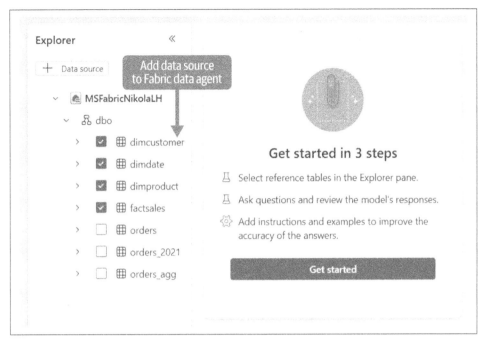

Figure 13-34. Adding a data source to Fabric data agent

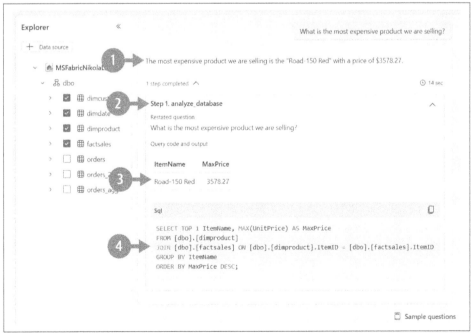

Figure 13-35. Fabric data agent response to a natural language question

Observe that the Fabric data agent cleverly interpreted the word "product" correctly and used into the item column from our dimproduct table, as we don't have a "product" column in the model. We can also expect answers to questions such as:

- Which customer placed the most orders?
- What product was sold more than three times on January 1, 2025?

However, if you try to search for some more sophisticated answers, by asking questions like these:

- Why is our productivity lower in Q3 2025 than in Q3 2024?
- What is the root cause of the orders spike in early 2025?

… it is not going to work. Please bear in mind that the final outcome of the Fabric data agent item is the query—SQL, DAX, or KQL. There is no SQL/DAX/KQL code with brain-like reasoning to *explain* something.

A Fabric data agent item can be configured to enhance the accuracy of the generated response by providing example queries. This is a well-known approach in generative AI, called *few-shot learning*, which enables guiding the Fabric data agent to generate the responses that match, or almost match, your expectations. The steps for providing example SQL queries are depicted in Figure 13-36.

Figure 13-36. Enhancing Fabric data agent with example SQL queries

You should first select the "Example queries" option (1) and then, in the Example queries window (2) choose to edit Example queries. Finally, in the dialog window (3), enter the example question and provide the SQL query that answers that question.

Another way to help the Fabric data agent generate the expected result is to use the "Data agent instructions" feature. The main goal of "Data agent instructions" is to provide definitions in plain English. Figure 13-37 displays the Data agent instructions workflow.

Figure 13-37. Helping Fabric data agent by providing instructions

Here are a few examples of Data agent instructions that you can use to fine-tune Fabric data agent–generated responses:

- Whenever we ask for "the most sold" products, the metric of interest is Sales Amount and not Order Quantity.

- The primary table to use is Fact Online Sales. Only use table Fact Reseller Sales when explicitly asked about resales.

- When asked about the marketing campaign impact, check the Sales Amount and not the number of units sold.

- Use the DimDate table and its attributes, such as Year, Month, or Day, to perform time-based analysis.

- When asked about customer demographics, join the `DimCustomer` table to relevant fact tables.

- `ListPrice` in the `DimProduct` table is the suggested selling price, while `UnitPrice` in the Fact Online Sales is the actual price at which the product was sold.

Once you are happy with the Fabric data agent item configuration, you can publish it to the workspace. Since it's a regular Fabric item, the Fabric data agent can also be shared with other users or group of users, as shown in Figure 13-38.

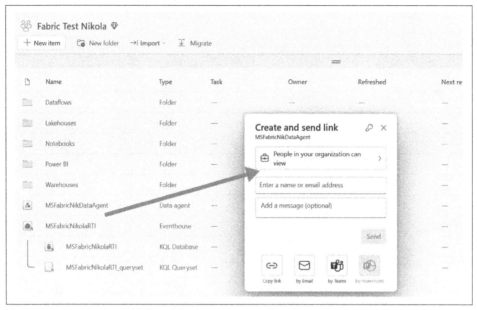

Figure 13-38. Sharing a Fabric data agent item with other users

Summary

If you made it to the end of this chapter without asking Copilot to summarize it, we salute you! By no means do we want to diminish the importance of AI and LLMs in today's world. On the contrary, we firmly believe that if we delegate more tasks and operations to AI, especially manual and repetitive tasks, we will not only become more efficient but have more time to spend on creative and strategic work.

A key takeaway from this chapter is this: generative AI models are only as accurate as the data they are fed, and it is always recommended that you check the output validity. Don't forget, this is just a Copilot, and you should still be the *pilot*.

Since Copilot and other AI features come with a cost, we are sure you'll enjoy reading the next chapter, where we cover the Microsoft Fabric pricing model in depth.

## PART III

Putting Fabric into Production

This section fills in the remaining gaps by addressing important topics that go beyond just understanding individual features. While knowing how each experience in Fabric works is essential, bringing everything together for a real-world production deployment requires a broader view.

We will cover key considerations such as pricing and security, ensuring you have the necessary information to plan and optimize your Fabric implementation effectively. Understanding cost implications will help you make informed decisions about resource allocation, while security best practices will provide the confidence needed to handle data responsibly.

Another crucial aspect we will tackle is choosing the right experience for the right use case. Fabric offers multiple ways to solve many data challenges, and it's not always immediately clear which approach is best. By clarifying when to use different components, we aim to remove uncertainty and provide guidance on how to design efficient, scalable, and maintainable solutions.

With these final pieces in place, you will have a complete picture of what it takes to move from learning Fabric's features to successfully applying them in production.

## CHAPTER 14

The Fabric Pricing Model

Now that we've explored all the features and experiences Fabric provides in Part II, let's kick off the final section of this book by taking a look at another interesting aspect of Fabric: licensing, or rather, pricing. Rather than sizing, deploying, and paying for a variety of individual services and offerings, with Fabric you are basically paying for a single product.

Fabric pricing consists of three components—compute, storage, and user licenses—as you see in Figure 14-1 (the same figure is in Chapter 1).

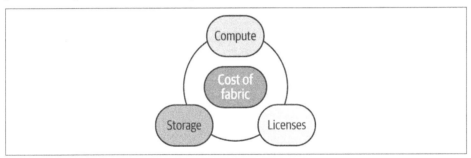

Figure 14-1. The three components of Fabric pricing

Compute and Capacities

When we talk about compute in Fabric, we talk about something called *capacities*. Capacities form the compute power of your entire Fabric deployment, no matter which specific offerings you're using, so the words *compute* and *capacity* are synonymous in the context of Fabric. Figure 14-2, for example, shows two capacities using different sizes in different regions.

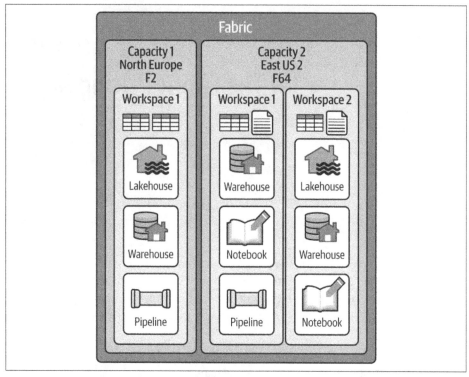

Figure 14-2. Capacity sizes and settings

Your entire Fabric environment can be based on a single capacity, or you can run multiple capacities that have different names, may sit in different regions, and may be different sizes. Depending on their sizes, they will have the ability to host a certain number of workloads at a time.

Capacity Types

There are three kinds of fabric capacities: Fabric, Fabric Reserved, and Fabric Trial (see Figure 14-3).

A regular Fabric capacity will be billed on a pay-as-you-go basis, so you only pay for the compute time your capacities are running, whereas with a reserved capacity, you make a commitment to pay for a certain amount of time in exchange for a discount.

Both Fabric and Fabric Reserved capacities use Azure billing. From a technical perspective, they are the same thing, so the differentiation is solely for billing purposes.

Trials give you access to almost the full feature set of Fabric at no cost for 60 days with the equivalent of an F64 capacity (more on that in the next section). The most important feature currently missing from trials is Copilots.

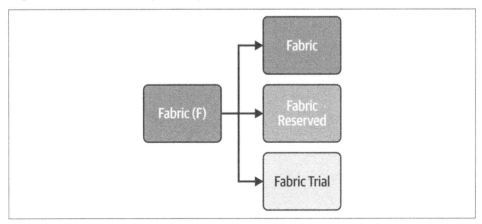

Figure 14-3. Fabric capacity types

While any capacity can be paused, this usually only makes sense for pay-as-you-go workloads because with a paused capacity, you will pay for it only while it is running; a reserved capacity will be billed 24/7 anyway. The process of pausing is for the capacity, not the workload. Therefore, unless you pause your capacity, you will still be billed even if there is no workload happening; in other words, you are billed for capacity uptime.

Capacity Sizes

Fabric capacities come in different sizes. As you may have come across in other cloud offerings, size determines the number of *capacity units* (CUs)—an equally abstract metric—and therefore the performance and size of workloads this capacity can provide.

The smallest size is an F2, which has two capacity units, followed by an F4 up to F2048, the largest size currently available, which has 2,048 capacity units.

To make this a bit more transparent: A day has 86,400 seconds. An F2 capacity has 2 capacity units so 2*86,400 seconds = 172,800 compute seconds available to you, while an F8 capacity has 8*86,400 resulting in 691,200 compute seconds available to you in a day (assuming you are running your capacity 24 hours a day). See Figure 14-4.

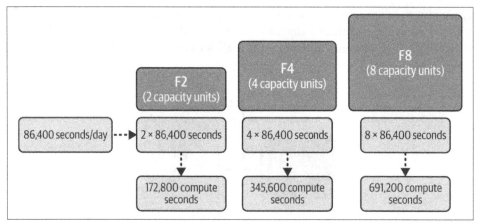

Figure 14-4. Meaning of capacity sizes

Unfortunately, there is no great guidance or general rule on how much can be achieved within a compute second because that is very workload (and offering) specific, so the best practice when it comes to sizing your environment is still to start with an educated guess and then work your way up or down from there.

What Exactly Is a Capacity Unit (CU)?

A CU is basically a made-up unit by Microsoft. It does not easily convert into memory, CPUs, or anything similar. Every offering in Fabric has its own translation of how it uses CUs or how they map into something more relatable. Those mappings are, however, not public for every offering and are also subject to change. At the time of writing, for example, 2 CUs would translate to one vCore for Spark or 0.25 vCores for Power BI. This means, when running an F2 capacity, without bursting (which we'll discuss in the next section), you could use one Spark vCore, but that would use your entire capacity. Especially with mixed workloads (lakehouse, warehouse, Power BI, etc.), you could easily end up in a situation with a very hard to predict requirement of CUs to support those workloads.

To better understand the consumption of your CUs, Microsoft has provided the Metrics app (*https://oreil.ly/hKT9G*), which we will discuss in more detail in Chapter 15.

 One important thing to note: in general, a higher number of CUs will not give you more compute power, only more compute time. So increasing the number of CUs will give you more concurrent compute resources but will not necessarily improve the performance of a single workload.

Capacity Bursting (and Smoothing)

Even the smallest capacities allow you to make use of a feature called *bursting*. Cool. What does that mean?

Let's assume you run an F8 capacity and you keep it running 24/7. Let's now make another assumption: you run a workload that would usually take 10 minutes to complete using your F8 capacity. Now, through bursting, Fabric *may* grant you additional compute power—more than you pay for—so this workload completes in 5 minutes, as if you had bought an F16 capacity (see Figure 14-5).

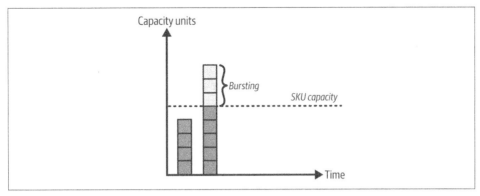

Figure 14-5. Bursting

So, is Microsoft gifting you free compute? Well, no. Think of it more as a credit line. Any extra compute that you consume through bursting will need to be recovered through its counterpart, *smoothing*, within 24 hours. In addition, bursting is not guaranteed, so if you are running in a region that is at capacity, there may simply not be any additional resources available to you, which will mean no bursting for your capacity.

How does that impact you? If you don't use the full compute units all the time, the smoothing will simply be recovered through the spare capacity you're not using, as shown in Figure 14-6.

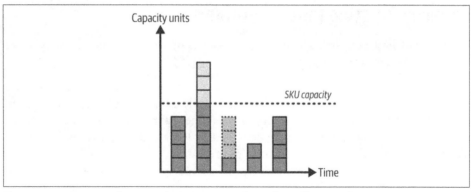

Figure 14-6. Previous bursting being recovered in a less idle period

If you consistently use all the compute units available to you, at some point, as illustrated in Figure 14-7, your capacity will be *throttled*. This means that, for example, while you're still paying for your F8 capacity, you may only get to use 4 CUs for a period of time.

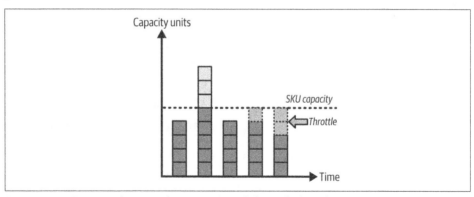

Figure 14-7. Previous bursting being recovered through throttling

And if you simply pause your capacity right after bursting? Then you'll continue to be billed until you've paid your dues, that is, until all the extra compute units used by bursting have been recovered. See Figure 14-8.

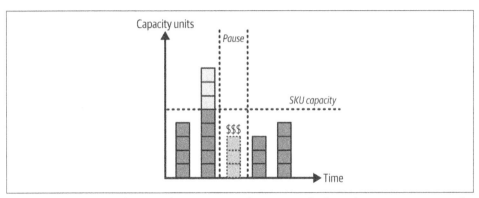

Figure 14-8. Previous bursting being recovered in a period where the capacity is paused

To help manage your CU consumption, you can also make use of a feature called *surge protection*. Surge protection helps manage compute consumption by limiting background job usage in a capacity. It is configured at the capacity level and serves to reduce throttling and rejections, though it does not replace scaling or optimization strategies. When enabled, two thresholds control its activation and deactivation. The *background rejection threshold* determines when surge protection becomes active by rejecting new background jobs once the 24-hour background percentage exceeds the set limit. Conversely, the *background recovery threshold* dictates when surge protection stops being active, allowing background jobs to resume once usage drops below the specified limit.

To enable surge protection, an admin role on the capacity is required. Go to the Fabric Admin portal, navigate to "Capacity settings," select a capacity, expand Surge Protection, enable it, set the Background Rejection and Background Recovery thresholds, and select Apply, as shown in Figure 14-9.

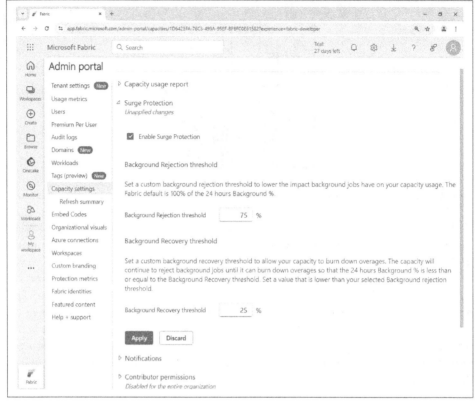

Figure 14-9. Enabling surge protection for a capacity

Capacity Limitations

Some features require a certain minimum SKU. Similar restrictions apply to other features. You can find an overview of current limitations at on the Microsoft website (*https://oreil.ly/fsUT-*). Unfortunately, that overview isn't always complete. so if you are relying on a specific feature, make sure to double-check its prerequisites in the documentation.

Storage

Storage pricing is straightforward. You simply pay per gigabyte for the storage you are using in OneLake. Storage will always be billed independently of compute, so even when you pause your capacity, you will pay for the storage used. You cannot pause your storage.

If you are making use of mirroring, which we elaborated on in Chapter 11, you can take advantage of free storage for your mirrored data. With mirroring, you receive free storage for replicas up to a certain limit based on the purchased compute capacity SKU you provision (1 TB per capacity unit). For example, if you purchase an F8 capacity, you will get 8 free terabytes worth of storage. OneLake storage is billed only when the free mirroring storage limit is exceeded, or the provisioned compute capacity is paused.

User Licenses

User licenses do not play a significant role within Fabric with one exception: Power BI. If you're not using Power BI within Fabric, or your capacity has a size of F64 or above, only report creators will need a Pro license. If you are using Power BI on a capacity that is smaller than F64, you will require a Power BI Pro license for every user that is using Power BI in workspaces within that capacity.

Otherwise, no paid user licenses are required (as long as you are strictly using Fabric capacities; there are other scenarios in the Power BI world that we don't get into in this book), and your workloads are being charged through the cost of capacities and storage alone. Every user accessing a workspace without a Power BI license will need a Free Fabric license though.

Networking

Charges for networking have been announced in the pricing calculator (*https://oreil.ly/5qcvH*) but are not implemented at the time of writing.

Regional Differences

As with all cloud services, keep in mind that prices vary by region and sometimes the differences are surprisingly big. Make sure to take a look at the Microsoft pricing page (*https://oreil.ly/AHZcz*) to get a full overview of Microsoft Fabric pricing applicable to you. Your choice of a region should, of course, also take latency as well as potential data residency restrictions into account.

Additional Pricing

In addition to the concepts described above, Microsoft has started to introduce alternative pricing options to the universal capacity model. Those include providing dedicated capacities for specific workloads (like a dedicated AI capacity) as well as, for example, a pay-per-use model for Spark (Autoscale Billing for Spark in Microsoft Fabric).

It is important to note that such options do not replace the capacity model but rather complement it to provide organizations with additional flexibility.

Summary

Microsoft Fabric follows a simplified pricing model with three main components: compute (capacities), storage, and user licenses. Compute power is measured in capacities, which dictate available resources for workloads. There are three types: Fabric (pay-as-you-go), Fabric Reserved (discounted commitment), and Fabric Trial (free for 60 days). Capacities range from F2 to F2048, with each size offering a specific number of CUs—an abstract metric determining available compute time rather than raw performance. Capacity bursting temporarily provides additional compute power but must be balanced within 24 hours through smoothing, potentially leading to throttling if resources are overused.

Storage in OneLake is billed separately per gigabyte, with mirroring providing free storage up to a certain limit based on compute capacity. Power BI users require Pro licenses for capacities smaller than F64, while other Fabric workloads are charged via compute and storage costs. Networking charges are expected but not yet implemented, and regional pricing differences exist, affecting cost, latency, and feature availability (e.g., Copilots in OpenAI-based services).

In our next chapter, we will talk about administration, governance, and monitoring in Fabric.

## CHAPTER 15

Administering and Monitoring Microsoft Fabric

Microsoft Fabric is a vast and complex platform. Regardless of marketing phrases about the "ease of use," "seamless integration," or "AI-powered experience," there are numerous challenges with maintaining this complex platform and ensuring that it aligns with your company's business goals, while at the same time adhering to organizational policies.

In this chapter, we'll examine why administering and monitoring Microsoft Fabric is essential for ensuring the reliability and performance of data workloads within the organization. As a unified data platform, Microsoft Fabric integrates multiple services and components discussed in the previous chapters. This multitude of services may sometimes represent a significant challenge to prevent unauthorized access, data breaches, and performance bottlenecks.

Effective Fabric administration ensures smooth workloads, while continuous monitoring through audit logs and performance analytics helps the organization to proactively identify and resolve issues, ensuring data integrity, optimal performance, and regulatory compliance. We'll also introduce various approaches for implementing effective monitoring in Microsoft Fabric, with the ultimate goal of maximizing the business potential and minimizing operational risk.

Data Governance with Microsoft Fabric

Before we introduce the key pillars of data governance in Microsoft Fabric, let's take a step back and explain what data governance represents. In a nutshell, data governance is a collection of policies, processes, features, and standards to ensure that data is secure, accurate, reliable, and available.

When we talk specifically about data governance in Microsoft Fabric, you can think of the set of capabilities and features to manage, protect, and monitor data to meet data governance and compliance requirements, as well as enhance the discoverability of sensitive organizational information. The majority of these capabilities and features are built-in, and you get them out of the box when you purchase a Fabric license, whereas some may require an additional service called Microsoft Purview.

Let's start with a high-level overview of the various data governance topics we are going to cover in this chapter:

Administering Microsoft Fabric
> You'll learn how to leverage the Admin portal to configure and manage your data estate.

Monitoring Microsoft Fabric
> You'll understand features for monitoring Fabric workloads and data estate.

Administering Microsoft Fabric

Let's kick it off by determining *who* in the organization can be a Microsoft Fabric admin. The Microsoft 365 user admin is the *capo di tutti cappi*[1]—they assign users to either the Fabric administrator or Power Platform administrator roles. Users in these two roles then have full control over the organizational Microsoft Fabric settings, except for licensing. After a user is assigned to the Fabric administrator or Power Platform administrator role, they can control and configure all the settings from the Admin portal.

Hierarchical Structure of Microsoft Fabric

Before we dive into individual settings in the Admin portal, let's first introduce a high-level infrastructure of Microsoft Fabric. As you can see in Figure 15-1, Fabric is structured as a hierarchy, starting from the tenant at the highest level, all the way to the individual items at the lowest level, such as notebooks, semantic models, lakehouses, and so on.

---

[1] *Capo di tutti cappi* (Italian) means "boss of all bosses." It's often used by law enforcement, the media, and the public in general to describe a Mafia boss who exerts significant influence on how the Mafia should be run.

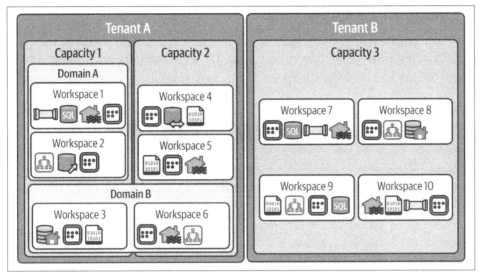

Figure 15-1. Hierarchical structure of Microsoft Fabric

Tenant

A tenant is a dedicated space for organizations to create, store, and manage Fabric items. Usually, there is a single Fabric tenant per organization, but there can be multiple tenants per organization. Each tenant consists of one or more capacities.

Capacity

Capacity represents a dedicated set of resources that is available at a given time to be used. Capacity determines the ability of a resource to perform an activity or produce an output. Different operations and items may consume capacity units at a given time.

Domain and workspace

A domain is a logical grouping of workspaces, whereas the workspace represents a collection of individual Fabric items that bring together various functionalities. We covered domains and workspaces in more depth in Chapter 3.

Please bear in mind that the domain can span multiple capacities. In Figure 15-1, domain B spans both capacities in Tenant A. Finally, Fabric items *are* the building blocks of the entire Fabric platform. These are the objects you create and manage in Microsoft Fabric. There are numerous item types, such as lakehouse, warehouse, KQL database, Dataflow Gen2, notebook, semantic model, and many more.

Working with the Admin Portal

Now that you are familiar with Microsoft Fabric core structure, let's explore the main tool for administering and governing Fabric. Table 15-1 summarizes various Admin portal settings and their descriptions.

Table 15-1. Settings in the Admin portal

Setting	Description
Tenant settings	Enable, disable, and configure Microsoft Fabric
Usage metrics	Explore the usage of Fabric workloads
Users	Manage users in the Microsoft 365 Admin portal
Premium Per User	Configure auto refresh and semantic model workload settings
Audit logs	Audit Fabric activities in the Microsoft Purview compliance portal
Domains	Create and manage domains
Tags	Create and manage tags to enhance data categorization and discoverability
Capacity settings	Manage Fabric (F) and Power BI Premium (P) capacities
Refresh summary	Schedule refresh on a capacity and view past refresh details
Embed codes	Manage embed codes for report sharing
Organizational visuals	Manage Power BI visual types accessible within the organization
Azure connections	Configure and manage connections to Azure resources
Workspaces	Manage workspaces
Custom branding	Adjust the look of Microsoft Fabric to match the organization's branding
Protection metrics	Monitor sensitivity label usage
Featured content	Manage promoted Power BI content (reports, dashboards, apps)

Let's now explore the Admin portal. Once you log in to Fabric using your admin account credentials, the portal can be accessed from the Settings icon in the top ribbon, as displayed in Figure 15-2.

Once in the Admin portal, you can navigate between the various settings specified in Table 15-1 by choosing the setting from the menu on the left-hand side. Figure 15-3 illustrates the Tenant settings user interface, with Microsoft Fabric–related settings on the top.

Each setting in the Admin portal can be configured in the following ways:

- Enabled, where you may choose between two options:
  - The entire organization
  - Specific security groups
- Disabled

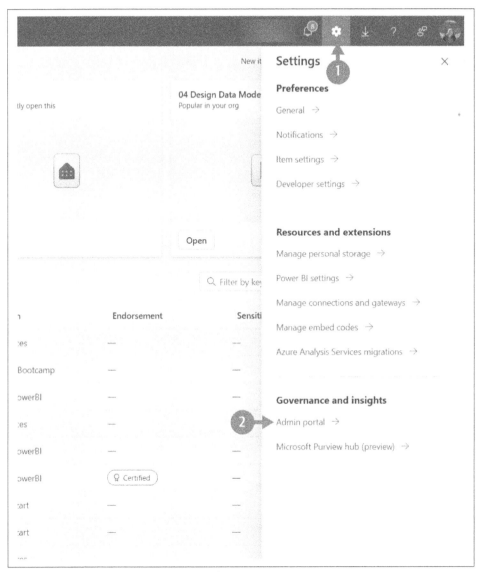

Figure 15-2. Accessing the Admin portal

There is also a checkbox "Except specific security groups," which is the opposite of "Specific security groups." When you check this option, the specified security groups *will not* be able to use a particular feature.

Figure 15-3. Tenant settings in the Admin portal

Probably the most important setting is the "Users can create Fabric items," and we'll soon come to explain why. A lot of organizations have been using Microsoft Power BI for years, long before Fabric was even an idea in someone's head at Microsoft. So, the fair question would be, What if I want only Power BI? There will inevitably be organizations that simply want to continue using their favorite BI tool, without expanding their workloads to Microsoft Fabric. For this scenario, Fabric can be disabled, either on the tenant or capacity level.

On the flip side, you may also enable Fabric workloads on either the tenant or capacity level. Please keep in mind that when Fabric is enabled on a tenant level, capacity admins can override this setting depending on the business needs and decide to disable Fabric workloads for a particular capacity.

The full list of the Tenant settings and their detailed description can be found on the official Microsoft Learn page (*https://oreil.ly/f6yhG*).

Under "Capacity settings," you can manage all the capacities in the tenant. Once you open a particular capacity, there are additional settings that can be configured, as shown in Figure 15-4.

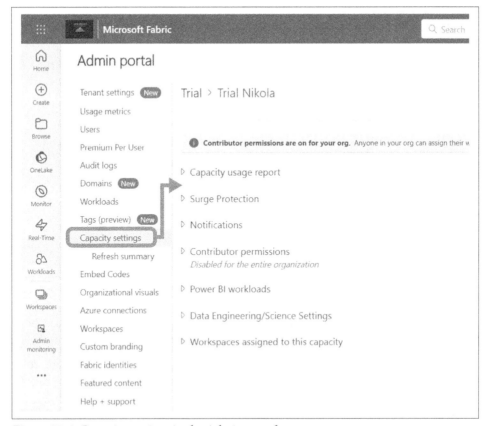

Figure 15-4. Capacity settings in the Admin portal

From this page, you can also create a new capacity, change the capacity name, add and remove capacity admins, resize the capacity, and so on.

On the Workspaces page, you'll find personal and group workspaces that exist in your organization. Here, you can configure numerous workspace properties, such as access or capacity, as well as obtain information about specific workspaces, as shown in Figure 15-5.

These are just some of the most important pages in the Admin portal. Microsoft Fabric administration is an extremely broad topic that goes way beyond the scope of this book. Therefore, please don't consider this section a definitive guide to administering Microsoft Fabric but just a quick guide to the core administrative tasks. If your day-to-day job requires performing administrative tasks in Fabric, we strongly encourage you to explore additional resources that provide a deeper level of understanding of each and every component in the Admin portal.

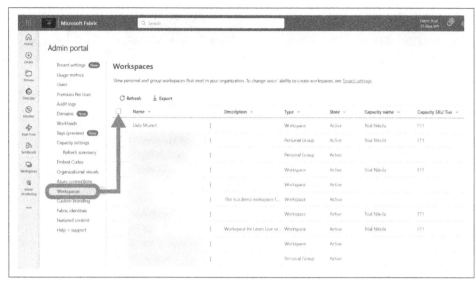

Figure 15-5. Managing workspaces from the Admin portal

A good starting point would be reading the official Microsoft documentation about the Admin portal (*https://oreil.ly/i6EIn*) and all the available options in the portal.

To wrap up this section, we'll provide you with an overview of the admin roles related to Microsoft Fabric. Figure 15-6 displays several roles that work together to administer Microsoft Fabric within the organization.

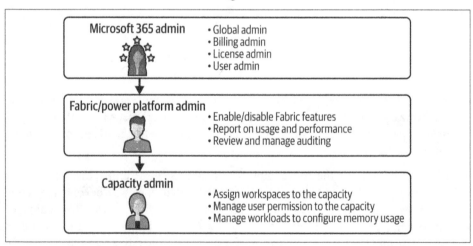

Figure 15-6. Admin roles related to Microsoft Fabric

Monitoring Microsoft Fabric

Setting the stage for proper data usage in Microsoft Fabric is, obviously, of paramount importance. Securing the data is one of the key aspects as well. Having the ability to classify and catalog data brings the entire experience to a whole new level. But we would not exaggerate if we said that monitoring Fabric is *icing on the cake*.

This is the part where all the pieces come together and the part that enables you to understand how your Fabric tenant *really* works. Microsoft Fabric offers several built-in capabilities to monitor, get insights, and act based on events in the tenant. Table 15-2 provides a high-level overview of the monitoring features and their intended use cases and the target audience.

Table 15-2. Monitoring features overview

Feature	Use case	Target audience
Monitor hub	Monitor Fabric activities from a central location	Developers and team members for monitoring scheduled workloads
Capacity metrics app	Monitor usage and consumption	Fabric administrators, capacity administrators, developers performing workload optimization
Microsoft Purview hub	Manage and govern data estate, particularly with respect to endorsement and sensitivity labels	Fabric administrators, data owners
Admin monitoring	A dedicated workspace for security and governance tasks, such as audits and usage checks	Fabric administrators

Monitor Hub

If you are searching for a central location to monitor various Fabric activities, look no further—the Monitor hub *is* the place to go. Any Fabric user can access the Monitor hub, although they will be able to see activities only for Fabric items they have permission to view. Figure 15-7 displays the Monitor hub main page.

The Monitor hub displays activities for the following Fabric items: pipelines, dataflows, data marts, lakehouses, notebooks, semantic models, and Spark job definitions. There are numerous options to rearrange the way the data is displayed; for example, you can filter the data based on different criteria, add or remove particular columns, or sort the data in a different order.

Figure 15-7. Monitor hub in Microsoft Fabric

Additionally, if you have proper permissions, you might be able to perform specific actions, as shown in Figure 15-8, where the user may access additional details or check historical runs of the selected item.

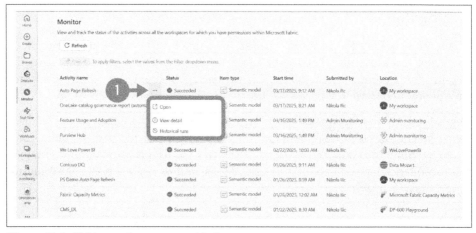

Figure 15-8. Taking action on a specific item

Capacity Metrics App

Microsoft Fabric Capacity Metrics app is a built-in application that enables monitoring of the Fabric capacity. To start using the Capacity Metrics app, you have to be a capacity administrator. The first step is to install the app from AppSource, which you can access from the AppSource web page (*https://oreil.ly/dM1dO*) or from the Power BI service by selecting Apps > Get apps > Microsoft Fabric Capacity Metrics app, as shown in Figure 15-9.

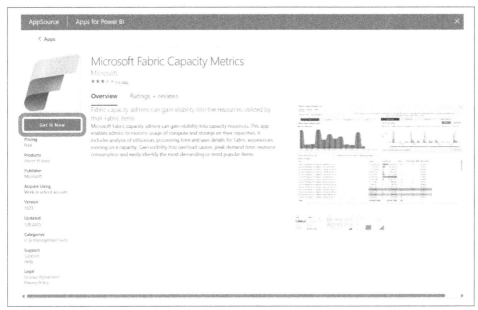

Figure 15-9. Installing the Capacity Metrics app from the AppSource

Once you install the app, you'll get access to an abundance of information. Let's try to break down the core metrics of the app. We'll start by exploring the Compute page of the generated Power BI report, which is shown in Figure 15-10.

Figure 15-10. Compute page of the Capacity metrics app

The multi-metric ribbon chart on the top left provides an hourly view of capacity usage. You can switch between the following metrics in the visual:

CU
> Capacity units processing time in seconds

Duration
> Processing time in seconds

Operations
> Total number of operations in the capacity

Users
> Number of unique users (including Service principals) who performed operations

The visual in the top right provides four information types:

Utilization
> This shows capacity units usage over time. It offers various metrics, including Background %, Interactive %, Background non-billable %, Interactive non-billable %, Autoscale CU % Limit, and CU % Limit. You can find more details about each of these metrics in the Microsoft Learn documentation (*https://oreil.ly/FUKy0*).

Throttling
> This shows delay and rejection over time. Throttling is based on the amount of future capacity consumption as a result of multiple smoothing policies. If you are not sure what smoothing is, we have you covered in Chapter 14.

Overages
> This shows the add, burndown, and cumulative carryforward percentages over time. It takes into account only billable operations.

System events
> This shows capacity events, such as the state of the capacity (Active, Deleted, Overloaded, Suspended), state change reason (e.g., Created, ManuallyResumed, AllRejected), and the time the capacity was paused or resumed. You can find more details about system events on the Microsoft Learn official page (*https://oreil.ly/qoCGv*).

Finally, the matrix visual at the bottom provides a tabular overview of various metrics for each item in the capacity. You can use slicers to narrow down the displayed data to a specific Fabric item (or multiple items), as well as customize the columns included in the matrix.

Let's now examine the Storage page of the Capacity Metrics app. The default view is shown in Figure 15-11.

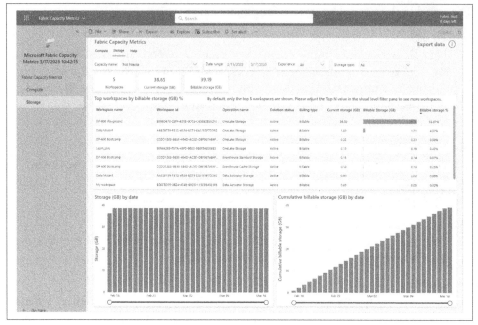

Figure 15-11. Storage page of the Capacity Metrics app

Card visuals on the top provide information about the number of workspaces, current storage in GB, and the billable storage in GB. The table visual in the middle shows storage information for the selected top *n* workspaces in the capacity. The two column charts at the bottom display the storage trend for the previous 30 days. If necessary, you can drill down into a particular day and see the data on an hourly level.

Microsoft Purview Hub

Microsoft Purview hub represents a centralized location in Fabric where Fabric administrators can manage and govern their organizational data estate. Microsoft Purview hub provides a set of built-in reports, providing insights about sensitive data, item endorsement, and domains. It's also a gateway to more advanced features of Microsoft Purview, such as Data Catalog, Information Protection, Data Loss Prevention, and Audit.

To access Microsoft Purview hub, you need to have a Fabric administrator role. Microsoft Purview hub can be accessed from the Settings option in the top ribbon, as shown in Figure 15-12.

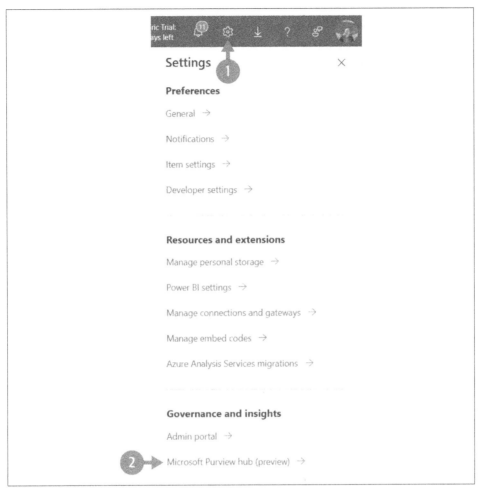

Figure 15-12. Accessing Microsoft Purview hub

Once you find yourself in the hub, you'll discover various built-in visualizations to help you understand the current data estate. The report provides numerous insights into sensitivity labels, endorsements, domains, and items explorer, as shown in Figure 15-13.

Figure 15-13. Built-in Power BI report in Microsoft Purview hub

In addition, you can access various Microsoft Purview capabilities, like Data Catalog, Information protection, and many more, directly from the hub.

Admin Monitoring Workspace

When you work as a Fabric administrator, wouldn't it be great if you had your own dedicated environment to monitor and manage Fabric workloads and usage? That's exactly what the Admin monitoring workspace enables you to accomplish.

The Admin monitoring workspace is automatically installed the first time an admin logs into Fabric and selects "Admin monitoring" from the workspaces. Since this is a workspace, the content can be shared with other users in the organization when needed.

Inside the Admin monitoring workspace, you'll find the built-in Power BI semantic model and a report called Feature Usage and Adoption. Let's explore this report in more depth. The Overview page, shown in Figure 15-14, enables you to identify daily activities and user trends, the most active capacities and workspaces, and activities by most or least active users.

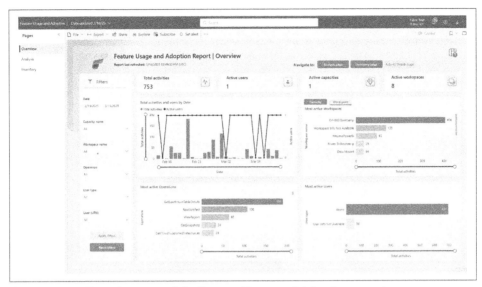

Figure 15-14. Overview page of the Feature Usage and Adoption report

Let's imagine for a moment that you work as a Fabric administrator for a large global retailer. You've configured a separate, dedicated capacity for each department in the organization. Your usual workflow might start with a look at the Overview page, where you identify that the Sales and Financials department capacities had more than 1,000 activities, whereas other capacities had fewer than 100. To obtain more insight into this behavior, you might navigate to the Analysis page of the report and use the decomposition tree visual to drill down and understand the details, as illustrated in Figure 15-15.

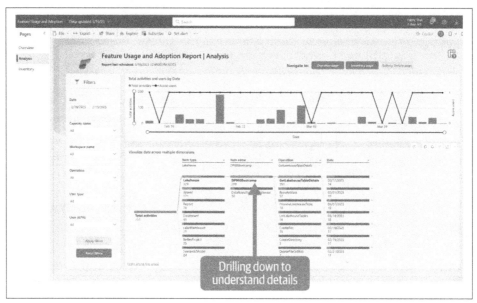

Figure 15-15. Analysis page of the Feature Usage and Adoption report

You can drill down even further by selecting a specific data point and then looking into the lowest level of detail, which shows every individual operation for the particular date. To expand on our previous example, you may identify the high number for the ViewReport action on the Sales and Financials capacities. Then, on the Activity Details page, you may discover that a new report was created last week that has been heavily accessed, causing the high number of activities on the capacity.

Finally, the Inventory page displays all the items in the Fabric tenant and provides information about their use. Data can be analyzed per workspace or per item type, while the decomposition tree visual at the bottom enables visualizing the data across numerous dimensions, as shown in Figure 15-16.

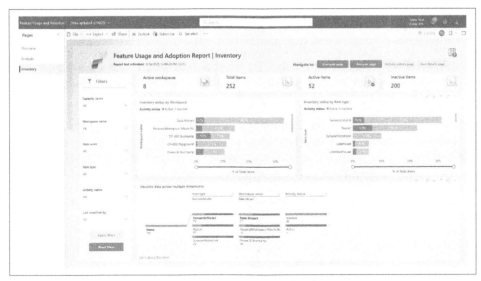

Figure 15-16. Inventory page of the Feature Usage and Adoption report

As on the Analysis page, the Inventory page enables you to drill down and obtain more detailed information by navigating to the Item Details page.

Table 15-3 provides information about the measures used in the Feature Usage and Adoption report and their definitions.

Table 15-3. Feature Usage and Adoption report measures and their definitions

Measure	Definition
Active capacities	The number of capacities with audit activity
Active users	The number of users who generated the audit activity
Active workspaces	The number of workspaces with audit activity
Activities	The number of audit activities generated
Items	The count of items displayed
Total activities	The number of audit activities generated (displayed only in card visuals)
Total items	The count of items displayed (displayed only in card visuals)

You can also use Fabric REST APIs to obtain this information, if you prefer developing your own custom solution.

Summary

We covered a lot in this chapter! Administration and monitoring in Microsoft Fabric is such a vast topic that we definitely only scratched the surface here. We did our best to equip you with the essential concepts and features to help you keep your Microsoft Fabric tenant in optimal shape.

Administration features in the Admin portal enable not only centralized management of workspaces, capacities, and other Fabric items but also the enforcement of efficient data government policies. Numerous built-in monitoring capabilities provide out-of-the-box solutions for the early detection of performance issues and operation failures.

In the next chapter, we'll discuss various features and options for securing Microsoft Fabric workloads.

## CHAPTER 16

Securing Microsoft Fabric

The need to keep data safe and secure is an ongoing concern, and Microsoft Fabric, as a unified data platform, is no exception. In real-world implementations, Microsoft Fabric handles vast volumes of sensitive information across a variety of workloads—data engineering, data warehousing, data science, and real-time intelligence. Without proper security measures—such as data access control, sensitivity labels, and similar—this sensitive data may be exposed to unauthorized access or breach.

In this chapter, we'll examine various options and features that enable the implementation of robust security policies to protect sensitive information.

Security represents a key aspect of any data analytics solution. Microsoft Fabric provides a wide range of security features to ensure that data is secured at rest and in transit, as well as to enable access and permission control of users and applications.

There are several aspects of security in Microsoft Fabric, so let's briefly introduce them:

Authentication
> Like other Microsoft SaaS solutions, such as Microsoft Office or OneDrive, Fabric relies on Microsoft Entra ID as its cloud-based identity provider. Entra ID enables easy connection from any device and any network.

Network security
> In various scenarios, you'll need to leverage data that resides outside of Microsoft Fabric. There are two directions to consider when configuring network security, inbound and outbound.

Inbound security handles securing the traffic coming into Fabric. Here, you can choose between Entra ID Conditional Access and private links:

- By implementing Entra ID Conditional Access, you can define a list of IP addresses for inbound connectivity to Fabric, use multifactor authentication (MFA), or restrict the traffic based on specific parameters, such as country or device type.

- Private links allow restricting access to the Fabric tenant from a VNet (Azure virtual network) only, while blocking all public access.

Outbound security enables connecting to external data sources and bringing the data into Fabric in a secure way. Let's explore different ways to connect to external data:

- Trusted workspace access is a Fabric workspace that uses workspace identity and can securely access Azure Data Lake Gen2 storage accounts with public network access enabled, from selected virtual networks and IP addresses.

- Managed private endpoints allow a secure connection to data sources, such as Azure SQL database, without exposing them to a public network.

- Managed virtual networks are virtual networks created and managed by Fabric for each Fabric workspace. They provide network isolation for Spark workloads, ensuring that Spark compute clusters are provisioned in a dedicated network.

- Data gateway enables secure connection to either on-premises data sources, using an on-premises data gateway, or to a data source that might be protected by a firewall or virtual network. In the latter scenario, you may use a VNet data gateway.

- Connecting to OneLake from an existing service may be useful when you need to connect to Fabric using an existing PaaS service, such as Azure Synapse Analytics or Azure Data Factory. In these scenarios, you can use Azure Integration Runtime (IR) or Azure Data Factory managed virtual network.

Securing data

When you store data in OneLake, all the data is encrypted at rest and stored in the tenant home region or in one of the capacities in a different region of your choice. This is a common requirement for organizations that conduct business across multiple regions.

Let's imagine a global retailer with headquarters in the US, selling its goods all over the planet. To comply with local regulations, the company must ensure that data remains stored at rest in different regions. This is called *data residency* in Microsoft Fabric. It's important to keep in mind that in these cases, the query execution layer, query caches, and item data assigned to a multi-geo workspace remain in the Azure region where they were created. However, some metadata is stored at rest in the tenant's home region.

Accessing data

Fabric items are stored in workspaces. Therefore, access control is implemented using workspace roles. However, there is the option to control the access at a more granular level, which we will examine in depth in the following section.

Protecting data

In synergy with Microsoft Purview Information Protection, you can apply sensitivity labels to your data to label it as general, confidential, or highly confidential. Once you apply sensitivity labels, they will follow the data automatically as it flows through various Fabric workloads—all the way from the data source to the end user—and keep sensitive data protected from unauthorized access. Sensitivity labels are part of the wider Data Loss Prevention (DLP) solution, which enables organizations to identify, monitor, and protect sensitive data across various locations.

Data recovery

Data recovery encompasses both disaster recovery and business continuity. Disaster recovery can be configured in the "Capacity settings" page of the Admin portal. When enabled, it creates a cross-region replication of the OneLake data. This feature may not be available in all regions. Additionally, you should be aware that disaster recovery, because it is geo-replication enabled, consumes more storage and transactions, which are billed as BCDR Storage and BCDR Operations, respectively (BCDR stands for business continuity disaster recovery), and can be found in the Microsoft Fabric Capacity Metrics app.

Secure Data Access in Microsoft Fabric

In this section, we will introduce various concepts and features to control data access in Microsoft Fabric. Let's first revisit the Fabric storage architecture. The cornerstone of the entire Microsoft Fabric platform is OneLake, a central storage repository for the entire organization, regardless of whether the organization chooses to use a lakehouse, warehouse, KQL database, or any other Fabric item for storing the data. In the end, all roads lead to OneLake, as we described in Chapter 3.

In simple words, OneLake is nothing more than a logical structure of files and folders, as depicted in Figure 16-1.

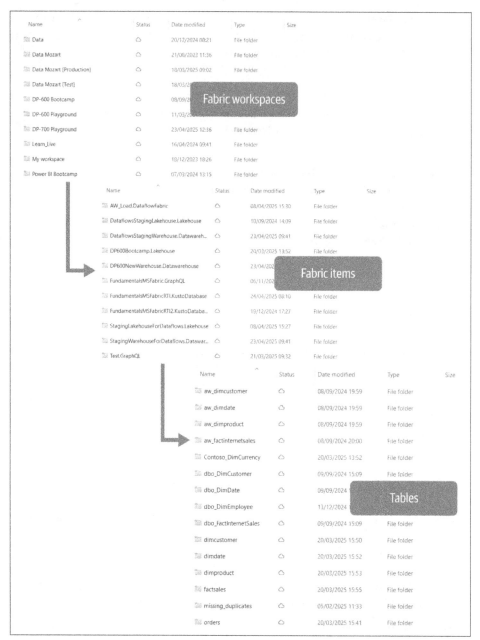

Figure 16-1. Physical representation of the OneLake structure

As you'll see, OneLake itself is at the top level of this hierarchy. Then, we have one or multiple workspaces that serve as containers for various Fabric items, such as lakehouses, warehouses, KQL databases, semantic models, and so on. When you go one level further and open, say, a lakehouse, there are a lot of folders inside, each representing an individual table. Finally, each table folder consists of one or more files.

Let's now examine the conceptual structure of OneLake, as shown in Figure 16-2.

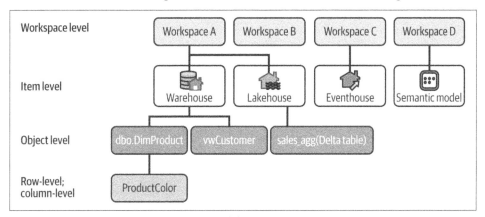

Figure 16-2. Conceptual representation of the OneLake structure

Understanding the conceptual structure of OneLake will help us break down how this structure impacts the data access control options in Fabric. Let's start from the top.

Workspace-Level Access Control

When you grant access to a workspace, a user (or a group of users) gets access to all the items in the particular workspace. Imagine the scenario where you have a workspace that contains 5 lakehouses, 2 warehouses, and 10 semantic models. The workspace role will enable the user to access all of these items. Of course, depending on the role itself, the user can perform a certain set of actions on top of the items, but the key thing to keep in mind here is that with workspace roles, *every single item in the workspace is accessible.* There are four workspace roles:

- Admin
- Member
- Contributor
- Viewer

Table 16-1, which is also available in Microsoft's official documentation (*https:// oreil.ly/koIil*), shows the capabilities of each workspace role.

Table 16-1. Fabric workspace roles and their capabilities

Capability	Admin	Member	Contributor	Viewer
Update and delete workspace	✓			
Add or remove people, including other admins	✓			
Add members or others with lower permissions	✓	✓		
Allow others to reshare items[a]	✓	✓		
Create or modify database mirroring items	✓	✓		
Create or modify warehouse items	✓	✓		
Create or modify SQL database items	✓	✓		
View and read content of data pipelines, notebooks, Spark job definitions, ML models and experiments, and eventstreams	✓	✓	✓	✓
View and read content of KQL databases, KQL querysets, and real-time dashboards	✓	✓	✓	✓
Connect to SQL analytics endpoint of lakehouse or warehouse	✓	✓	✓	✓
Read lakehouse and data warehouse data and shortcuts[b] with T-SQL through TDS endpoint[c]	✓	✓	✓	✓
Read lakehouse and data warehouse data and shortcuts[b] through OneLake APIs and Spark	✓	✓	✓	
Read lakehouse data through Lakehouse explorer	✓	✓	✓	
Write or delete data pipelines, notebooks, Spark job definitions, ML models and experiments, and eventstreams	✓	✓	✓	
Write or delete eventhouses,[d] KQL querysets, Real-Time Dashboards, and schema and data of KQL databases, lakehouses, data warehouses, and shortcuts	✓	✓	✓	
Execute or cancel execution of notebooks, Spark job definitions, and ML models and experiments	✓	✓	✓	
Execute or cancel execution of data pipelines	✓	✓	✓	
View execution output of data pipelines, notebooks, and ML models and experiments	✓	✓	✓	✓
Schedule data refreshes via the on-premises gateway[e]	✓	✓	✓	
Modify gateway connection settings[e]	✓	✓	✓	

[a] Contributor and Viewer roles can also share items if they have an explicit Reshare permission

[b] Additional permissions are required to read the data from the shortcut destination

[c] TDS endpoint is a Tabular Data Stream protocol that emulates a SQL data connection. It allows querying data sources using the T-SQL language.

[d] Additional permissions are required to perform certain operations in eventhouses

[e] Permissions on the gateway are also required

Item-Level Access Control

If you need to enable a specific user or group of users to access a particular item or a subset of items in the workspace, but not necessarily all the items in that workspace, you should grant them access by sharing the item. With this approach, the user has restricted access to a workspace—they don't even need any of the workspace roles—and can access only the shared item.

Depending on the item type (lakehouse, warehouse, KQL database), the set of permissions might differ. Whenever you share the item with the user, it will automatically grant them read permission for that item.

Figure 16-3 shows item-level access control options for a lakehouse item.

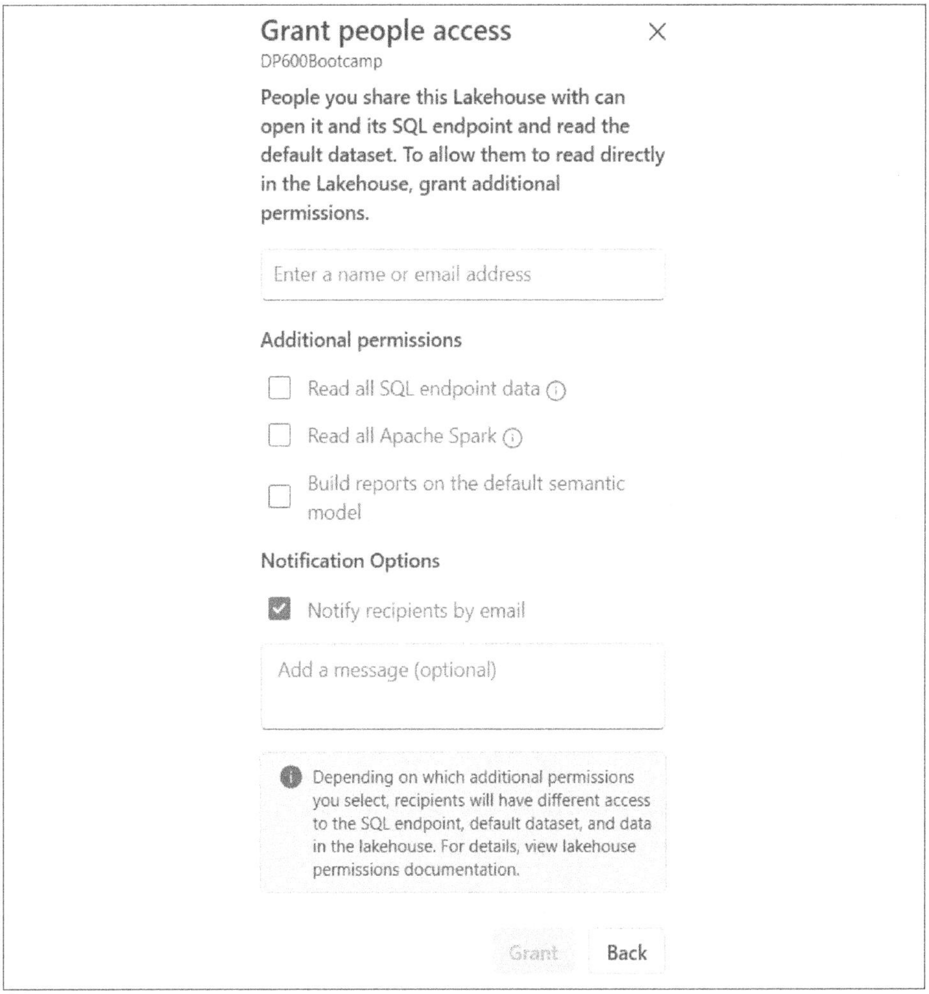

Figure 16-3. Item-level access for a Fabric Lakehouse

When you want to share a KQL database item, the workflow is slightly different because sharing is available only by creating and sending a link, as shown in Figure 16-4.

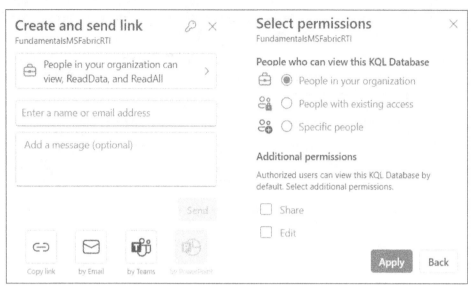

Figure 16-4. Item-level access for a KQL database

Table 16-2 lists the effects in place for each of the granted permissions.

Table 16-2. Permission options when sharing a lakehouse

Permission granted	Effect
Read	Discover the item in the data hub, open it, and connect to the warehouse or SQL analytics endpoint of the lakehouse
Edit	Edit the item or its content
Share	Share the item and grant permissions up to the permissions they have
Read All with SQL analytics endpoint	Read data from the SQL analytics endpoint of the lakehouse through TDS endpoints
Read All with Apache Spark	Read lakehouse data via OneLake APIs and Spark; read lakehouse data via Lakehouse explorer
Build	Build new Power BI content based on the semantic model
Execute	Execute or cancel the item execution

When you want to share a warehouse item, the options are slightly different, as you'll notice in Figure 16-5.

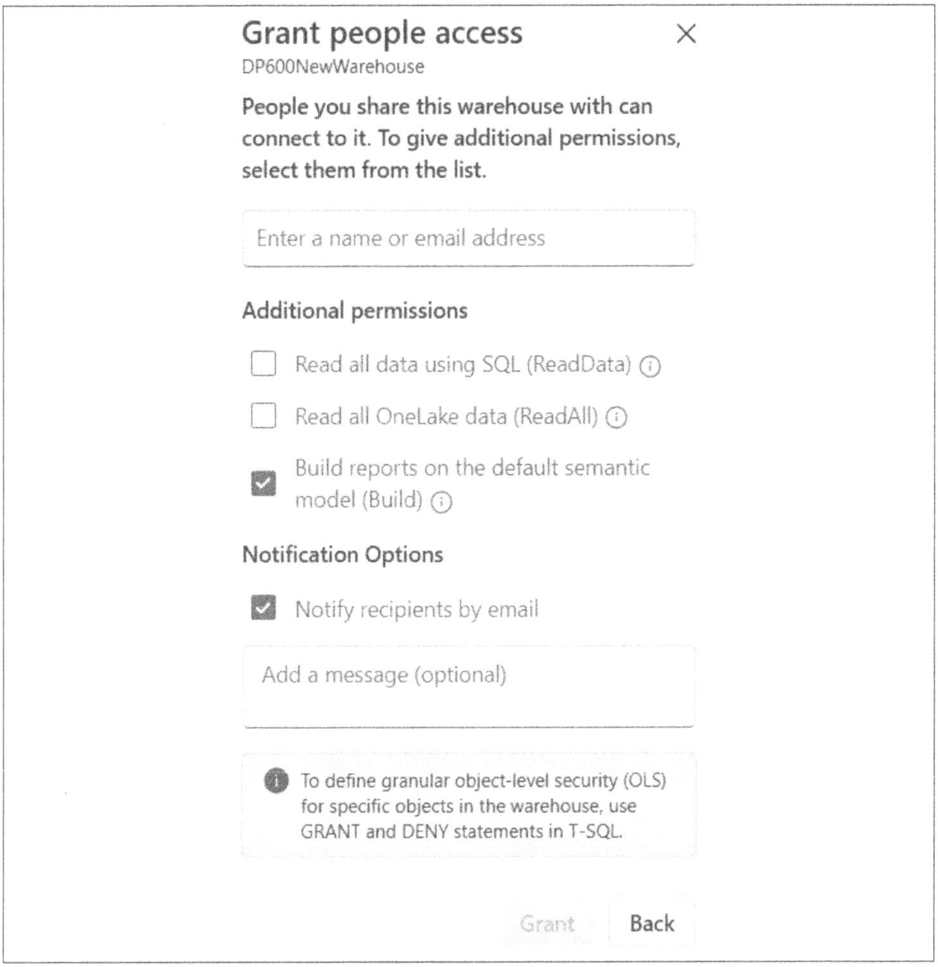

Grant people access   ✕

DP600NewWarehouse

People you share this warehouse with can connect to it. To give additional permissions, select them from the list.

> Enter a name or email address

Additional permissions

☐   Read all data using SQL (ReadData) ⓘ

☐   Read all OneLake data (ReadAll) ⓘ

☑   Build reports on the default semantic model (Build) ⓘ

Notification Options

☑   Notify recipients by email

> Add a message (optional)

ⓘ To define granular object-level security (OLS) for specific objects in the warehouse, use GRANT and DENY statements in T-SQL.

Grant   **Back**

Figure 16-5. Item-level access for a Fabric warehouse

Let's examine the permission model of the warehouse. If nothing is selected, the user will have read permission, which allows connecting to the SQL analytics endpoint, but doesn't allow querying data unless they are granted explicit permission using the T-SQL GRANT statement:

Read all data using SQL (ReadData)

The user can read all the objects in the warehouse. If you need to apply more granular control, you can do this using the T-SQL GRANT/REVOKE/DENY statements. This permission is equivalent to the "Read all with SQL analytics endpoint" permission on a lakehouse.

Read all OneLake data (ReadAll)
> The user has read access to the underlying Parquet files in OneLake. ReadAll should be provided only in scenarios where the user needs full access to the warehouse files.

Build reports on the default semantic model (Build)
> The user can create Power BI reports on top of the default semantic model.

You can also manage the access directly. Once you click on the three dots next to the item name and choose "Manage permissions," you'll go to a dedicated page as shown in Figure 16-6. This page provides not only an overview of all the users and their permissions on the selected item but also the possibility to add new users if needed, as well as to grant or revoke permissions for the existing user.

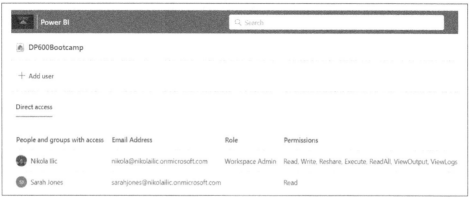

Figure 16-6. Manage permissions page

Row-Level Security

As its name suggests, row-level security allows you to control access to particular rows in a Delta table. Let's imagine your company is running a business in multiple regions (US, Europe, Asia) and you have analytics teams in each of these regions. The requirement is to restrict access so that US analysts can see only US sales data, analysts from Europe see only European sales data, and so on.

 Just to make this clear from the beginning: here *we are not talking about the row-level security (RLS) for Power BI semantic models* but rather examining the RLS feature for Fabric Warehouse and the SQL analytics endpoint of the Lakehouse. Don't confuse these two, as they are configured and managed completely independently.

To be able to implement row-level security, you need to either be an Admin, Member, or Contributor in the workspace where the item resides *or* have elevated permissions on the warehouse or SQL analytics endpoint of the lakehouse.

In the following code snippet, we show how to implement RLS using T-SQL language. The first step is to define roles and predicates: *roles* determine *who* can access the data, whereas *predicates* define *which* data can be accessed:

```
-- Creating schema for Security
CREATE SCHEMA Rls;
GO
-- Creating a function for the analyst evaluation
CREATE FUNCTION Rls.tvf_location(@analyst AS varchar(50))
    RETURNS TABLE
WITH SCHEMABINDING
AS
    RETURN SELECT 1 AS tvf_location_result
WHERE @analyst = USER_NAME();
GO
-- Using the function to create a Security Policy
CREATE SECURITY POLICY LocationRls
ADD FILTER PREDICATE Rls.tvf_location(analyst)
ON MySchema.MyTable
WITH (STATE = ON);
GO
```

To wrap up, it's important to keep in mind that the analyst must be part of the MySchema.MyTable.

Object-Level and Column-Level Security

With *object-level security*, we can control access to specific database objects: tables (*https://oreil.ly/mkjjS*), views (*https://oreil.ly/g2FlD*), or stored procedures. This way, we ensure that a user, or group of users, can access only those objects to which they've been granted permission. For those of you coming from the SQL Server world, this might sound familiar (because it is): by using GRANT, DENY, and REVOKE commands, we can implement object-level security in the Fabric warehouse as well.

Similar to the previous section, don't confuse object-level security (OLS) for Power BI semantic models with the object-level security feature for the Fabric warehouse and SQL analytics endpoint of the lakehouse.

In the following code snippet, we are granting the users that belong to the SalesAnalysts group permission to query the data from the Sales table:

```
GRANT SELECT ON dbo.Sales TO [SalesAnalysts];
```

Column-level security (CLS) works in a similar manner, but it allows for more granular access control, since you can grant access to specific columns. In the following code snippet, we grant permissions to users in the `SalesAnalysts` group to query the data from the columns `CustomerKey`, `FirstName`, `LastName`, and `Email`:

```
GRANT SELECT ON dbo.Customer (CustomerKey, FirstName, LastName, Email)
    TO [SalesAnalysts];
```

If the user who belongs to the `SalesAnalysts` group tries to execute a query that retrieves data from columns other than those specified, it will return an error.

 Please be aware that it is possible to circumvent granular Fabric warehouse security rules. If a user is granted ReadAll permission when the warehouse is shared, they will be able to see all data in a specific table. Therefore, make sure to double-check if various data access rules are in collision and always implement them by sticking with the principle of least privilege.

Additionally, bear in mind that when you implement RLS/OLS/CLS in a warehouse or the SQL analytics endpoint of a lakehouse, and you use Direct Lake semantic models for Power BI, all queries will, by default, *fall back to DirectQuery mode*. If you want to learn more about Direct Lake mode for Power BI semantic models, please refer to Chapter 9, where we cover Direct Lake in depth.

Folder-Level Access Control

Let's wrap up this section by understanding how to control access on the lowest level of the OneLake hierarchy—individual folders. This is implemented through the OneLake Data Access Roles feature, which can be accessed directly from Lakehouse explorer, as displayed in Figure 16-7.

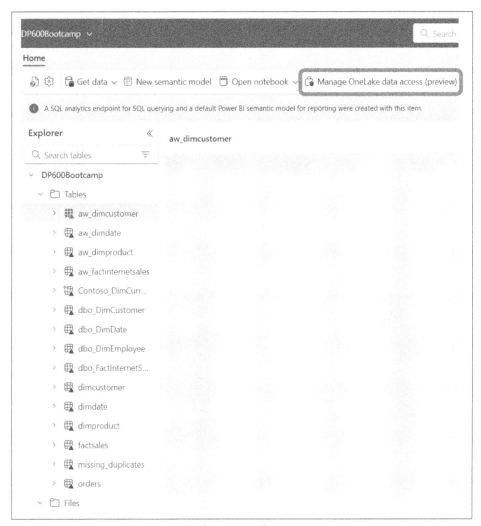

Figure 16-7. Accessing the OneLake data access feature

The process of configuring the access is fairly straightforward, as shown in Figure 16-8. First, we need to create the role. Then, we choose which folders or individual files should be accessible to this role. Finally, we assign the role to a user or group of users.

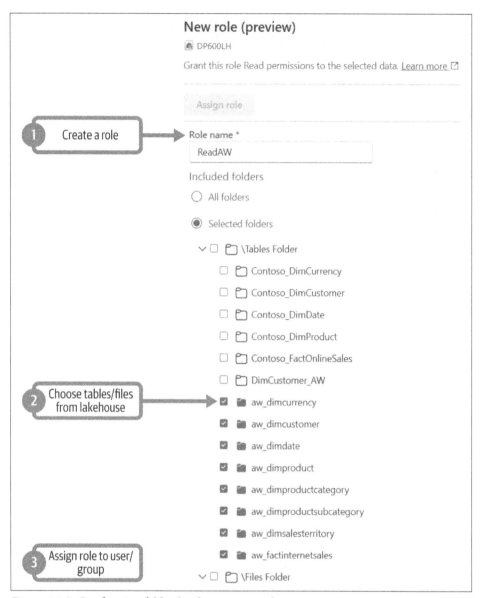

Figure 16-8. Configuring folder-level access control

However, there are a few important considerations when implementing OneLake data access roles:

- These roles apply only to users accessing OneLake directly.
- When you start configuring the OneLake data access role, before you create any new role, be aware that there is already a DefaultReader role defined for the

selected lakehouse, which was generated when the lakehouse was created. By default, this role grants access to all folders in the lakehouse to users with ReadAll permission. Hence, make sure that you don't have the same user or group of users assigned to the DefaultReader and any custom role, because these users will then be able to see all the lakehouse folders.

- You can leverage the current set of lakehouse permissions when assigning users to a group. It's enough to choose the option "Add users based on Lakehouse permissions," and we can immediately add users who already have particular permissions on the lakehouse, as shown in Figure 16-9.

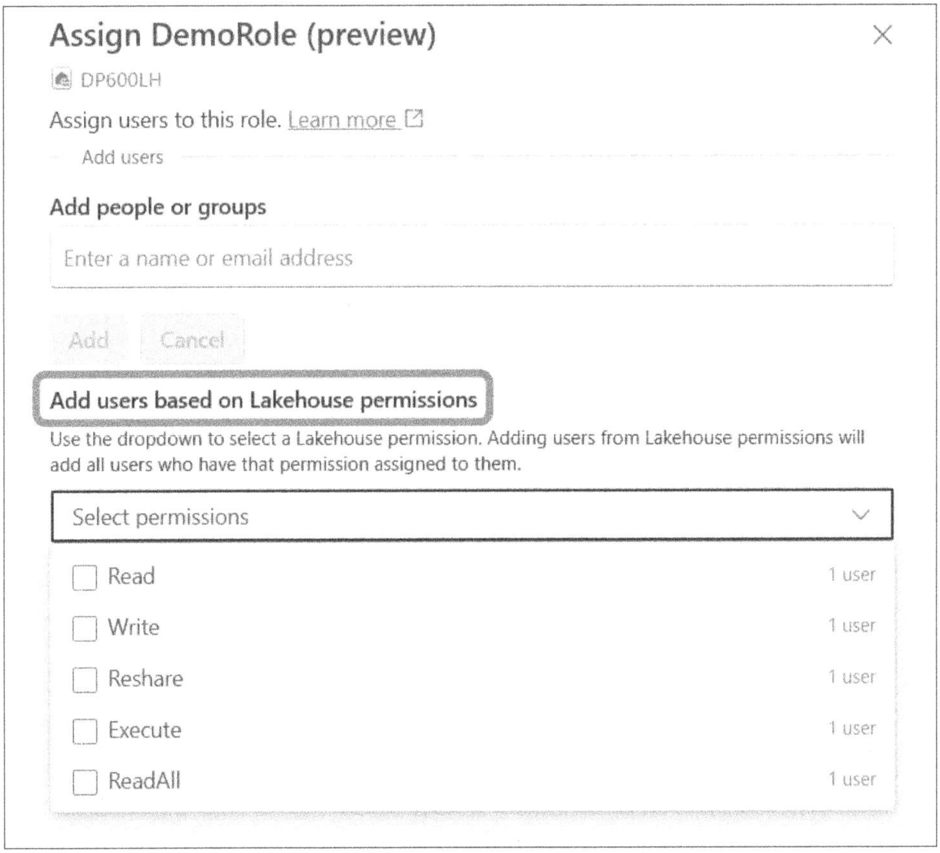

Figure 16-9. Assigning users to a role based on their lakehouse permissions

To summarize, Figure 16-10 depicts how OneLake role-based access control (RBAC) is evaluated in the imaginary scenario of the user requesting to read the data from Folder A in Lakehouse B in the Fabric workspace.

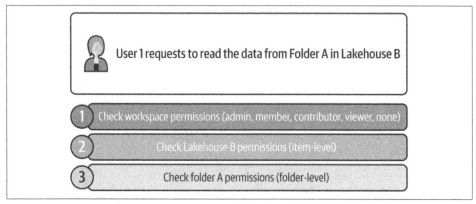

Figure 16-10. OneLake RBAC permissions evaluation process

Shortcuts Security Model

Before we dig into explaining the shortcuts security model in Microsoft Fabric, let's first make a connection between two key terms to understand different shortcut paths:

- *Target path* refers to the location that a shortcut points to.
- *Shortcut path* refers to the location where the shortcut appears.

Figure 16-11 illustrates the difference between these two paths.

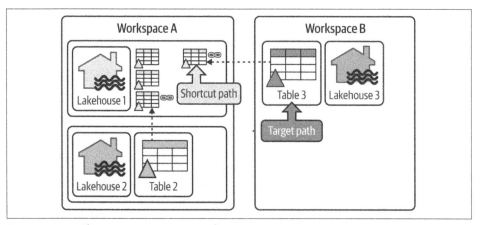

Figure 16-11. Shortcut versus target path

Let's first examine the OneLake RBAC for internal shortcuts. Just as a reminder, internal shortcuts are objects that point to other locations inside OneLake. For any folder in the lakehouse, RBAC permissions always inherit permissions to all internal shortcuts where this folder is defined as a target path. Simply said, the user must have read permission in the target location. Defining RBAC permissions is not allowed in the shortcut path; they have to be specified on the folder in the target path, as shown in Figure 16-12.

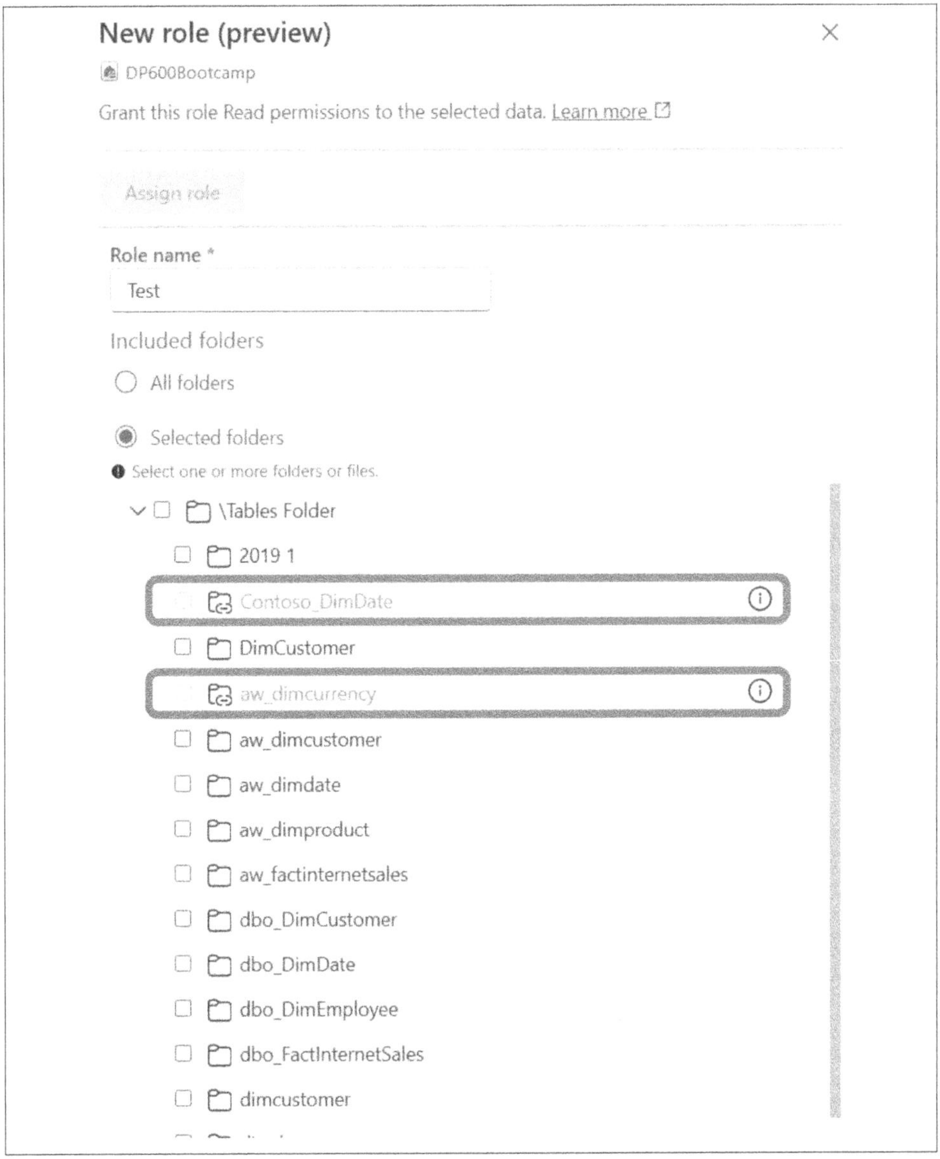

Figure 16-12. Defining RBAC permissions on the folders in the target path

RBAC permissions can be defined for external shortcuts as well. Again, as a quick reminder, external shortcuts are OneLake objects that point to storage locations *outside* OneLake, such as ADLS Gen2, Dataverse, Amazon S3, Google Cloud Platform, and so on. When defined, these permissions will be applied *on top* of the delegated authorization model enabled for the external shortcut.

Let's imagine the following scenario: User1, who has access to the target path, created a shortcut pointing to the Amazon S3 storage. After that, another user, User2, tries to access the data in the OneLake shortcut. Table 16-3 outlines all the possible outcomes.

Table 16-3. RBAC permissions with external shortcuts

S3 authorization for User1	OneLake RBAC authorization for User2	Can User2 access data in the OneLake shortcut?
Yes	Yes	Yes
No	No	No
No	Yes	No
Yes	No	No

Common Security Scenarios

In this section, we introduce common security scenarios that you may need to implement when working with Microsoft Fabric and explain how to ensure that you follow the recommended security practices in each instance. Table 16-4 shows which tools might be used based on the traffic direction.

Table 16-4. Common security scenarios and tools to ensure security

Traffic direction	Scenario	Tools
Inbound	Fabric endpoints protected from the public internet	Fabric is, by default, protected from the public internet; for additional protection, use Entra conditional access policies for Fabric and/or enable private links on the tenant level
Inbound	Fabric may be accessed only from the organizational network and/or from specific devices	Entra conditional access policies for Fabric
Inbound	Enforce MFA when accessing Fabric	Entra conditional access policies for Fabric
Outbound	No-code/Low-code data ingestion from on-premises data sources	On-premises data gateway with Dataflow Gen2 and/or pipelines
Outbound	No-code/low-code data ingestion from data sources in Azure behind private endpoints	VNet gateway with Dataflow Gen2 and/or pipelines
Outbound	Code-first data ingestion using notebooks from data sources in Azure behind private endpoints	Fabric notebooks with Azure private endpoints

Data Discovery and Trust

Getting your head around all the data assets in an organization can often be a daunting task. This is particularly the case in large enterprises, where discovering data assets is rightly considered an area to master on its own. To overcome this challenge, many organizations implemented a centralized inventory of all data assets called a *data catalog*.

The data catalog leverages metadata (data *about* data) to establish an informative and searchable inventory of all the organizational data assets. These assets may include, but are not limited to:

- Structured data
- Unstructured data
- Reports and query results
- Data visualizations and operational dashboards
- Machine learning models

A data catalog enhances capabilities to collect and enrich the metadata making it easier to identify and use properly. Data catalogs provide numerous benefits:

Better data understanding
> Improved context enables data analysts and other data professionals to find detailed data descriptions and understand the business relevance of the particular data.

Enhanced operational efficiency
> Regular business users can access and analyze data faster, while IT professionals can focus on high-priority tasks.

Reduced risk
> Data analysts can work with data with more confidence.

Better data for better analysis
> Data professionals can confidently respond to challenges and provide business answers based on the appropriate and trustworthy data.

Now that you know what data catalog in general is, let's examine how this concept is implemented in Microsoft Fabric.

OneLake Catalog

The OneLake catalog represents a centralized location that enables you to search and explore various Fabric items, as well as govern the data you own. Once you open OneLake from the menu on the left, there are two key areas inside the OneLake catalog: Explore and Govern. Figure 16-13 displays the Explore tab content.

Figure 16-13. Explore tab of the OneLake catalog

The Explore tab provides a list of all the Fabric items you have access to. In addition, you can filter the displayed data based on different criteria, such as Data, Insights, Processes, Solutions, and Configurations, thus narrowing down displayed results based on your specific needs.

You may also explore particular items in more detail, as shown in Figure 16-14, where we're taking a thorough look into one of the Power BI semantic models.

Here, you can find not only a general overview of the item, such as tables that are part of the model or endorsement type, but also the item lineage—both upstream and downstream dependent items, monitoring, and permissions. Therefore, we can easily think of the Explore tab in the OneLake catalog as a one-stop shop for understanding a particular Fabric item.

The Govern tab provides insights about the governance status of all the Fabric items you own and recommended actions you might consider taking to improve the governance status of the data. Figure 16-15 displays the main Govern tab content.

Figure 16-14. Detailed overview of a Fabric item in the OneLake catalog explorer

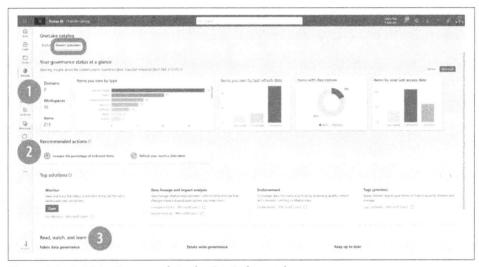

Figure 16-15. Main Govern tab in the OneLake catalog

There are three main areas to examine in the Govern tab:

1. *Insights*

   Provides a visual overview of the governance status of your data.

2. *Recommended actions*

   Shows actions you can take to enhance the governance status of your data, as well as guidance to help you accomplish them.

3. *Tools and learning resources*

   Provides a list of resources you may explore to help better understand and manage your data from the governance point.

Within the Insights area, once you click on the "View more" button, you'll go to a detailed overview of your data estate. This includes more granular information in a dashboard-like representation where you can examine the "Sensitivity label coverage" and "Discover, trust, and reuse" insights.

Endorsement

When you have high-quality, trustworthy data and content, you probably want to make it easier for users to identify that content. This is where the Endorsement feature comes in, enabling you to clearly label particular items with a badge.

There are three available endorsement badges in Microsoft Fabric, as displayed in Table 16-5.

Table 16-5. Endorsement options in Microsoft Fabric

Endorsement type	Description	Which items can be endorsed?	Who can endorse items?
Promoted	Item creator thinks the item is ready for sharing and reuse	Any Fabric item except Power BI dashboards	Any user with write permission on the item
Certified	Authorized reviewer certifies that the item meets the organization's quality standards and is ready for use across the organization	Any Fabric item except Power BI dashboards	Users defined by the Fabric administrator
Master data	Data in the item is a core source of organizational data (single source of truth)	Items that contain data (e.g., lakehouses, warehouses, semantic models)	Users defined by the Fabric administrator

Please keep in mind that Certified and Master data endorsement types are available only if the Fabric administrator enabled them in the Admin portal. In addition, the Certified option may be delegated to domain administrators, which allows having different reviewers for each domain.

Once endorsed, Fabric items appear in the list with the assigned badge, as shown in Figure 16-16.

☐	Name	Type	Owner	Refreshed	Location	Endorsement
⊞	OneLake catalog governance repo...	Semantic model	Nikola Ilic	3/17/25, 8:21:21 AM	My Workspace	—
🏠	DP600Bootcamp	Lakehouse	Nikola Ilic	—	DP-600 Bootcamp	—
⊞	We Love Power BI	Semantic model	Nikola Ilic	2/22/25, 10:07:16 AM	WeLovePowerBI	⊘ Promoted
⊞	07 Create Reports	Semantic model	Nikola Ilic	2/21/25, 8:49:13 AM	WeLovePowerBI	♡ Certified
⊞	End-To-End Collisions NYC grey	Semantic model	Nikola Ilic	11/13/24, 12:37:11 PM	Data Mozart	—
⊞	04 Design Data Model	Semantic model	Nikola Ilic	2/27/25, 2:58:26 PM	WeLovePowerBI	—

Figure 16-16. Endorsement badges for Fabric items

Tags

When the built-in endorsement badges are not sufficient, you can expand the item metadata by implementing tags. *Tags* are customizable text labels defined by Fabric administrators. Based on the specific organizational needs, the Fabric admin may create tags such as FY 2025, Marketing—Events, Sales—US 2024, and so on. These tags can then be applied to Fabric items so that users can search for and find the data based on the specific tag.

Figure 16-17 illustrates the workflow when implementing Tags in the organization.

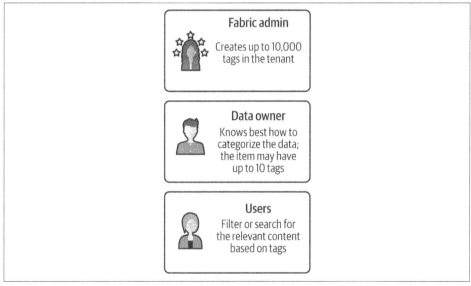

Figure 16-17. Workflow for implementing tags in Microsoft Fabric

Sensitivity Labels

Sensitivity labels represent a key component in enabling your organization to meet compliance and governance requirements. The main purpose of sensitivity labels in Microsoft Fabric is to protect sensitive data against unauthorized access.

Sensitivity labels require using an additional, non-Fabric solution. Say hello to Microsoft Purview. In a nutshell, Microsoft Purview is a set of services and features for data governance, data security, and risk and compliance. Sensitivity labels are defined in Microsoft Purview Information Protection and then applied in Microsoft Fabric to specific Fabric items.

Please bear in mind that Microsoft Purview (unlike Microsoft Purview hub, which we discussed in Chapter 15) *is not* part of Microsoft Fabric; thus, it requires separate licensing and pricing.

Figure 16-18 shows how to apply a Confidential sensitivity label to a Fabric lakehouse.

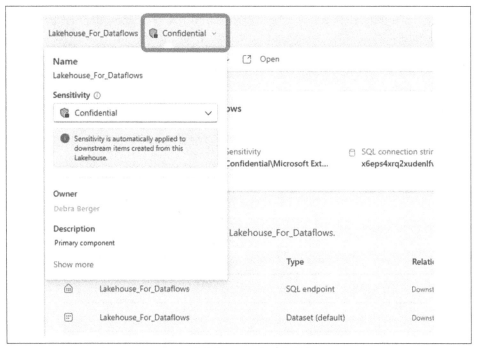

Figure 16-18. Applying a sensitivity label to a Fabric lakehouse

There are three areas where sensitivity labels may be leveraged to control access:

Fabric tenant
This scenario relies on sensitivity labels associated with Microsoft Purview protection policies. When the user logs in to the Fabric tenant and tries to access the protected item, their access is controlled by that protection policy.

Power BI Desktop
This scenario relies on sensitivity labels associated with Microsoft Purview publishing policies.

Supported export paths
This scenario relies on sensitivity labels associated with Microsoft Purview publishing policies. The following export paths are supported: export to Excel, PDF, and PowerPoint; Analyze in Excel; PivotTable in Excel with a live connection to Power BI semantic model; and download to Power BI Desktop file (*.pbix*).

You can find more information about using sensitivity labels for information protection in Microsoft Fabric in the official documentation (*https://oreil.ly/f5sUX*).

Summary

By implementing various security features, you are ensuring that your sensitive data is protected from unauthorized access and compliant with regulatory requirements. The topics discussed in this chapter are no means an exhaustive list of features and best practices relevant to keeping your data secure, reliable, and maintainable. And this is especially true considering the number of updates and enhancements Microsoft implements in each product development iteration. Therefore, we strongly encourage you to consider this chapter a starting point in your Fabric security journey and stay up-to-date with the latest features in this area.

In the next chapter, we will explore core concepts and capabilities for implementing CI/CD workflows in Microsoft Fabric.

## CHAPTER 17

CI/CD in Microsoft Fabric

Continuous integration (CI) and *continuous deployment* (CD) are crucial concepts in the modern software development workflow. When implemented properly, CI/CD processes enhance the software or data delivery workflow and enable faster, more reliable, and more frequent releases, ensuring high code quality and developer efficiency.

If we take a look into CI/CD concepts with our Fabric lens off, we might conclude that CI represents the practice of regularly integrating (merging) code with the rest of the organization and that CD is a set of practices to always keep your application in a deployable state, usually implemented through a pipeline, which ensures that all changes go through a series of test environments before culminating in a production deployment.

CI/CD Workflow Options

Before we examine particular features and concepts for implementing effective CI/CD workflows in Microsoft Fabric, let's first take a step back and explain how these concepts fit into the big picture of the more generic lifecycle management concept. In a nutshell, *lifecycle management* enables an effective workflow for releasing products quickly by continuously delivering up-to-date content into production, while maintaining the ongoing development of new features and bug fixes and ensuring they are deployed using the most efficient delivery method.

We can identify three main components of lifecycle management in Microsoft Fabric:

- *Git integration* is a CI part of the workflow.
- *Deployment pipelines* are a CD part of the workflow.
- *Fabric APIs* enable automation and programmatic management of CI/CD processes.

In the following sections, we'll examine these components in more depth.

Git Integration

Git integration enables developers to back up and version their work, revert to previous stages if needed, collaborate with others or work individually using Git branches, and apply familiar source control tools to manage Fabric items.

Explaining general Git and version control concepts is beyond the scope of this book. Therefore, we will *assume* that you are already familiar with Git basics and focus on examining how Git integration can be implemented in Microsoft Fabric.

If you are not familiar with Git in general, here is a list of resources you may find helpful:

- "What is Git?" (*https://oreil.ly/CTLoO*)
- "What is version control?" (*https://oreil.ly/464Ws*)
- "Basic concepts in Git integration" (*https://oreil.ly/OeaP2*)
- "Manage branches in Microsoft Fabric workspaces" (*https://oreil.ly/R1DI2*)

Microsoft Fabric supports the following Git providers: Git in Azure Repos, GitHub, and GitHub Enterprise. Most Fabric items support Git integration. Even in those scenarios where the workspace or Git repository contains unsupported items, it can still be connected, but the unsupported items will be ignored during the integration process.

Let's now examine the entire process of Git integration. As a prerequisite, you first need to set up either an Azure DevOps or GitHub account. Then, we need to connect the Fabric workspace with a Git repository. This is done from the workspace settings, as shown in Figure 17-1.

Figure 17-1. Setting up Git integration for the Fabric workspace

Once you provide all the necessary information, such as project name, Git repository, and branch, the synchronization process starts automatically. After you connect to the repository, you can see the Git status of each item in the Fabric workspace, as shown in Figure 17-2.

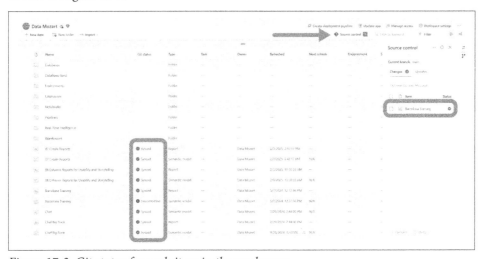

Figure 17-2. Git status for each item in the workspace

Each item may have one of the following statuses:

- Synced
- Conflict (the item was changed in both the workspace *and* the Git repository)
- Unsupported item

- Uncommitted changes in the workspace

- Update required from Git

- Item identical in both places but needs to be updated to the last commit

In Figure 17-2, you may notice that there is one uncommitted item in the workspace—a Power BI semantic model. This happened because we made some changes to the item, so the Git integration process automatically labels the item as Uncommitted and also flags the warning in the "Source control" button in the top ribbon. From here, we can commit changes directly to the repository in Azure DevOps.

The same will happen if someone uploads a new version of the file to the Git repository or makes changes to the file directly inside the Git repository. The Git integration process will again display the warning and provide you with the option to update the content in the workspace, as shown in Figure 17-3.

Figure 17-3. Update required status for the item that was changed directly in the Git repository

As you may conclude, when you make changes in the Fabric workspace, you can synchronize them with the Git repository using the Changes option in the Source control window. On the flip side, when new commits are made in the Git repository branch, you may synchronize them with the workspace content using the Updates option in the Source control window.

There are several recommended practices when developing Microsoft Fabric content in the shared environment. The key thing to be aware of is that when you are developing in the shared environment, it will affect all users in that workspace. Therefore, you should either use an isolated environment (i.e., a separate workspace) or use client tools such as Power BI Desktop or VS Code for development purposes. In addition, development should be done in a separate branch instead of the main branch to ensure that multiple developers can work in parallel on the feature without impacting the main branch.

If you still prefer developing directly in the Fabric web interface, you can isolate your work by clicking the "Source control" button and then choosing the "Branch out to new workspace" option, as shown in Figure 17-4.

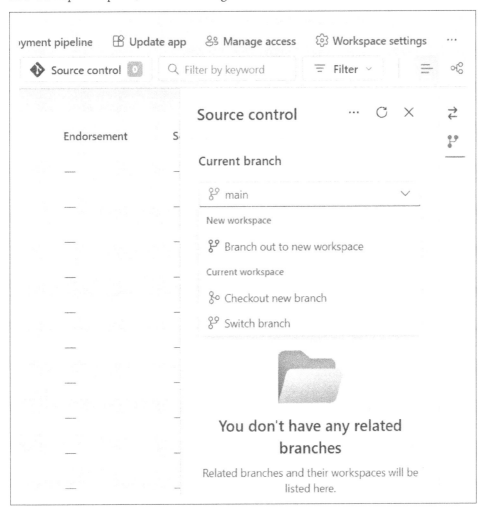

Figure 17-4. Creating an isolated branch in another workspace

Let's wrap up by examining required Fabric permissions for common actions in a Git repository. Table 17-1 lists popular actions and necessary Fabric workspace roles.

Table 17-1. Common actions and their required workspace roles

Action	Fabric workspace role
Connect/disconnect workspace to/from Git repository	Admin
Sync workspace with Git repository	Admin
Switch branch in the workspace	Admin
View Git connection details	Admin, Member, Contributor
See workspace Git status information	Admin, Member, Contributor
Update from Git	• Contributor in the workspace (write permission on all items) • Item owner (in cases where the tenant switch blocks updates for non-owners) • Build permission on external dependencies (if any)
Commit workspace changes from Git	• Contributor in the workspace (write permission on all items) • Item owner (in cases where the tenant switch blocks updates for non-owners) • Build permission on external dependencies (if any)
Create new Git branch from Fabric	Admin
Branch out to another workspace	Admin, Member, Contributor

When the items *in the workspace* have been changed, you should *commit* changes to the Git repository. If more than one item has changed, you can pick individual items to commit.

When the items *in the connected Git branch* have been changed, you should *update* the items in the workspace. The Update command always updates the entire branch—you can't pick individual items to update.

Deployment Pipelines

Deployment pipelines are the out-of-the-box Microsoft Fabric solution for CD. The main reason to use deployment pipelines is to enable efficient and flexible, automated movement of Fabric items through the various development lifecycle stages.

Although you may define between 2 and 10 stages in a pipeline, the general idea is to have stages for development, test, and production. Once you create a pipeline, it will contain these three core environments. From there, you may add, delete, or rename stages per your needs.

Let's briefly introduce the key principles for each of the core environments:

Development

You should use this environment for designing, reviewing, and playing around with the Fabric content. You can start small, using minimal amounts of data for development, and once you confirm that the content is ready for review, you can push it to the next stage.

Test

This is a preproduction environment, where you should test and verify that the content meets certain criteria. In this stage, you should run tests on larger, more realistic data volumes but also test items you plan to share with users, such as the Power BI App, to confirm it's fully ready. Once you confirm that the content is at the level necessary to meet end users' expectations, you'll push it to the final stage.

Production

This is the final version of the content, and it needs to provide the highest possible level of quality and accuracy.

Before we examine some of the key concepts and inner workings of deployment pipelines, let's first explain how to create a deployment pipeline in Microsoft Fabric. A pipeline can be created from the Workspaces window, as shown in Figure 17-5.

After you've created a pipeline, you have to add the content you plan to manage in the pipeline. This is done by assigning a workspace to the specific pipeline stage, unless you are creating a pipeline directly from the particular workspace, in which case the workspace will be automatically assigned to the pipeline. Please bear in mind that a workspace can be assigned to only one deployment pipeline at a time.

Once we assign the workspace to the development stage, we'll get a warning if there are any unsupported items. Figure 17-6 shows the dialog for deploying items from the development to the test stage.

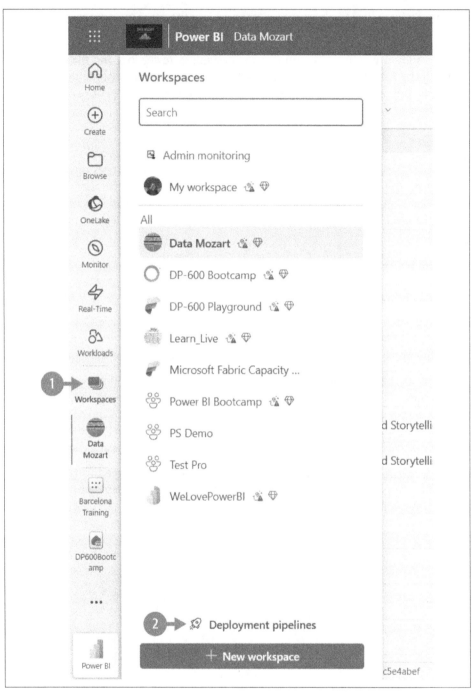

Figure 17-5. Creating a deployment pipeline

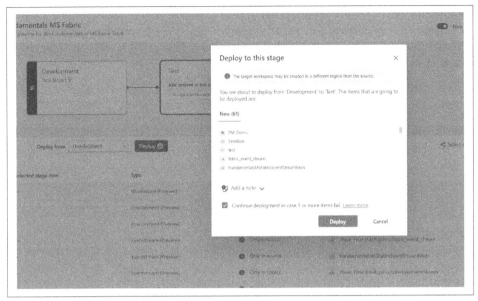

Figure 17-6. Deploying items from the development to the test stage

A Word of Warning About Lakehouse Deployment

At the time of writing, deployment pipelines for the majority of Fabric items are still in preview. This means that the way the deployment process works, as well as supported functionalities, might change when the feature becomes generally available.

This also means that the behavior of the deployment process might differ from item to item. A good example is the lakehouse item. If nothing is specified during the deployment pipeline configuration, a new *empty* lakehouse will be created in the target stage, while the notebooks are remapped to reference the new empty lakehouse. If you configure a pipeline to reference an existing lakehouse in the target stage, a new empty lakehouse with the same name will still be created, but the notebooks' references will be preserved and will point to the existing lakehouse if configured.

It's possible that the aforementioned behavior will not be relevant by the time you are reading this book. Therefore, when you set up deployment pipelines, make sure to check the list of currently supported Fabric items (*https://oreil.ly/sojrc*) and their specific features in the Microsoft documentation.

If you haven't assigned an existing workspace to the test stage, Fabric will automatically create a new workspace with the same name as the one in the previous stage and append the suffix [Test]. As a prerequisite, you need to select the items that should be deployed; otherwise, the new workspace will not be created. Similarly, if you haven't assigned an existing workspace to the production stage, a new, automatically created workspace will be assigned the suffix [Production]. The user who deploys the content automatically becomes the owner of the cloned semantic models and the only admin of the newly created workspace.

When moving content between the stages, you may choose among these three options:

Full deployment
    Deploys all the content from the source to the target stage (e.g., from the development to the test stage).

Selective deployment
    You can pick individual items that should be deployed to the target stage.

Backward deployment
    Deploys content from the target stage to the source stage (e.g., from the test to the development stage).

Let's now introduce several important concepts in deployment pipelines.

Autobinding

During the deployment process, deployment pipelines will check for any dependencies between the items being deployed. For example, a Power BI report always depends on the semantic model item. If the linked item exists in the target stage, deployment pipelines will automatically connect the deployed item to the dependent item in the target stage. For example, if you are deploying a Power BI report from the development to the test stage, and the report is connected to the semantic model Sales that was previously deployed to the test stage, the report will automatically connect to the Sales semantic model. However, if the Sales semantic model doesn't exist in the test stage, the deployment will fail. The potential failure can be resolved by choosing the "Select related" option for the deployment.

In some scenarios, you might want to avoid autobinding. For example, if you develop a pipeline for organizational semantic models and another pipeline for reports, you might prefer to have all the reports linked to semantic models in the production stage. Autobinding can be avoided by defining a parameter rule (see "Deployment rules" on page 359).

Item pairing

Item pairing is associating an item in one stage with the same item in another stage. Pairing might occur in two ways:

Deployment
> When an unpaired item is copied from, let's say, the development to the test stage, a copy of the item is automatically created in the test stage and paired with the item from development.

Assigning a workspace to the deployment stage
> When a workspace is assigned, the pipeline will try to pair the items by the item name and type. If there are two or more items with the same name and type in the stage, then the folder location will also be taken into account. Table 17-2 considers various scenarios for item pairing.

Table 17-2. Item pairing in different scenarios

Development	Test	Item pairing
Item name: Report1 Item type: Power BI report	Item name: Report1 Item type: Power BI report	✓ Items are paired
Item name: Report1 Item type: Power BI report	Item name: Report1 Item type: Power BI report Item name: Report1 Item type: Power BI report	⊖ No pairing (duplicates identified); deployment fails
Item name: Report1 Item type: Power BI report Folder location: Folder1	Item name: Report1 Item type: Power BI report Folder location: Folder2	⊖ No pairing, but deployment succeeds
	Item name: Report1 Item type: Power BI report Folder location: Folder1	✓ Items are paired
	Item name: Report1 Item type: Power BI report	⊖ No pairing, but deployment succeeds

Deployment rules

When you are implementing deployment pipelines, different stages may have different configuration settings. For example, each stage may have a different database or different query parameters. Also, the development stage might be used only to query sample data from the database, while the test and production stages query the entire database.

Configuring *deployment rules* enables you to allow changes to content when you deploy content between the stages. For example, if you want a semantic model in a production stage to point to a production database, you can define a rule for that semantic model. The rule is defined in the production stage, under the specific semantic model.

Once you define the rule, content deployed from test to production will inherit the value from the deployment rule, and will always apply it as long as the rule is unchanged and valid.

Figure 17-7 displays the workflow for defining deployment rules for the production stage.

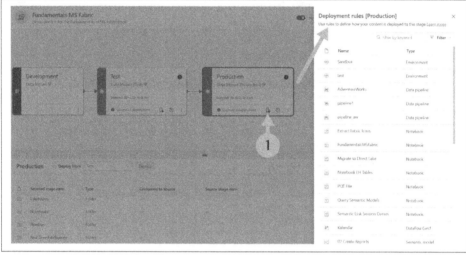

Figure 17-7. Defining deployment rules for the specific stage

Once you select the particular Fabric item, you'll be able to set deployment rules for both data source and parameters (if you have any parameters defined). Figure 17-8 illustrates the data source rule definition for the Power BI semantic model so that it connects to another database when deployed to the production stage.

For notebooks, you may also specify the default lakehouse rule. You should always check the list of supported items and deployment rules (*https://oreil.ly/v-Or2*) in the official Microsoft documentation.

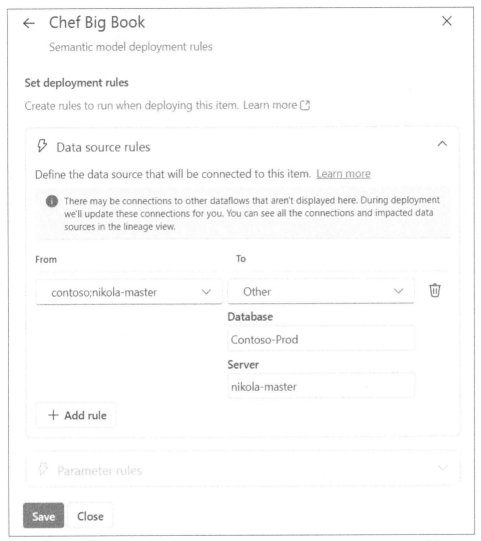

Figure 17-8. Defining data source deployment rule for a Power BI semantic model

Copy item properties between the stages

When you deploy content between stages, not all item properties will be copied to the target stage. Table 17-3 shows which item properties are copied or not copied during the deployment process.

Table 17-3. Item properties copied between the stages

Copied	Not copied
Data sources	Data
Parameters	Permissions for a workspace or specific item
Report visuals	Workspace settings
Report pages	Personal bookmarks
Dashboard tiles	App content and settings (needs to be done manually)
Model metadata	Role assignment[a]
Item relationships	Refresh schedule[a]
Sensitivity labels[b]	Data source credentials and endorsement settings[a]

[a] Semantic model property.
[b] Labels are copied when a new item is deployed, when an existing item is deployed to an empty stage, or when the source item contains a sensitivity label and the target item doesn't.

Deployment pipeline permission model

Deployment pipelines rely on their own permission model, although it's still interconnected and highly dependent on the workspace permission model. There are two possible ways to allow users to work with deployment pipelines—through the Pipeline admin role, which is the only role specifically used for deployment pipelines, or via workspace roles *in combination* with the Pipeline admin role. As you may conclude, the Pipeline admin role is required for all the operations related to the deployment pipeline.

Table 17-4 displays the deployment pipeline permission model.

Table 17-4. Deployment pipeline permission model

Role	Permission
Pipeline admin	• View a pipeline • Share a pipeline with others • Edit and delete a pipeline • Unassign a workspace from a stage • No permissions on the workspace content
Workspace Viewer (and Pipeline admin)	• Consume content • Unassign a workspace from a stage
Workspace Contributor (and Pipeline admin)	The same as Viewer plus: • Compare stages • View semantic models • Deploy items (must be at least Contributor in both source and target workspaces)

Role	Permission
Workspace Member (and Pipeline admin)	The same as Contributor plus: • View workspace content • Update semantic models • Configure semantic model deployment rules
Workspace Admin (and Pipeline admin)	The same as Member plus: • Assign a workspace to a stage

Recommended Practices for Lifecycle Management

Let's wrap up this section by introducing the recommended practices when implementing lifecycle management in Fabric. We'll follow the common workflow, starting from content preparation and then moving through the three main stages: development, test, and production.

Table 17-5 displays the list of recommended practices for each part of the workflow.

Table 17-5. Recommended workflow practices

Stage	Recommended practices
Content preparation	• Separate development between teams • Plan a permission model • Connect different stages to different databases • Use parameters to change configuration settings between stages
Development	• Back up work into a Git repository • Roll back changes • Use an isolated environment (workspace) to work
Test	• Simulate the production environment • Configure deployment rules with a real-life data source • Check related items to avoid breaking changes • Update data items • Test the Power BI app if needed
Production	• Define who can deploy to production • Set deployment rules • Update the production Power BI app if needed • Deploy using Git integration

Automating CI/CD Workflows with Fabric REST APIs

Fabric REST APIs enable the automation of numerous Fabric procedures and processes, improving efficiency and productivity. When it comes to CI/CD REST APIs specifically, you can leverage them for different actions and operations, such as committing the changes from the workspace to the connected Git repository, updating the workspace with commits made to the Git repository, checking which items have incoming changes, deploying the deployment pipeline content between stages, and many more.

Since Microsoft constantly updates the list of available REST APIs, we suggest you always check the list of currently supported REST APIs for the specific task. In the official Microsoft documentation, you can find a list of all deployment pipelines APIs (*https://oreil.ly/Dn-qF*) as well as a list of all Git-related APIs (*https://oreil.ly/l37Ds*).

Summary

We are not exaggerating when we say that CI/CD workflows are critical for successful Microsoft Fabric implementation. This is because they enable automated, consistent processes for developing, testing, and deploying analytics solutions.

By establishing CI/CD processes, organizations ensure consistent quality and reduce the space for manual errors, while at the same time increasing the overall data platform quality and agility. Microsoft Fabric environments often assume tight collaboration among data engineers, data analysts, and developers, working simultaneously on notebooks, data pipelines, semantic models, and other Fabric items. With Git integration and deployment pipelines, Microsoft Fabric provides out-of-the-box solutions for implementing effective CI/CD workflows. Moreover, implementing CI/CD processes promotes DevOps and DataOps principles by automating repetitive tasks, enforcing quality gates, and establishing continuous feedback loops. This is of paramount importance in enterprise-grade environments, where any inconsistency or delay may significantly affect the decision-making process.

In the next, final chapter of the book, we put all the pieces of the Microsoft Fabric puzzle in the right place and provide you with clear guidance about "when to choose what" in Fabric.

## CHAPTER 18

Fabric Decision Guide: When to Choose What

You've come a long way by reading this book so far, and you should be well equipped with a thorough understanding of the individual Microsoft Fabric components.

We like to think about this chapter as a puzzle. You know the feeling when you start building a jigsaw—you are very aware of each piece and what's displayed on it. Not only that, but there are probably pieces that seem to be the right shape to fit here and there in the jigsaw. But, are these pieces really in the right spot? Or, should you use another one? Consider this chapter the final jigsaw: you know each and every individual piece, and we will now help you put all of these pieces into the right place.

How to Pick the Right Option

Microsoft Fabric is all about the options. As you've seen up to this point in the book, the same task can often be completed in multiple ways. And it doesn't necessarily follow that one way is better than the other. Sometimes, it boils down to the skill set of the individuals in your organization performing the data task, or maybe it's just a personal preference. Sometimes, however, these decisions might have a larger impact on the entire data platform workload. Therefore, it is of paramount importance to understand the implications of choosing Option A versus Option B to complete Task XYZ in Microsoft Fabric.

In the following sections, we'll do our best to provide you with guidance on the most common Fabric dilemmas. Please bear in mind that the list of dilemmas is not definitive—we simply handpicked some of the challenges that Fabric practitioners face most frequently and where we believe that such guidance would make the lives of these practitioners much easier in their day-to-day work with Microsoft Fabric.

> ### Generally Recommended Practices and Edge Case Scenarios
>
> Before we proceed, an important disclaimer: the guidance we provide here is based on both our experience with implementing Microsoft Fabric in real-world scenarios and Microsoft's recommended practices.
>
> Please keep in mind that this guidance relies on *generally recommended* practices (we intentionally avoid using the phrase *best practices*, because the best is very hard to determine and agree on). The word *generally* means that the practice we recommend should be used in *most* of the relevant scenarios, but there will always be edge cases where the recommended practice is simply not the best solution. Therefore, you should always evaluate whether the generally recommended practice makes sense in your specific use case.

Choosing an Analytical Engine

All Microsoft Fabric roads lead to OneLake! You learned that mantra in Chapter 3. However, which road is the right one for *you*, dear reader? Should you pick a lakehouse, a warehouse, or maybe an eventhouse for storing your data in OneLake? There are numerous factors to take into account, so let's explore three that we consider most relevant: data volume, supported data types, and supported programming languages.

In this section, we'll break down the key considerations for choosing the optimal path.

Data Volume

Although there is no single number that differentiates *small* from *big* data, and you'll probably find dozens of opinions in the various resources on the web or other books, we often refer to big data as an extremely large and diverse collection of data that continuously grows over time. However, for the sake of setting boundaries when making decisions, we'll consider big data anything above 5 TB of stored data with 100+ GB of ingested data per day.

When choosing the optimal analytical engine in Microsoft Fabric, there is no such thing as the minimum amount of data suitable for warehouse versus lakehouse, or vice versa. In theory, you could store only a handful of data records in any of the analytical stores in Fabric, but you'll start reaping the benefits of massively parallel processing (MPP) architectures, which are implemented in both Fabric lakehouse and Fabric warehouse, only with large amounts of data. Explaining the details of MPP is beyond the scope of this book, but you can find more details in the TIBCO glossary (*https://oreil.ly/EqJP5*).

To wrap up, data volume shouldn't be a determining factor when deciding which analytical engine to use, as each lakehouse, warehouse, and eventhouse scales to support petabytes of data if necessary.

Supported Data Types

When choosing a storage option in OneLake, you'll need to first consider the data type. Table 18-1 outlines the supported data formats for three Fabric analytical storage types.

Table 18-1. Supported data formats per analytical storage

Supported data format	Lakehouse	Warehouse	Eventhouse
Structured	Yes	Yes	Yes
Semi-structured	Yes	Limited (JSON)	Yes
Unstructured	Yes	No	Yes

As you can see in Table 18-1, both lakehouses and eventhouses support all data formats. So, the fair question would be, When should I use a lakehouse over an eventhouse? The short answer is that whenever you need to handle any type of streaming or event-based data, choose an eventhouse. A few examples of event-based data are telemetry and log data, time series data, and data collected from IoT devices.

The long answer is more nuanced and depends on numerous factors, such as:

Using data downstream
It's important to consider how you plan to use the data downstream. For example, if you are using Direct Lake mode for Power BI semantic models, data must be available in Delta format, which is not supported in eventhouses. We cover Direct Lake mode in depth in Chapter 9. Luckily, there is a feature in Fabric Eventhouse, "OneLake availability," that allows replicating eventhouse data in Delta Parquet format in OneLake. Keep in mind, however, that the synchronization between the eventhouse data and Delta-replicated data sometimes may take a while.

Optimizing storage cost
Generally speaking, storage is more expensive for eventhouses than for lakehouses, since eventhouses use OneLake Cache Storage (*https://oreil.ly/7ah96*) to provide the fastest query response times at an additional cost.

Processing streaming data
Eventhouses are optimized for processing streaming data (indexing and partitioning happen automatically), whereas processing streaming data using a lakehouse will force the creation of multiple small Parquet files that must be vacuumed and optimized later, which can lead to increased capacity unit

consumption. Explaining the vacuum and optimize operations is out of the scope of this book, but you can read more about them in the Microsoft documentation (*https://oreil.ly/VCY7z*).

Supported Programming Languages

This is undoubtedly a key factor, not only when deciding about the analytical engine but also when designing the entire Fabric architecture. The reason is obvious—let's imagine that the entire data team in your organization consists of hard-core T-SQL developers. Would you force them to learn another programming language (Python, for example)? Or would you rather choose a Fabric component that plays to their strengths?

Table 18-2 shows supported programming languages for both read and write operations.

Table 18-2. Supported programming languages per analytical storage

Operation type	Lakehouse	Warehouse	Eventhouse

Read	• Spark
	  – PySpark
	  – Spark SQL
	  – Scala
	  – R
	• T-SQL
	• Python
		• T-SQL	• KQL
			• T-SQL

Write	• Spark
	  – PySpark
	  – Spark SQL
	  – Scala
	  – R
	• Python
		• T-SQL
		• Python (using pyodbc library)
			• KQL

Let's stop for a moment and examine the importance of the selection you make based on the information in Table 18-2. Imagine that you're implementing a medallion architecture in Microsoft Fabric. (We cover the medallion architecture in detail in Chapter 5.) In accordance with the recommended practice of building a star schema dimensional model in the final layer (gold/curated), you'd need to apply various data transformations to implement business rules and logic. If your data engineers or analytics engineers are feeling comfortable writing T-SQL, you should probably choose a warehouse for this layer, since T-SQL can't be used for inserting, updating, or deleting data in a lakehouse or eventhouse.

On the flip side, if the majority of the data team is proficient with Python or any language that can be used to manipulate the data using the Spark engine, you'd probably go all the way with a lakehouse. Although, in full honesty, the road between T-SQL and Spark SQL is not that long, in case you plan to leverage SQL skills while using a lakehouse.

Supported Data Ingestion and Data Access Methods

Data can be ingested into Microsoft Fabric using numerous tools or accessed by leveraging particular features such as shortcuts. (We covered shortcuts in Chapter 3.) Therefore, a decision on which analytical engine to use might also depend on the ingestion option you choose or feel most comfortable with.

We provide a decision guide on various data ingestion options in a later section ("All Roads Lead to OneLake—but Which One Is the Right Road?" on page 380). Here in Table 18-3, we just want to help you understand which ingestion methods are supported in regard to the selected analytical engine.

Table 18-3. Supported data ingestion/data access methods per analytical storage

Data ingestion/access method	Lakehouse	Warehouse	Eventhouse
Pipeline	Yes	Yes	Yes
Dataflow Gen2	Yes	Yes	Yes
Eventstream	Yes	No	Yes
Spark connectors	Yes	Yes, but limited	Yes, but limited
T-SQL commands	No, except when executed using Python pyodbc library	Yes	No
KQL commands	No	No	Yes
Shortcuts	Yes	Yes, but only as a source	Yes

Access Control

In Chapter 16, we examined various options for securing the data in Microsoft Fabric. The availability of particular access control features may also impact the decision about the analytical engine you want to use. Table 18-4 shows how each access control feature can be implemented in a lakehouse, warehouse, or eventhouse.

Table 18-4. Available access control options per analytical storage

Access control feature	Lakehouse	Warehouse	Eventhouse
Object-level security	Yes	Yes	Yes, via restricted view access policies
Row-level security	Yes, via SQL analytics endpoint	Yes	Yes
Column-level security	Yes, via SQL analytics endpoint	Yes	No

OneLake Interoperability

"What if I choose a lakehouse for my silver layer and a warehouse for the gold layer? Can I combine the data from them?"

"I've already configured my eventhouse to store the streaming data generated by our IoT devices. How can I mix and match this data with the existing data from a lakehouse or warehouse?"

These are some of the questions we're often asked by customers considering or already using Microsoft Fabric. In this section, we'll provide an overview of the interoperability between various analytical engines in Fabric, as shown in Table 18-5.

Table 18-5. Interoperability features per analytical storage

Interoperability feature	Lakehouse	Warehouse	Eventhouse
Data stored in OneLake	Yes	Yes	Yes, when the Eventhouse "OneLake availability" is enabled
Data stored in Delta format	Yes	Yes	Yes, when the OneLake Integration property is enabled
Source for shortcuts	Yes	Yes	Yes, when the OneLake Integration property is enabled
Target for shortcuts	Yes	Yes, via cross-database queries	Yes
Cross-lakehouse/warehouse/ eventhouse queries	Yes	Yes	Yes, when the OneLake Integration property is enabled

Scenario-Based Decision Guide

Based on all of the criteria and typical analytical requirements discussed above, we identified a few common scenarios you might face when deciding which Fabric component to pick for a particular use case. Table 18-6 illustrates the *level of suitability* of each analytical engine for the scenario in the scope. A 5-star rating means that the particular engine is a good fit for the specific use case. A 3-star rating means that the required scenario may be accomplished by using the particular analytical engine, but with some limitations or considerations. Finally, a 1-star rating means that we don't recommend using the particular engine for that specific use case.

For the sake of clarity, here is a brief overview of each of the scenarios identified in Table 18-6:

Operational reports with low data latency
> The emphasis is on providing low latency and high concurrency for small-to-medium volumes of structured data.

Enterprise data warehousing

The emphasis is on providing scalability for storing and analyzing medium-to-high volumes of structured, semi-structured, or unstructured data.

Implementing a medallion architecture

This refers to a design pattern where data goes through multiple layers (such as bronze, silver, and gold or raw, validated, and curated) on its way from ingestion to being consumption-ready. In real life, there are dozens of scenarios where a medallion architecture is implemented by combining multiple analytical engines. One of the most common is using a lakehouse for the bronze and silver layers and a warehouse for the gold layer. Of course, this is not set in stone, and depending on the specific use case, you may use a lakehouse-only or warehouse-only approach when implementing a medallion architecture. On the flip side, the eventhouse would be a good fit when implementing a medallion architecture for streaming data.

Implementing data marts

The emphasis is on providing efficient analytical capabilities for structured data as a subset of an enterprise data warehouse focused on a particular line of business, department, or subject area.

Real-time analytics

The emphasis is on providing efficient processing and analytical capabilities for the data as soon as it becomes available. In streaming data scenarios, an eventhouse is the most obvious choice, although you might also pick a lakehouse in some cases where query concurrency is not a concern.

Handling arbitrary unstructured data

A lakehouse is a no-brainer here because of its support for all data types.

Table 18-6. Scenario-based level of suitability

Scenario	Lakehouse	Warehouse	Eventhouse
Operational reports with low data latency	★★★	★★★	★★★★★
Enterprise data warehousing	★★★★★	★★★★★	★★★
Implementing a medallion architecture[a]	★★★★★	★★★	★★★★★
Implementing data marts	★★★★★	★★★★★	★
Real-time analytics	★★★	★	★★★★★
Handling arbitrary unstructured data	★★★★★	★	★★★

[a] When a single analytical engine is used across all medallion layers

We'll wrap up this section with Figure 18-1, which shows a high-level decision tree for the analytical storage engine. Please keep in mind that it shows a simplified overview based on the common scenarios we've examined, and it's by no means a definitive guide to choosing the optimal analytical engine. In addition, we would also like to emphasize that combining multiple engines should be an option you consider when you need to incorporate diverse analytical workloads across the data platform.

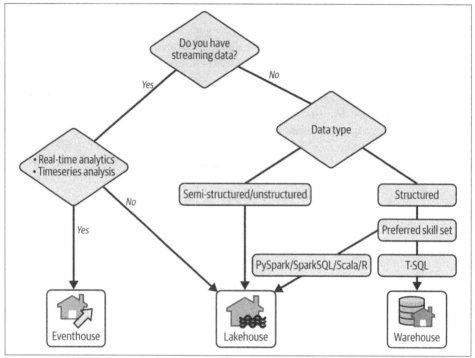

Figure 18-1. Decision tree for choosing the optimal analytical engine

Mirrored Azure SQL Database Versus SQL Database

You learned about mirroring and SQL databases in Fabric in detail in Chapters 11 and 10, respectively. And, if you wondered after reading those two chapters what the difference is between the mirrored Azure SQL Database and SQL database in Fabric, we don't blame you. These two are "children" of the same "mother"—Azure SQL Database.

From a purely conceptual and technical point of view, there is very little difference between the mirrored Azure SQL Database and the SQL database in Fabric. In both cases, your operational data is replicated in near real time and stored in Delta format in OneLake, using the same technology under the hood.

The key difference, and the key factor that you should consider when choosing between these two, is *who* is taking care of the operational database itself. If you choose mirroring for Azure SQL Database, since we are talking about a PaaS offering, *you* are in charge of the database—security, number of vCores or DTUs (database transaction units as a blended measure of CPU, memory, reads, and writes), cost management, scalability, and so on. On the flip side, as a SaaS offering, the SQL database in Fabric is managed as part of the entire Fabric ecosystem. This means it automatically scales and integrates with the development and analytics framework in Fabric and costs are included in your Fabric bill.

 Mirrored Azure SQL Database or SQL database in Fabric. Which one is better? We're afraid there is no correct answer to this question, as it would be the same as trying to answer the question, is it better to sit in the back seat of a self-driving car or drive the car yourself?

Figure 18-2 depicts the key difference between the mirrored Azure SQL Database and the SQL database in Fabric.

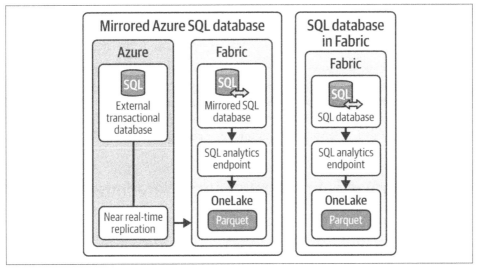

Figure 18-2. The key difference between the mirrored Azure SQL DB and SQL DB in Fabric

Let's wrap up this section by introducing two real-life scenarios that might help you choose between the mirrored Azure SQL Database and the SQL database in Fabric.

Scenario 1: Web Application with Operational Data

Task

You are a developer tasked with creating a web application to store operational data. You need an easy and straightforward database setup and management process. One of the requirements is enabling integration of the operational data with other analytical workloads, where the master data is managed within the Fabric warehouse. What should you choose?

Solution

You should choose SQL database in Fabric, since creating a database is one click away and Microsoft Fabric automatically handles database management. Additionally, by creating a near real-time replica of the transactional data, you'll have the data readily available for cross-querying with other Fabric analytical storage engines, such as a lakehouse or warehouse.

Scenario 2: Big Data Containing Sensitive Information

Task

You are a developer tasked with creating a .NET application that should support a large amount of data (10+ TB). Additionally, since the application will handle sensitive information about credit card numbers, you need to ensure that the data is always encrypted.

Solution

You should choose Azure SQL Database and configure mirroring of the database to Fabric. Since the SQL database in Fabric supports only up to 4 TB of storage, it won't meet the requirement regarding the amount of data. In addition, Azure SQL DB has an "Always Encrypted" feature, which is not available in the SQL database in Fabric. Hence, to fulfill this requirement, you must choose the Azure SQL DB.

SQL Database in Fabric Versus Fabric Warehouse

If you are a hard-core T-SQL person, you'll probably feel at home while reading this section. If you haven't skipped previous chapters, especially Chapter 5, you are probably aware that T-SQL can be used for read-only operations over the data stored in a lakehouse via a SQL analytics endpoint. However, we owe you clarification about *data-writing* possibilities using the T-SQL language.

There are two Fabric items that support the CRUD (create, read, update, delete) set of operations using T-SQL: Fabric warehouse and SQL database in Fabric. Therefore, the fair question would be, When and why should I choose one over the other?

Before we dive into exploring scenarios, Figure 18-3 provides a decision tree based on the common requirements when working with structured data.

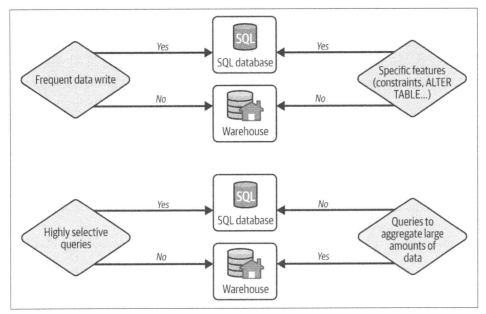

Figure 18-3. SQL database versus warehouse decision tree based on the common requirements

Let's now examine a few use cases based on the requirements you might face when choosing between the SQL database in Fabric and a warehouse.

Scenario 1: Aggregating Big Data for Analytical Reports

Task

You are an analytics engineer tasked with designing a solution to support complex business reporting requirements. The end users must be able to perform analysis over large amounts of data, where most of the queries should be able to efficiently support aggregating the data per different attributes. The acceptable data latency in reports is up to 12 hours.

Solution

You should choose the Fabric warehouse. The warehouse relies on the MPP paradigm, which provides an efficient solution for queries performing aggregations over huge amounts of data. Additionally, since there is no requirement for frequent data writes, choosing a warehouse would make more sense.

Scenario 2: Near Real-Time Operational Reporting with Enforced DatabaseEnforced Database Constraints

Task

You are a database developer tasked with designing a solution for storing the data in a high concurrency database that guarantees strongly enforced foreign keys for relational integrity. The end users should be able to create reports that combine the data from this database and other Fabric analytical engines, namely a lakehouse, but occasionally they will also need to run a few near real time operational reports that retrieve specific database records.

Solution

You should choose the SQL database in Fabric, because, unlike the Fabric warehouse, it provides enforced constraints (primary keys, unique keys, etc.). The requirement to combine the data with other Fabric items could be fulfilled by the automatic data replication from the SQL database to OneLake. Finally, SQL database in Fabric is not constrained by latency and is optimized for highly selective query patterns, which are commonly present in operational reporting scenarios.

Direct Lake Versus Import Mode for Semantic Models

For Power BI professionals reading this book, this is probably one of the most exciting sections. Since the introduction of Microsoft Fabric and the Direct Lake feature, there have been many ongoing debates on the topic of this section. If you are not sure what the difference is between Direct Lake and Import mode, please refer to Chapter 9, where we cover all semantic model storage modes in more depth.

While our intention here is to provide thorough guidance about choosing between Direct Lake and Import mode, this is by no means a definitive guide, nor do we want to proclaim the winner in this battle. In the end, maybe it's not even a fair battle, as Import mode has been here since Power BI was introduced a decade ago, whereas Direct Lake is still very much a work in progress. However, our goal is to provide clear guidance and examine potential use cases for both Import and Direct Lake based on common sense and experiences from real-life Direct Lake implementations at the time of writing this book. Apparently, as the adoption of Fabric grows over time, there will be more Direct Lake reference points to compare.

 While there is no doubt that Direct Lake *is* an amazing feature, it is by no means a solution that fits every scenario, nor is it a direct replacement for Import and DirectQuery storage modes. Both Import and DirectQuery are here to stay—Direct Lake is just another option that supplements the old-guard Power BI storage mode.

We ask you to take a look at Figure 18-4, which shows a decision guide for using Import versus Direct Lake mode. After that, we will elaborate on particular decision points and provide further explanation when necessary.

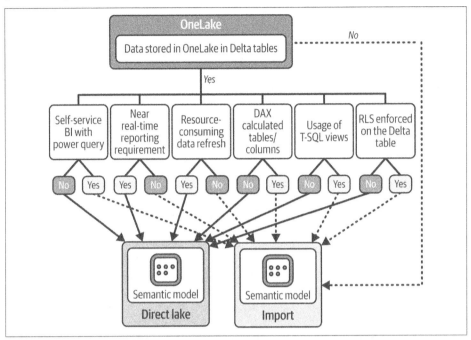

Figure 18-4. Direct Lake versus Import mode decision tree based on the common requirements

Let's break down Figure 18-4 and provide additional context for particular decisions. The key decision-maker is the storage location or, if you want to be more precise, the storage format of the data. One of the prerequisites for using Direct Lake is that the data be stored in Delta format. We want to emphasize the following point here: data doesn't necessarily need to be *physically* stored in OneLake. If you are, for example, leveraging shortcuts to a Delta table stored in ADLS Gen2, Dataverse, or any other supported external storage location, as long as the data is stored in the Delta format, it can be part of the Direct Lake semantic model. However, keep in mind that the best possible performance of Direct Lake storage mode semantic models is achieved by applying V-Order to Delta tables, which is not applied to Delta tables stored outside Microsoft Fabric.

Finally, if your data sources reside in workspaces that are in a different region than the workspace where you store semantic models, you can't use Direct Lake, because creating a Direct Lake semantic model in a workspace that is in a different region of the data source workspace is currently not supported.

Let's now examine the main consideration points from Figure 18-4 using an already familiar scenario-based approach.

Scenario 1: Self-Service BI with Power Query

Task

You are a seasoned Power BI developer with strong experience in transforming and preparing data using Power Query. You are aware of Dataflow Gen2 capabilities to leverage the Power Query skill set in Fabric, but the centralized IT department manages the lakehouse, and you don't have permission to modify Delta tables.

Solution

You should choose Import mode because it supports data preparation using Power Query, whereas Direct Lake models don't allow using Power Query at all.

Scenario 2: Near Real Time Reporting Requirement

Task

You are developing a sales report in Power BI that requires the data to be available in the report as soon as it lands in OneLake. The maximum tolerance for data latency is five minutes.

Solution

You should choose Direct Lake storage mode. When using Direct Lake mode, the data is retrieved from OneLake and loaded into memory at query time. This ensures that the latest data will always be available in the semantic model. Import mode, however, is not suitable for near real time reporting requirements because you'd need to refresh the data on a high cadence. Depending on the semantic model size, you may not be able to refresh frequently enough to fulfill the business requirement.

Scenario 3: Resource-Consuming Data Refresh Process

Task

You are an analytics engineer in a large global corporation who is building a complex semantic model. It's initially around 20 GB in size and is expected to grow over time. Since the older data is also subject to change, incremental refresh is not an option. The data in the report should be refreshed every four hours.

Solution

You should choose Direct Lake storage mode. When refreshing the Import mode semantic model, the system needs available memory that is approximately double the size of the model—in our scenario, approximately 40 GB. This is because the system keeps the read-only copy of the model available for querying while the data refresh process runs. The entire process is described on the Microsoft website (*https://oreil.ly/5pLX-*).

A full refresh of a large semantic model is very resource consuming, both in terms of capacity units and time. When using Direct Lake mode, the refresh process (also known as framing) refreshes metadata only. This means that even for large semantic models, a refresh operation should not take more than a few seconds.

Scenario 4: Using DAX Calculated Tables/Columns

Task

You are a Power BI developer who is proficient with the DAX language. In the company you work for, data preparation and transformation are performed by a dedicated team of data engineers. The Fabric warehouse is managed by the IT department, and you don't have permission to modify Delta tables. To extend a relatively small semantic model for the HR department, you need to implement business logic, which assumes creating additional calculated tables and columns based on the existing model tables.

Solution

You should choose Import mode. DAX calculated tables and columns are calculated and persisted when the model is refreshed. Since there is no data refresh in Direct Lake mode (only metadata is refreshed), these types of model objects are not supported in Direct Lake. Although this will produce the desired outcome in this specific scenario, for the sake of sticking with generally recommended practices, we suggest avoiding the use of DAX calculated tables and columns. Instead, implement the transformation logic as upstream as possible—in this case, by applying the calculation logic in the Delta table in Fabric warehouse.

Scenario 5: Using T-SQL Views

Task

You are a Power BI developer tasked with creating a Power BI semantic model for the financial department in your organization. Your analytics engineer colleague, a seasoned T-SQL professional, implemented the entire logic for the serving (gold) layer using T-SQL views. You need to leverage these views in the semantic model.

Solution

You should choose Import mode. Although T-SQL views can be used in Direct Lake semantic models, all queries that retrieve the data from views will automatically fall back to DirectQuery storage mode, which may impact the report queries' performance. You can learn more about the DirectQuery storage mode and the Direct Lake fallback behavior in Chapter 9.

Scenario 6: RLS/OLS Enforced in the Warehouse/SQL Analytics Endpoint of the Lakehouse

Task

You are a Power BI developer tasked with creating a Power BI semantic model for the sales department in your organization. The data source for the model is Delta tables in the Fabric warehouse. Your company applies strict data access policies, which assume that access is granted using T-SQL commands to enforce RLS and OLS on the Delta table stored in a warehouse.

Solution

You should choose Import mode. Although implementing both RLS and OLS on the Delta table in the warehouse will not prevent using these tables in Direct Lake mode, all queries will automatically fall back to DirectQuery storage mode, which may impact the report queries' performance. Please don't confuse this type of RLS and OLS with features of the same name that are implemented on the semantic model level. When applied on a semantic model level, both RLS and OLS are supported in Direct Lake mode.

All Roads Lead to OneLake—but Which One Is the Right Road?

In Chapter 3, we first introduced the phrase "all roads lead to OneLake." You may recall that one way or another, all organizational data ends up in OneLake. When we say "one way or another," we refer to the fact that data can be both ingested and stored in OneLake and/or be made accessible via different OneLake data access mechanisms, such as shortcuts, for example.

However, even if we can unequivocally agree that all roads lead to OneLake, this doesn't necessarily mean that any of these roads should be taken without some up-front thinking and consideration.

We'll explain this by using a simple analogy. Imagine that we are based in Salzburg, Austria. And we promised our kids we'd take them on a trip to Disneyland in Paris, France. We can reach Paris in a multitude of ways:

- We can take a plane and reach Paris very quickly. It would probably take no more than five hours in total, and, moneywise, this is probably the most expensive option. Let's say it would cost about $2,000.

- We can drive a car from Salzburg to Paris. This option would probably take approximately 12 hours, but it would cost us about $1,000.

- We can ride a bicycle from Salzburg to Paris. This option would take more than 50 hours, but it would cost us only $200.

Now, which option is the best? Well, it depends! If you don't have the money, then a plane is not an option. If you don't have a skilled driver, then a car is not an option. What if you have a fear of flying or are not allowed to fly for whatever reason? Then, no amount of convenience would make you choose that option. Also, you probably don't want to expose your kids to a 50-hour bicycle ride—but, hey, what if they are professional cyclists? There are, of course, many more considerations and "ifs" to take into account, but we hope you get the point: the final decision will depend on numerous factors.

The same applies to the roads that lead to Microsoft Fabric OneLake. The goal of this section is to provide high-level guidance to help you choose the path that makes the most sense for your organization and the data workloads you need to perform.

What Is Covered in This Guidance?

As in other sections in this chapter, we are *not* focusing on providing a definitive guide that covers every single scenario. The reason is simple—there are so many different use cases and so many determining factors that it would be utterly arrogant if we proclaimed that in the next few pages, you'd find the answer to every scenario.

Therefore, we are covering conceptual differences between various data ingestion/data access options. Performance-wise, we will just provide a few basic hints, without explicitly telling you to use, say, a notebook instead of Dataflow Gen2 due to *the notebook's better performance*. Don't forget our analogy about the trip to Disneyland: what good will it do you if the notebook performs better but you don't know how to code in a notebook?

Dataflow Versus Notebook Versus Pipeline Versus Mirroring Versus Shortcut

Now that we've laid the groundwork setting expectations in regard to performance and possible limitations, let's examine what's in the scope of our guidance. We've intentionally omitted the eventstream item; as its main purpose is to ingest streaming data into OneLake, it should always be your preferred choice when you have requirements for handling streaming data. In batch data scenarios, the selection is more nuanced, as you may notice in Figure 18-5. As usual, we will provide an extended explanation below, including your favorite (at least we *hope* it's your favorite) scenario-based approach.

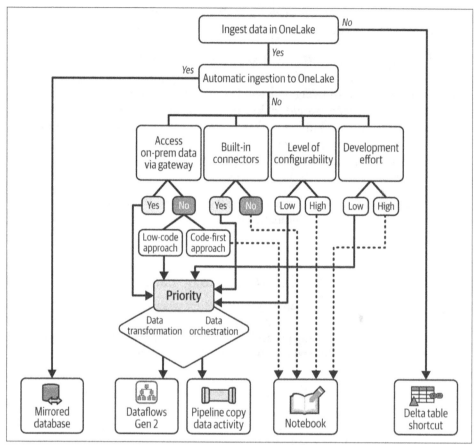

Figure 18-5. All roads lead to OneLake—but which one to choose?

Let's break down key findings from Figure 18-5. First and foremost, you need to decide whether you want to ingest the data and physically store it in OneLake or access data that is stored outside OneLake (and will stay outside OneLake), but still make it available for Fabric workloads. Next, in case you plan to implement the automatic ingestion solution, the mirroring feature would be the obvious choice, assuming the data source is supported for mirroring. In most cases, a decision between using mirroring (*https://oreil.ly/XuqKP*) and shortcuts (*https://oreil.ly/-JEHz*) depends on the sources supported for each of these features.

We'll give you a simple example: if you need the data stored in the Azure SQL Database to be available in OneLake (but without you having to implement an ingestion process), you must use mirroring, since shortcuts don't support this data source. However, if your data resides in, say, Google Cloud Storage and you want that data available in OneLake without physically moving it, you have to use shortcuts, because there is no mirroring for Google Cloud Storage.

A decision about when to use each of the ingestion methods is significantly more complex and requires a lot of up-front planning. The key consideration is, Do you or your team prefer a low-code/no-code approach or a code-first approach?

Answering this question may immediately push you away from using notebooks, for example. Even if you don't know how to code and hire proficient data engineers to build a solution using notebooks, bear in mind that this type of solution will probably require more development effort for continuous monitoring and optimization. Although notebooks provide a higher level of configurability than Dataflow Gen2 or data pipelines, with great power comes great responsibility. In many cases, a possible performance gain may result in higher maintenance costs over time. While low-code solutions are very much "set it and forget it," Spark-related workloads require continuous monitoring and optimization. However, truth be told, low-code solutions often don't provide the same level of transparency as, for example, notebooks when you need to troubleshoot potential issues.

 It is by no means our intention to scare you off from using notebooks. On the contrary! We firmly believe that notebooks provide the most power and flexibility of all ingestion methods in Fabric and, when configured and managed properly, may provide the best possible performance. It's just that using Spark and notebooks requires a specific skill set and data engineers with strong technical expertise.

Scenario 1: Ingesting Data As Is from On-Premises Data Source

Task

You are a seasoned Python data engineer tasked with ingesting data to OneLake from a large table stored in the on-premises SQL Server database. To adhere to the company's data security policies, on-premises data sources can be accessed only via an on-premises data gateway. The data should be ingested in the Fabric lakehouse staging area as is, without applying any further transformations during the ingestion process.

Solution

You should choose "Copy data activity" in the data pipeline. Although your primary skill set (Python) would enable you to comfortably use notebooks in Fabric, connecting to a SQL Server database via an on-premises data gateway is not supported with notebooks. Since the primary use case of Dataflow Gen2 is to apply various data transformations, and there is no such requirement in the task, you should proceed with the Copy data activity in the pipeline, which provides the highest throughput for copying the data between the source and destination.

Scenario 2: Customizing the Data-Writing Process

Task

You are a data engineer tasked with ingesting data to Fabric lakehouse from a bunch of CSV files stored in ADLS Gen2. Since the files vary significantly in size and number of rows, you need to customize and configure various data-writing options, such as V-Order, the number of rows per file, and the number of rows within row groups in the Parquet file.

Solution

You should choose notebooks. Neither Dataflow Gen2 nor Copy data activity in the data pipeline offers a way to customize the data-writing process—it is automatically handled in the background. On the other hand, you can use Python to configure the V-Order behavior, as well as the minimum and maximum number of rows per row group and the maximum number of rows per file. Generally speaking, notebooks provide full flexibility in customizing the data-writing process.

Scenario 3: Transforming Data for the Serving Layer

Task

You are an analytics engineer tasked with building a semantic model for the serving layer. The model will be used by numerous data analysts for creating Power BI reports. Before you transitioned into the analytics engineer role, you worked as a data analyst yourself, and you feel most comfortable using Power Query to shape and transform the data. You need to ensure that after the Dataflow Gen2 successfully runs, a semantic model is immediately refreshed.

Solution

You should choose Dataflow Gen2 activity and add it to the data pipeline orchestration workflow. Dataflow Gen2 provides a low-code, Power Query–based user interface, which allows you to perform all kinds of data transformations. Dataflow Gen2 can be run either as a standalone item or as a part of the data orchestration workflow. To efficiently fulfill the business requirement, you should add the Dataflow Gen2 activity, with all the transformation logic applied, to a pipeline canvas and then add the semantic model refresh activity to the pipeline; the refresh activity will be executed after the Dataflow Gen2 activity is successfully completed.

To wrap up this section, you won't be wrong if you conclude that choosing the appropriate data ingestion method, in the end, represents a trade-off between the simplicity and straightforwardness of GUI-based options (Dataflow Gen2, data pipeline) and potential performance gains you may get by leveraging the full power of notebooks. Do you want to click rather than code? Quite possibly, but there's a cost to having the code abstracted for you by a GUI. However, in many scenarios, this cost is well worth it if you are not yet proficient with Spark-related workloads.

To V-Order or Not to V-Order?

In previous sections, we discussed when to use a particular Microsoft Fabric feature or item to complete a specific task. In this section, we are taking a slightly different approach. Instead of examining whether you should choose feature A or feature B to complete task C, we want to wrap up this chapter by exploring a single Fabric feature—which is by default turned on—and in which scenarios, if any, you might want to consider disabling that feature. The feature in the spotlight is called V-Order.

V-Order is a proprietary Microsoft algorithm that applies some special techniques when writing data to Delta Parquet files in OneLake. The main reasoning behind V-Order is that subsequent data-reading operations should be more performant. By default, all Fabric workloads write data applying V-Order. Consequently, any Fabric analytical engine that reads data from the OneLake can potentially benefit from V-Ordered Delta Parquet files.

It's important to keep in mind that V-Ordered Delta tables are still just Delta tables. Hence, any engine that is capable of reading regular Delta tables can also read the data from a V-Ordered Delta table.

Before we examine specific scenarios in which you might consider modifying the default behavior, let's first explain the various techniques incorporated in the V-Order operation.

Sorting

> During the writing process, data is reshuffled and sorted so that similar values are grouped together to increase the data compression rate. Sorting may include one or multiple columns of the table.

Row group distribution

> A single Parquet file consists of multiple row groups. A row group represents a subset of the data, determined by the row group size. V-Order optimizes the data distribution within these row groups to enhance data compression and enable efficient data pruning. *Data pruning* means that during the query execution, the engine can skip scanning unnecessary row groups.

Encoding

> By applying two special encoding algorithms, dictionary encoding and run-length encoding (RLE), data is additionally compressed and replaced with

shorter, numeric values (dictionary encoding) or the count of repeating values (RLE). Figures 18-6 and 18-7 illustrate the logic behind both dictionary encoding and RLE, respectively.

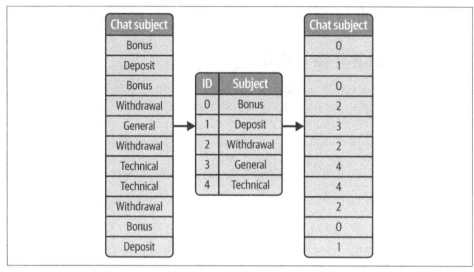

Figure 18-6. Dictionary encoding without reshuffling

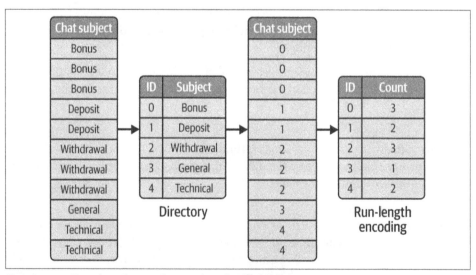

Figure 18-7. Run-length encoding with reshuffled data

As you may rightly assume, the RLE algorithm provides the best possible compression rate. However, it requires the data to be sorted in a specific order; the more buckets of repeating values, the higher the compression. That's why V-Order applies special sorting during the data-writing process.

But, there is no free lunch, and this special sorting comes with a price. Obviously, the engine that writes the data needs more time and compute resources to reshuffle and sort the data than if it simply dumped it in OneLake in a random order.

Now that you know what V-Order is and how it works under the hood, let's examine how various workloads in Fabric may benefit from it. The biggest beneficiary is Power BI and its new Direct Lake feature. (We covered Direct Lake in depth in Chapter 9.) The reason is simple—when V-Ordered, data in Delta Parquet files is stored in almost the same way as in the native Power BI database called VertiPaq, an in-memory database used to store data when using Import mode for semantic models. When using Import mode, VertiPaq applies the same encoding types we previously examined, dictionary and run-length encoding. Hence, having the data sorted in advance using the same encoding logic immensely helps in Direct Lake scenarios. In numerous real-life implementations, we've noticed that cold-cache Direct Lake queries (the initial query that is run *before* the data is loaded into VertiPaq memory) perform 20% to 50% better on V-Ordered tables than on regular, non-V-Ordered Delta tables.

Other beneficiaries are the Fabric warehouse and SQL analytics endpoint of the lakehouse. These two are powered by the same engine, so technically there should be no difference in performance between the warehouse and SQL analytics endpoint of the lakehouse. In the end, the SQL engine in Fabric is also based on Microsoft's Verti-Scan technology, which applies similar encoding and compression algorithms as VertiPaq. Based on multiple tests and benchmarks we performed, the query performance increased by approximately 10% to 15% when the V-Ordered table was used.

What about lakehouses? Can the Spark engine also benefit from V-Order? Well, if you are to believe Microsoft's official documentation, yes. However, in our tests and in real-life use cases, the Spark engine either performed worse with V-Ordered tables, or, at best, performed slightly better, but that was before we incurred the increased cost of the V-Order data writing process. Again, the reason why Spark doesn't benefit from V-Order is simple—unlike VertiPaq and the SQL engine, which are built to get the best out of data sorted in a specific order, Spark is not based on the same architecture. Of course, you may find particular cases when the V-Ordered table performs better than the non-V-Ordered table, but generally speaking, the Spark engine doesn't rely too much on the key advantages that V-Order provides for VertiPaq and the SQL engine.

Figure 18-8 displays a decision tree to be used when making the case for disabling the default V-Order behavior.

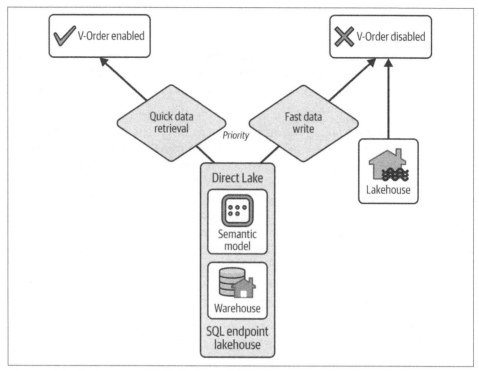

Figure 18-8. Decision tree for V-Order enablement

Obviously, this is a simplistic decision tree. In reality, a decision is way more nuanced and depends on multiple factors. Here is a simple example: let's agree that V-Ordered tables in the Fabric warehouse will provide a 10% improved query performance. You might be (rightly) wondering, Is it worth sacrificing 10% to 20% more time and capacity units for the data-writing process to apply V-Order to these tables? Sounds like a bad deal, right? But, what if you have hundreds or even thousands of ad hoc SQL queries running every day to retrieve the data from those tables? In this scenario, it's probably worth it to apply V-Order. If you decide to disable V-Order for Fabric warehouse workloads, please be aware that enablement is done on the warehouse level, not the individual database or table level. Hence, if you're building your Fabric architecture with warehouses only, you might consider disabling the V-Order feature in the staging warehouse, while keeping it enabled in the curated/gold warehouse.

> A word of warning, though: disabling V-Order on the warehouse level is an irreversible operation. So please make sure that you are doing the right thing by changing the default V-Order behavior. It is strongly recommended that you create a copy of the warehouse and test the impact with the V-Order feature disabled.

Below, we provide a set of code snippets you might find helpful when dealing with the V-Order feature. In our examples, we are using Spark SQL, but you can also use other Spark languages, such as PySpark, Scala, and SparkR.

Check the V-Order configuration in the Spark session:

```
%%sql
SET spark.sql.parquet.vorder.enabled
```

Disable V-Order writing in the Spark session:

```
%%sql
SET spark.sql.parquet.vorder.enabled = FALSE
```

Enable V-Order writing in the Spark session:

```
%%sql
SET spark.sql.parquet.vorder.enabled = TRUE
```

Check the V-Order configuration on a warehouse:

```
SELECT [name], [is_vorder_enabled]
FROM sys.databases;
```

Disable V-Order on a warehouse:

```
ALTER DATABASE CURRENT SET VORDER = OFF;
```

You can read more about the process of controlling the V-Order writes in the Microsoft documentation (*https://oreil.ly/n0ee3*).

Summary

Congratulations! You've made it to the end of this book. Thank you for joining us on this journey through Microsoft Fabric. We traversed a high-level overview of the platform, with OneLake as its central storage repository, and the core Fabric components and workloads. We've also explored strategies for choosing the best tool for the job at a time when Microsoft Fabric continues to evolve at an extraordinary pace.

Microsoft Fabric is a vast topic. While it was hard to go deep into each and every individual component, we hope that we've succeeded in creating a user guide that will enable data engineers, analytics engineers, data analysts, data scientists, and, let's be a little bit immodest, any data professional, to find their way in a product that is growing at an unprecedented rate. We strongly encourage you to continue learning and exploring on your own. As you discover interesting topics and concepts in this book, be curious and don't hesitate to try them. Additionally, identify domain experts who can help you on your Microsoft Fabric journey. Of course, do your best to stay up-to-date with all the latest changes and announcements about Microsoft Fabric.

However, don't lose your critical nose for every single shiny new product feature—take all the promises with a healthy grain of salt.

What's coming next for Fabric? The good news is that Microsoft is investing heavily in this new platform, so you can expect a lot of new features to be introduced, as well as fine-tuning of the existing ones as the product matures. Last but not least, many of *you* may play a pivotal role in determining what comes next. Technology is defined not only by those who create it but also by those who use it and adopt it.

Finally, we wish you an exciting journey with Microsoft Fabric! We decided to work with Microsoft Fabric and write this book, not just because *Microsoft Fabric is a cool new product out there* but because we wanted to share our excitement about using Fabric in real life. If we've managed to convey this excitement to you, we consider our mission successful.

Index

deploying ML models as, to support non-technical teams, 122
provided by OneLake, 57
retail, Fabric solutions for, 9
RLS (see row-level security)
roadmap (Fabric), 10
role-based access control (see RBAC)
row-level security, 332
    enforced in warehouse/SQL analytics endpoint of lakehouse, 380

S

SAMI (System Assigned Managed Identity), 225
scalability
    of data lakes, 41
    of OneLake, 45, 48
scenario-based decision guide, 370-372
schedules, running data pipelines via, 86
Schema explorer
    of GraphQL item, all mutation operations available for tables with primary key, 245
    of GraphQL item, CREATE mutations available in, 241
schemas
    adding to lakehouse, 99
    in Fabric data warehouses, 113
    schema-on-write for data warehouses, 108
securing data, 324
security
    advanced, in OneLake, 45
    data discovery and trust, 341-347
    secure data access in Fabric, 325-341
        common security scenarios in Fabric and tools, 340
    securing Fabric, 323-325
        aspects of security, 323-325
    security metadata stored in OneLake, 51
    SQL databases in Fabric, 205
selective deployment, 358
self-service BI with Power Query, 378
Semantic Link, 125-134
    augmenting gold layer with, 132
    creating bridge between data science and business intelligence, 126
    evolution of collaboration between data science and BI workloads, 126

hidden gem of Fabric, 125
leveraging to optimize Power BI semantic models quickly, 126
migrating existing semantic models to Direct Lake, 132
optimizing semantic models with Best Practice Analyzer rules, 130
translating semantic models into different languages, 131
visualizing dependencies in semantic models, 128
semantic model storage modes, views and, 114
semantic models, 8
    composite models built on top of, 176
    creating Direct Lake on OneLake semantic model, 179
    default versus custom, 180
    defining data source deployment rule for, 360
    Direct Lake semantic model in Power BI service, 272
    Direct Lake versus Import mode for, 376-380
    DirectQuery versus Import mode, 174
    memory footprint of Import versus Direct Lake semantic models, 191
    Monitor hub displaying activities for, 311
    preparing semantic model for Copilot, 270
    refreshing or framing Direct Lake semantic model, 186
    SQL, DirectLakeBehavior for Direct Lake, 197
    syncing with OneLake, 183-184
semi-structured data, 49
sensitive data, protecting, 325
sensitivity labels, 325, 346
    areas in which they may be used to control access, 347
sensor data, 50
sentiment analysis, 123
shortcut database (KQL) versus OneLake shortcuts, 145
shortcut path, 338
    RBAC permissions not defined in, 339
shortcuts, 5

About the Authors

Nikola Ilic is an independent consultant and trainer focusing on Power BI and Microsoft Fabric. Since he lives in the beautiful city of Salzburg, which is well-known as the birthplace of Wolfgang Amadeus Mozart, Nikola was brave enough to use the composer's last name as part of his nickname—and that's why Nikola "makes music from the data"! When his head is not in charts and numbers, Nikola enjoys spending time with his wife and two kids, watching football, and cooking.

Ben Weissman is running a small consultancy firm, focused on data warehousing, business intelligence, and data analytics. His unofficial job title is "data passionist" to emphasize his never-ending curiosity for data and insights. His non-data time is dedicated to his daughter, his partner, good food, and exploring the world.

Colophon

The animal on the cover of *Fundamentals of Microsoft Fabric* is the great black-crested cockatoo (*Probosciger aterrimus*). Also known as the palm cockatoo or the goliath cockatoo, the great black-crested cockatoo can be found in the rainforests and woodlands of New Guinea, the Aru Islands, and Cape York Peninsula in Queensland, Australia.

The great black-crested cockatoo is one of the largest of all cockatoos in existence (and the largest parrot in Australia), measuring about 24 inches from head to tail and weighing 2–2.5 pounds. Although its feathers are naturally black, they often take on a smoky gray hue due to a fine white powder produced by its down feathers, which helps keep the plumage healthy and well maintained. Beneath each eye, it has a small, featherless patch revealing red skin that can shift in shade depending on the bird's emotions.

One unique feature of the black-crested cockatoo's striking appearance is that it has one of the largest beaks of any parrot. Not only does the bird use this beak to crack open hard nuts and seeds that would be difficult for other birds, but it can break off and bite sticks until they reach a desirable size. This cockatoo uses the sticks to "drum" on hollow trees or stumps, with each bird creating a unique rhythm. It is believed that the male cockatoos drum to protect their territory or attract a female, while the females drum to secure or reinforce their bond with a male cockatoo.

The cover illustration is by José Marzan Jr. based on an antique line engraving from Lydekker's *Royal Natural History*. The series design is by Edie Freedman, Ellie Volckhausen, and Karen Montgomery. The cover fonts are Gilroy Semibold and Guardian Sans. The text font is Adobe Minion Pro; the heading font is Adobe Myriad Condensed; and the code font is Dalton Maag's Ubuntu Mono.

O'REILLY®

Learn from experts.
Become one yourself.

60,000+ titles | Live events with experts | Role-based courses
Interactive learning | Certification preparation

 **Try the O'Reilly learning platform
free for 10 days.**

www.ingramcontent.com/pod-product-compliance
Lightning Source LLC
Jackson TN
JSHW071235030825
88679JS00009BA/230